Betsy Sherid

BETSY SHERIDAN'S JOURNAL

Letters from
Sheridan's sister
1784–1786
and
1788–1790

Edited by
William LeFanu

Oxford   New York
OXFORD UNIVERSITY PRESS
1986

Oxford University Press, Walton Street, Oxford OX2 6DP

Oxford New York Toronto
Delhi Bombay Calcutta Madras Karachi
Kuala Lumpur Singapore Hong Kong Tokyo
Nairobi Dar es Salaam Cape Town
Melbourne Auckland

and associated companies in
Beirut Berlin Ibadan Nicosia

Oxford is a trade name of Oxford University Press

First published 1960 by Eyre and Spottiswoode
First published as an Oxford University Press paperback 1986

British Library Cataloguing in Publication Data
Sheridan, Elizabeth
Betsy Sheridan's journal: letters from
Sheridan's sister 1784-1786 and 1788-1790.
1. England—Social life and customs—
18th century
I. Title II. LeFanu, William
942.07'3 DA485
ISBN 0-19-281874-0

Printed in Great Britain by
Richard Clay (The Chaucer Press) Ltd
Bungay, Suffolk

Contents

Illustrations

The Linley Sisters, *c*.1772, by Thomas Gainsborough. By permission of the Governors of Dulwich Picture Gallery.

'Sheridan Threatening Sir Sampson Wright', 1778, by Gillray. *British Museum*

Henry LeFanu *and* Alicia Sheridan. *Miniatures in the editor's possession*

'The Prince's Secret Wedding', 1786, by Gillray. *British Museum*

Principal Characters

THE SHERIDAN FAMILY

THOMAS SHERIDAN 1719–1788 'My Father'.
His wife Frances Chamberlain died in 1766.
> *Their children:*
> CHARLES 1750–1806. He married Letitia Bolton; their children were Charles, Tom, and Letitia.
> RICHARD BRINSLEY 1751–1816 'Dick'. He married Elizabeth Linley in 1773; their son TOM was born in 1775.
> ALICIA 1753–1817. She married Joseph LeFanu in 1781.
> ELIZABETH 1758–1837 'Betsy'. She married Henry LeFanu in 1789.

THE LEFANU FAMILY

WILLIAM LEFANU 1708–1797 'The Old Gentleman'.
His wife was Henriette Raboteau 1709–1789.
> *Their children included:*
> JOSEPH 1743–1825 'Mr L.'. Alicia Sheridan's husband; their children were TOM born 1784 and BESS born 1787; Joseph's son by his first wife, who died in 1778, was WILLIAM born 1773.
> HENRY 1747–1821 'Harry'. Afterwards Betsy's husband.
> PETER 1749–1825. He married Betsy's first cousin Frances Knowles – FANNY – whose mother was Thomas Sheridan's sister.

[ix]

THE LINLEY FAMILY

THOMAS LINLEY 1733–1795.

His wife was Mary Johnson 1729–1820.

Their children:

ELIZABETH 1754–1792 'Mrs S.' Wife of Richard Brinsley Sheridan.

MARY 1758–1787 'Mrs Tickell'. She married Richard Tickell in 1780, their children were Betty, Dick, and Sammy.

JANE 1768–1806 'Jenny'. She married Charles Ward in 1800.

OZIAS 1765–1831.

TOM Linley (1756–1778) was drowned when he was 22; MARIA died early in 1784 aged 21; and WILLIAM (1771–1835) was still a boy in the period of the Journal.

Editor's Note

This journal, it is her own name for it, was kept by Sheridan's younger sister Elizabeth (Betsy) from September 1784 to September 1786 and from July 1788 to March 1790. It was sent in the form of weekly letters, while she was in England, to her elder sister Alicia LeFanu in Dublin. It has never till now been printed at length.

The Journal is not quite complete, for Betsy occasionally refers to a letter which has not survived, and there are a few gaps in the weekly sequence. The large gap, 1786–1788, occurred because the sisters were then in Dublin together.

The Journal is printed from the original letters which, with a few exceptions, have descended to me from my great-great-grandmother Alicia, for whom they were written. Letters 36, 37 and the second part of 58 are taken from Moore's *Memoirs of the Life of Sheridan*, published in 1825. Moore borrowed the originals of these from Alicia's son, but instead of giving them back to Thomas LeFanu he put them with the Sheridan family papers. Evidently Moore borrowed a few others which he did not use, for letters 42, 44 and the first part of 58 were printed by Fraser Rae in his *Sheridan* of 1896, from the originals which he found among the Sheridan papers at Frampton Court. I have not traced where these five originals went after the Frampton papers were dispersed, but Mr Cecil Price of Aberystwyth has kindly given me transcripts of 44 and the beginning of 42, which are fuller than Rae's versions. These transcripts had belonged to Lady Wavertree, a granddaughter of Sheridan's grandson Brinsley Sheridan of Frampton.

Betsy wrote each day's instalment of her Journal with hardly a paragraph and punctuated only with dashes. I have supplied paragraphs and punctuation, but left her spelling untouched. I have, however, made some omissions. I have left out many of the formal openings and most of the endings with conventional greetings to relations and friends. To save postage the letters were usually addressed to Charles Sheridan at Dublin Castle, differentiated by having two seals, or to Joseph LeFanu's colleague at the Custom House, J. E. Madden: these addresses have been omitted. The letters sent through Charles often contain abuse of him, but Betsy evidently trusted him to honour her two seals. I have also left out the signatures: usually 'E. Sheridan' or 'E.S.' and after her marriage 'E. Lefanu'.

Comments on Alicia's Dublin news have mostly been omitted, and discussion of ailments and moods has been drastically curtailed. I have also removed a number of passages and four whole letters which deal only with business arrangements and contain no news or gossip.

The name Elizabeth Sheridan was shared by Sheridan's sister and his wife between 1773 and 1789. Mrs R. B. Sheridan, however, was usually called Eliza, though her own sister Mary Tickell called them both Betsy, and Eliza sometimes used this name of herself.

Although Betsy's dating was sometimes careless, it has been possible with the help of postmarks to date each letter precisely. Where a letter has both English and Irish postmarks the Irish one is usually six days later than the English. The corrected dates are printed at the heads of the letters.

WILLIAM LEFANU

September 1959 Shottesbrook, Boreham, Chelmsford

Introduction

Sheridan's image looks at us from a hundred distorting mirrors. Every memoir of his age records some escapade or improvisation, while Gillray's ruthless cartoons trace the decline from the young idler in Brighton Pavilion to the claret-sodden politician on the Westminster hustings with his hat squashed over his ears.

Sheridan himself, looking back six weeks before he died, spoke of the time 'when the horizon looks clear and beautiful, and the grass beneath you assumes a brighter green'. He had found and read his own draft of the four-day speech in which he indicted Warren Hastings twenty-eight years before. It was his political successes he remembered, not the theatrical triumphs of ten years earlier still. Yet the author of *The School for Scandal* and the battered old statesman whom Byron found the most amusing talker in London are better known than the Sheridan of his great years. While he sauntered through the London palaces of the Whig grandees or made the round each summer of their country houses from Chatsworth and Wynnstay to Crewe Hall and Delapré Abbey, he found time for strenuous parliamentary work and detailed preparation of enormous, closely argued speeches.

Sheridan was elected M.P. for Stafford in 1780 when he was twenty-eight. His ability was rewarded with an under-secretary-ship as early as 1782, but it was only in 1788, when the King went mad, that his party had their first chance of real power. In the eight years since his election he had made himself a name for hard work and brilliant speech, and had moved into the innermost group of Charles Fox's friends in the Devonshire House circle. Through the months of the Regency crisis in the winter of 1788–89 he was Fox's most active lieutenant and the confidential adviser of the Prince of Wales: 'when a head is wanted they have recourse to *his*; every difficult negotiation, every mistake to be rectified is put upon him'.

Through these months of thrilling hopes Sheridan's younger sister Betsy was living in his house and writing a regular Journal to their married sister Alicia LeFanu in Dublin. She had begun the habit of this weekly Journal four years earlier, when she came back to London after living for several years in Ireland. Her father had written when she joined him that he had been leading 'the disagreeable life of an old bachelor; with Betsy I find some of my old domestic sensations renewed; her good spirits, good humour, and good sense make home very comfortable'.

From the autumn of 1784 to the summer of 1786 she kept house for her father in London or went with him to Bath and Tunbridge Wells, always writing this record of her daily life for Alicia. In London they lodged with his old servant William Thompson, and at the watering places stayed in similar private lodgings, usually joining the common dining-room of the house. Though she saw Sheridan often and his wife nearly every day when she was in London, the early Journal is chiefly concerned with her father's affairs: his lectures, his writing, and his quarrels with his sons. But she has plenty to tell Alicia about her own amusements: looking at the first balloons or listening to the Handel Commemoration music in Westminster Abbey, and naturally Alicia in Ireland expects a full description of the latest English fashions.

Then there is a break of twenty months when Betsy went to Dublin with her father. They came back to England in July 1788, and at once she resumed her Journal, but within a month her father died. Sheridan and his wife now welcomed her, at first in the country and later in Bruton Street. She lived with them till her marriage nearly a year later. The second part of the Journal describes this year in vivid detail and continues through the first months of her married life.

Betsy's Journal was read by Tom Moore, and he acknowledged the help Betsy herself gave him with his *Life of Sheridan*, for she outlived her brother by more than twenty years. Moore and later biographers have quoted phrases or passages from the Journal which give intimate glimpses of Sheridan and his wife, but the Journal has never till now been printed at length. The two halves of it, read together, give a much more enlightening and complete picture of the background of Sheridan's life in his greatest years than can be gathered from the fragments his biographers have used. It is, besides, an amusing human document in itself. Betsy appears as a direct, independent character, quiet but quick-witted, though a little given to introspection and imaginary illnesses. She has plenty of friends and an eye for comedy, and is a naturally easy writer with an occasional telling phrase. She was well able to take her place in the smartest world of fashion, when caught up in it, but glad to get away from it when she could.

*   *   *

Sheridan's father wanted him to go the Bar, and for a few months before his marriage – he was only twenty-one – he worked seriously with 'Messrs Coke, Blackstone and Co.' as he wrote to his friend Tom Grenville. When he married in April 1773 he needed ready money and turned to journalism and play-writing. Journalism seemed a quicker step towards politics than the struggle at the Bar, but the success of his plays took him half-unwillingly into his father's footsteps in the theatre. *The Rivals* made his name in the spring of 1775, and *The Duenna* had an unprecedented run of seventy-four nights the following autumn. Dr Johnson pronounced that 'the author of the two best comedies of the age must be a remarkable man', and had him elected to his famous Club. More practically, Sheridan had impressed Garrick. Garrick shared the monopoly patent of Drury Lane Theatre with a sleeping partner, Willoughby Lacy.

[3]

His brilliant and businesslike management had raised the value of his monopoly to £70,000. When Garrick retired in 1776 he sold his half-share to three partners: Sheridan, Sheridan's father-in-law Linley, and James Ford, a fashionable ladies' doctor. Sheridan borrowed £1350 to pay for his small share. Two years later he took over the mortgage of Lacy's half-share and sold his own original one-seventh to his two partners. Thus by a complicated series of mortgages and loans he had acquired for nothing the control of a very valuable property; for Garrick, Linley, and Ford all recognised Sheridan as the director of the theatre. By 1791, when he decided to enlarge it, Drury Lane was worth £150,000. Even before completing the purchase he had enormously enhanced the prestige of his theatre by producing *The School for Scandal* in May 1777. No new play had ever been so brilliantly cast, and Garrick himself directed the rehearsals. The shout of applause that greeted the fall of the screen on the first night still echoes in theatrical memories. Lady Teazle was taken by Mrs Abington, the most admired actress in London from whose manners and clothes great ladies copied theirs. Maria would have been played by the enchanting young 'Perdita' Robinson, but she was expecting a baby. The rest of the cast were well up to this high standard.

Michael Kelly the singer told Sheridan years later 'You write no plays, because you fear the author of *The School for Scandal*.' It would indeed have been a triumph to have matched that best comedy of two centuries which he wrote at twenty-five, for what can match it between *The Way of the World* and *The Importance of Being Earnest*? Yet Sheridan disliked the theatre: Drury Lane was his capital, a very sound and profitable investment till it disappeared in flame and smoke, but he never sat through a play, and always resented the imputation that his father had been merely an actor. After he had entered Parliament politics commanded all his energy and interest; wine and high society were 'my stimulus to further effort and my reward for work well done'. The detailed management of the theatre was left to his associates.

[4]

Drury Lane brought Sheridan a five-figure income, but he chose to live like a millionaire. Perhaps his wife best understood the ramification of loans behind the theatre's finances and often pressed him to pay off his mortgages, though she shared his love of extravagant living and did not know all his borrowings. Betsy records in October 1788: 'It is true my Brother is the purchaser of Dr Ford's share but he does not chuse to have it generally known. The Duke of Norfolk did not lend him the money, but who did is equally a secret to Mrs S. and myself. She declares she is often astonished at the points apparently impossible which he accomplishes.'

*   *   *

Elizabeth Linley was the most admired singer of her day, but from the beginning of their married life she and Sheridan agreed that she should no longer sing in public – he would not be 'Mrs Sheridan's husband'. All the more eagerly high society crowded to their musical parties. Two great ladies, rich fashionable beauties, Mrs Crewe and Mrs Bouverie, welcomed Elizabeth as a friend. She and Sheridan were often at their London parties or staying with them at Crewe in Cheshire or Delapré near Northampton. Sheridan's name was never linked with any woman of the theatre in that notoriously loose-living age, though the most distinguished actresses gladly played in his productions. His friendships and love-affairs were with women of the great world; his attachment to Frances Crewe, his Amoret, was prolonged and probably serious.

The year after the Sheridans' marriage a new star of the first magnitude rose on English society. Lady Georgiana Spencer was only seventeen when she married the Duke of Devonshire in 1774. Horace Walpole wrote that the young Duchess 'effaces all, without being a beauty'. She had every other charm: wit, intellect, enthusiasm, and unaffected good nature, added to great position and uncounted wealth. Her circle for all its brilliance and influence was most easy and natural. The Sheridans met her almost at once, but it was not till six years later in 1780 that they became friendly. Sheridan by then had decided to enter politics and the Duchess persuaded her father Lord Spencer to use his influence at Stafford to bring Sheridan into Parliament. Sheridan's friendship with Georgiana and his long love-affair with his 'dearest T L' – her sister Lady Duncannon – became for some years the deepest interest of his life. Betsy's adverse opinion of these fine ladies, as she records it in her Journal, will surprise and amuse those who think of Devonshire House as the flower of the English eighteenth century: grandeur mitigated by radical enthusiasm, wealth by Bohemian ease. The Journal ends, several months after Betsy had left what she calls 'the raree show of the great world' with a bitter reference to Lady Duncannon's excessive attachment to Sheridan.

*   *   *

Politics was the pastime and perquisite of the great Whig families. When Sheridan entered Parliament the brilliance of the young Charles Fox promised them a chance of righting the calamities which seemed to be overwhelming Britain. Only twenty-one years after the famous 'year of victories' which had conquered Canada and India, the American colonies had broken away and the power of France seemed more threatening than ever. India and Ireland were dangerously disaffected, while at home Parliament and the people chafed under the personal rule of an intransigent King. The unpopularity of George III and Queen Charlotte was widespread: their parsimony and obstinacy were openly ridiculed and caricatured. Betsy speaks slightingly of the Queen, as a commonplace of conversation.

In Sheridan the Whig party acquired a new Member who proved his usefulness by hard work on the matter of Bills and persuasive wit and skill in debate. While the Whigs were in office in 1782–83 Fox brought in his India Bill, which anticipated the reforms of seventy years later, but was far too radical to be accepted by the Court or the City. Out of office again, largely through the King's intrigue, they were occupied in criticising Pitt's commercial negotiations with France. Sheridan's mastery of the detail of national finance in these debates astonished everyone who knew his carelessness of his own affairs, but built him a solid parliamentary reputation. Outside the House politics became almost a riot in the Westminster election of 1784, when the Duchess of Devonshire canvassed extravagantly for Fox and the war of cartoons reached its libellous extreme. The bye-election of 1788 was scarcely less violent; Betsy mentions the excitement when Sheridan seized the Bow Street magistrate who called out the Guards.

The problem of India was tackled again by the Whigs in 1787 by attacking the great governor Warren Hastings who had come home with a reputation for efficiency and ruthlessness. Sheridan spoke all through the night of 7 February 1787 in the Commons, on the motion to impeach Hastings before the Lords, and carried the House with him. This dazzling performance had to be repeated in a different form in June 1788, when the trial had begun in Westminster Hall. Sheridan now secured an even greater triumph. His speech ran over four days and set out with detailed evidence the charges of oppression and corruption which the Whigs brought against Hastings. While London rang with this triumph, Betsy and her father came back from Ireland.

For their defiance of the King's prerogative the Whigs had secured an ally in the young Prince of Wales. He might have been most valuable to them, if they could have trusted him. The Prince came of age in 1783, and we can see from the Tunbridge gossip which Betsy repeats that at first he shared the public unpopularity of the Royal family. In society, however, his personal affability made him very welcome, particularly to the King's opponents among the young Whigs. Fox and Sheridan were soon his closest friends. A blunt Tory Member tried to make political capital in the spring of 1787 out of the Prince's marriage with Maria Fitzherbert, who was a Roman Catholic. The Prince had denied it to Fox, who in good faith denied it in the House in the Prince's name. Sheridan had the unenviable double task of satisfying Mrs Fitzherbert that the Prince had not deceived her and the House of Commons that Fox had not lied. This he somehow achieved, and Mrs Fitzherbert at least remained grateful to him. The charm of Sheridan's conversation captivated men and women alike. He did not climb into the world of the exclusive Whigs; from his boyhood at Harrow and at Bath he attracted its most brilliant members to himself. Jack Townshend, the gayest and wildest of young aristocrats, and Tom Grenville, the most gentle and scholarly of that starched and place-hunting family, became his friends in boyhood and remained his friends for life. The Prince of Wales was in his early twenties when he met Sheridan at Devonshire House; thirty years later Charles Greville the diarist was with them both at Brighton for three weeks and noticed that 'Sheridan never took the least more liberty in the Prince's presence than if it had been the first day he had ever seen him, while the Prince always showed by his manner that he thought Sheridan a man any prince might be proud to have as his friend'. Harriet Duncannon and her sister the fabulous Georgiana, Harriet Bouverie, Frances Crewe, and Maria Fitzherbert were no less willing than their husbands or brothers to number Sheridan among their closest friends. We see them all at his house through Betsy's not uncritical eyes.

The great opportunity for the Whigs and the Prince to help each other came in the autumn of 1788 when the King lost his reason. If his illness were prolonged and the Prince became Regent, the prospect of power and patronage for the Whigs seemed illimitable. The Journal shows Sheridan's life from the inside of his own house at the very time when his hopes were highest and his position as the personal link between the Prince and the Whig leaders, and as a secret negotiator with the Lord Chancellor about terms for the Regency, made him one of the most influential men in the country.

But the Queen and the Court party prevaricated till the King recovered, and then all parties vied in celebrating his restoration to responsibility. Horace Walpole cynically remarked that nothing makes a King so popular as losing his head. A comic turn of affairs, in which Sheridan was unwittingly involved, was that the Irish Parliament invited the Prince to assume the Regency at the very moment when it was too late. The Journal describes the discomfiture of the Irish Delegates in London.

*   *   *

Betsy had grown up in a wandering life without a settled home. She was born in Henrietta Street, Covent Garden in 1758. Her father Thomas Sheridan had been a successful actor-manager in Dublin till his theatre was wrecked in a political riot in 1756. Like many Anglo-Irishmen since Captain Macmorris he 'did not know another man as good as himself'. His attempt to establish himself as an actor in London was thwarted by the pride which made him refuse contracts and insist on profit sharing. With Garrick at the height of his popularity there was no room for an actor who would not take second place. Garrick in spite of his easy pre-eminence was always jealous of rivalry.

Thomas Sheridan was an earnest person, too conscious of his social and intellectual rights. He had been a scholar of Westminster and Trinity, Dublin, and now began to advocate a thorough reform of education. Books on elocution, lectures on oratory, recitals of Milton and Dryden took the place of his productions of Shakespeare but brought him more fame than income. He followed the fashionable world to Bath or Scarborough, took an expedition to Edinburgh, and made several tours of acting and lecturing in Ireland. In London he had his place in literary society, entertained Johnson and Boswell, and knew many of the people with whom Boswell's assiduity has made us all familiar. Boswell professed to like Thomas Sheridan, but he reports the many unkind and unjust things which Johnson said of him. In consequence, Johnson's characterisation 'Sherry is dull, naturally dull' has stuck to his memory. Betsy's picture of her father is partial on the other side, and she

[9]

gives us the idea of a generous, intelligent person, kindly to her and sensible in ordinary affairs, though peevish and ill-tempered from illness and failure, and peculiarly obtuse and bitter in his relations with his sons.

When his theatre was wrecked and his fortune disappeared with it, he had had to give up the fine house he had built for himself in the fashionable north side of Dublin and to mortgage his little country place, Quilca in Co. Cavan, where Swift and Stella had stayed with his father. His affairs were taken in hand by friendly trustees, the first of whom was a Huguenot merchant and banker, William LeFanu, who had come to Dublin as a young man and prospered in the close-knit Huguenot community which played a large part in the business and professional life of Dublin in the reign of George II.

Thomas Sheridan hoped to recoup his losses in London, and his wife's success contributed to their hopes. Her novel *Sidney Bidulph* appeared in 1761, was very popular and was praised by Johnson. Her play *The Discovery* was produced by Garrick in February 1763. Garrick and Thomas Sheridan took the leading parts and the play was a success, though Boswell thought it acted heavily. The next winter he went back to act in Dublin, where his 'Hamlet' was particularly acclaimed, but most of the quite considerable profits went to his creditors. In 1764 he took his family abroad, but Mrs Sheridan died at Blois in 1766.

Thomas Sheridan then came back from France with his elder boy Charles who was sixteen, and his two daughters Alicia of thirteen and Betsy who was only eight. The second boy Richard Brinsley, whom they all called Dick, was fifteen. He had been at Harrow while the others were in France, spending his holidays with various friends and relations in or near London. He now rejoined the family. After some desultory years in London they moved to Bath. There the young Sheridans renewed their friendship with the Linleys, whom they had known when they were all children. Thomas Sheridan the Irish gentleman would not make friends with the self-made music-master Thomas Linley and his vulgar wife, though willing enough for their beautiful eldest daughter to sing at his lecture recitals.

Elizabeth Linley's voice and training had already brought her to the first rank as a singer. The world was at her feet, and Thomas Linley, who was an excellent man of business, had no wish for more than acquaintance with the impoverished Irish actor and his half-educated family. His own children, 'all geniuses' as young Tom Linley ingenuously said, were rigorously trained as singers and musicians. How Charles the elder Sheridan boy thought himself in love with Elizabeth, how she was pursued by rich admirers, and eloped with Dick Sheridan when she was seventeen and he twenty, is general knowledge. After a forced separation they married two years later. As Tom Moore said, marriage was no sedative to them, but part of the romance of their lives for twenty years.

Charles Sheridan made his career in Irish politics. He was ambitious and able like his younger brother, but without Dick's charm or brilliance. Irish politics of the eighteenth century, where everything was subordinate to English decisions, seem now peculiarly unreal. Government office, which Charles achieved in his early thirties, was more a road to affluence and position than to real political power. Charles used his under-secretaryship to secure himself a good salary and, when he went out of office, a large pension for his wife. She was reputed a beauty in Dublin society, but did nothing to engage the affection of his sisters. Their dislike of Charles grew from real experience of his overbearing and penurious treatment. When Alicia and Betsy were living in Dublin after 1776, while their father stayed in London, Charles had charge of their affairs.

In 1781 Alicia married Joseph LeFanu, a son of her father's Huguenot friend. Joseph held a post in the Irish Customs Office, but was chiefly interested in books and the theatre. After a short visit to England, Alicia spent her married life in Dublin. She was a typical cultivated eighteenth-century lady, her round of little duties enlivened with letter-writing, versifying, and amateur theatricals. She even wrote a play which was produced and printed in Dublin. Her letters to Betsy have not survived, but a few letters which she wrote to Sheridan and his second wife show her to have been somewhat earnest and affected in manner, probably more like her father than the rest of his family. But in earlier years she had been a close friend of Sheridan's first wife, the most unaffected of women.

Betsy stayed on in Charles's household for three years after Alicia's marriage. It is clear from her resentment that he treated her like a poor relation. His father, too, while proud of Charles's success and glad to show his clever political pamphlets to influential people, felt bitter disappointment at his aloof superiority and unwillingness to promote Thomas's schemes for reforming Irish education. Charles's selfishness was obvious to outside observers. Mary Linley, Betsy's contemporary who had known them all since childhood, wrote before Betsy came back to London: 'Charlie's behaviour is what I expected long ago; I am only surprised she could stay so long.' The Journal shows that his family saw him as the original of Joseph Surface. In sententious self-righteousness he wrote letters of advice and rebuke to his famous brother, and we read in the Journal that he sent large packets, veritable pamphlets stitched together, of abusive recrimination to Betsy and Dick, trying to make mischief between them. Dick's reaction was characteristically charming and inconsequent.

The division of Ireland between two nations, the Protestant ascendancy and the oppressed Catholics, meant that the privileged minority formed a fairly homogeneous group: to belong to it was enough, inequalities of birth or wealth were of much less account than in England. Under the effervescent surface of Irish society, with its wild extravagance and exuberance, there was in the mid-eighteenth century a sober, cultivated group of professional people in Dublin, to which Thomas Sheridan had made his contribution by improving the standards of his theatre and educating his audience, however unsuccessfully, to respect it. This was a time of much building, when Dublin both north and south of the river was laid out in wide streets and noble squares, and small country houses began to go up in the villages round. Betsy often suggests to Alicia that she should go out to the country air of her cousins' houses, Annefield in Co. Kildare, or Hillbrook at Castleknock north-west of the city. Both sisters were inordinately concerned with their health and their states of mind.

The Huguenot community, which provided a leaven of cultivation for this professional life, in its second generation was readily assimilated into Anglo-Irish society, into the world of officials, lawyers, and clergymen trained at Trinity College. Such were the sons of Thomas Sheridan's trustee and banker 'good Mr LeFanu'. The eldest and youngest sons were clergymen; between them came Joseph who married Alicia Sheridan and Henry who married Betsy, the writer of the Journal. The Huguenots were not puritans; strict in religious observance and their sense of social duty, they enjoyed the good things of civilisation. Joseph LeFanu was an addict of the theatre and a lifelong friend of George Colman the distinguished London manager. Colman even put on one of Joseph's plays at Covent Garden. Joseph was a young widower with a boy of eight when Alicia married him in 1781. It was probably their shared interest in the theatre which drew him and Alicia together, for she alone of his children inherited her father's love of acting. Joseph and Alicia both acted for many years in the amateur theatre which the Dublin Huguenots supported. Henry LeFanu is a shadowier figure than his brother. He was a Captain in the 56th Foot and had distinguished himself at the siege of Gibraltar in 1779, but when Betsy met him at her sister's house he was a half-pay officer with a small allowance from his father. Their quiet attachment runs in an undertone through the Journal till their marriage in 1789. Betsy thought her father-in-law very miserly. She had thirty years of happy but never prosperous married life, and lived on as a widow till she was seventy-nine.

*   *   *

The early part of the Journal shows Betsy picking up the threads of old friendships among the families with whom she felt naturally at ease. She was twenty-six and had been away from London for eight years when she came back in 1784. The Angelo girls, daughters of the fashionable court fencing-master, are her particular friends. The Linleys, the 'nest of nightingales', her sister-in-law's family, welcome her 'to a bad dinner, not to make a stranger of me'; they had been friends since childhood. The Morrises, sons of her father's doctor, are frequently with her in the park or at the play; she wonders if she is wise to refuse George Morris's affection. It is amusing to speculate what her life might have been as the wife of a successful London physician, for George followed in his father's practice and improved it, while his brother Edward distinguished himself at the Bar.

Much of the theatrical gossip which she sent from London must have been gathered specially for Alicia, whom she considered an excellent actress. Betsy herself had little more than the ordinary amateur's interest in 'the play' and frequently forgets to say what play she saw, though she often went to Mrs Sheridan's box at Drury Lane. Actors and actresses of course she discusses with familiarity. Many of them had been her father's friends. John Henderson is often mentioned at the beginning of the Journal. He joined in one of Thomas Sheridan's seasons of poetry recitals at the Freemasons Hall. Betsy cordially disliked having to attend these displays of her father's virtuosity. The genial Henderson's rendering of 'John Gilpin' – Betsy promises to get Alicia a copy of Cowper's ballad – must have been a better bait for the audience than her father's formidable elocution.

Thomas Sheridan claimed Mrs Siddons as his own discovery, and called her his daughter. Betsy and he had seen her during Garrick's last season in December 1775; her Portia had struck them no more than it struck the rest of the audience, though Garrick and Henderson both admired her acting. Thomas Sheridan saw her again by chance at Bath in 1777 and was so much impressed this time that he offered to give her lessons, and he was considered the best trainer of young actors. By his advice she was engaged again for Drury Lane in 1782, when her success was outstanding. Alicia and Betsy welcomed her in Dublin the next season, but by 1784 when Betsy came back to London her father resented Mrs Siddons's familiarity and talked of her 'narrowness of spirit'.

The Linleys had made a success of their concerts at Bath and elsewhere, had grown quite affluent and moved to London, but there was still no affection between Thomas Sheridan and Thomas Linley. Indeed their relationship was more difficult than before. Thomas Sheridan had been manager of Drury Lane for his son from 1778 to 1781, but his meticulous, dictatorial methods had proved impossible with the actors. Dick Sheridan ended his father's contract and had not been forgiven. Thomas not only resented Dick's marrying beneath him, as he considered it; but that Linley had taken his place at Drury Lane and that Dick was clearly more at ease with his father-in-law than with him rankled in his irritable soul. There is an amusing account of the antagonism between him and Linley in a letter to Mrs Sheridan, who was in the country, from her sister Mary, written soon after Betsy had arrived from Ireland in the autumn of 1784:

'At supper', Mary wrote, 'my father said William Thompson had been speaking to him to have our Box for old Mr Sheridan, Betsy, and a young lady from the country. My mother fired up – you know how well she loves the old gentleman – that *your* Box was very much at his service and she should be happy to have Miss Sheridan's company with us. This I own I thought very reasonable, especially at so short notice and that notice only conveyed through William Thompson without deigning to send even a note about it. But my father grew peremptory and rude – so then up speaks my little i and settles it in an instant, for I cannot say I felt very much pleased to be turned out of the Box merely to give old Surly Boots a convenient seat, because the Boxes being so near there was quite room for Betsy with us, and

[15]

the Country Cousin and old Crusty may sit together; so my Mother is gone to the House to settle it all.'

When Betsy and Mary renewed their friendship in the autumn of 1784 Mary had been four years married to Richard Tickell, Sheridan's closest friend and collaborator in the theatre and in political journalism. 'You know how I love Tickell', Betsy wrote to Alicia, 'and Mrs Sheridan I believe not much more partial.' Tickell was a young barrister, whose early brilliance showed as much promise as Sheridan's, but he made little mark in the world. His life ended soon in disaster. He was found dead in 1793 below the windows of his rooms at Hampton Court, rooms which he had lent to Betsy and her husband for a few weeks when they married in 1789.

Mrs Sheridan welcomed Betsy with real affection. She was already the friend of the most fashionable women in London. At the same time she was keeping the accounts of Drury Lane, which Sheridan never troubled about except when he wanted ready money, helping her father with the theatre's music, and clearly as happy with her brothers and sisters as if she had never left that enchanted family. Tragedy which slowly destroyed the most brilliant of the Linleys had already struck: Tom the most accomplished musician of them all, Mozart's boyhood friend, had been drowned when he was twenty-two, and Maria, a singer like her sisters, had died of consumption at twenty-one. Mary Tickell kept Elizabeth supplied with the liveliest family gossip whenever she was out of London. Betsy too gives amusing glimpses of the Linley family.

Much of Betsy's time between 1784 and 1786 was spent at Bath and Tunbridge Wells. Dublin society overflowed to the English watering places, and many of the acquaintances she discusses with Alicia are Irish or have Irish connexions. At Bath, she says, people talk French to hide their brogues. Her gossip of the reigning beauties and their clothes, and her accounts of the petty incidents of a wonderfully idle life are entertaining still. She tells Alicia of walks and assemblies, the circulating library at Tunbridge whose stock never changes, the

[16]

fields at Bath where people walk among the cows in their best town clothes. Betsy turns away when her father is too affable to a reprobate old peer. Her father has no objection to a mild flirtation, for which Charles would have rebuked her. A plot is formed to silence a bore at the dinner-table, and there are continual games of whist or piquet in her father's overheated room.

*   *   *

Four years later, when she came to live with Mrs Sheridan in 1788, much had changed. Mary Tickell had been dead a year, and Mr Linley had had a stroke. Mary had called him a 'croaker' and now he was continually depressed. Mrs Sheridan had adopted Mary's three small children, all much younger than her own Tom. Betsy describes the trouble which she took with them, and the hours which she gave to copying her father's music or Sheridan's confidential political papers. Her life at the same time was as full as ever of frivolous entertainment, and already the consumption which had killed Maria and Mary was clearly attacking her. Her life 'would kill a horse', but 'amusement she says is the way to banish disagreeable reflections'. Even the search for health became an amusement, when all the smart world went to be hypnotised by Dr Mainauduc.

Of these brilliant last years of Elizabeth's short life Betsy's Journal gives the most intimate picture that remains. Here we can see the family circle at Bruton Street among whom Sheridan entertained his glittering grandees. Elizabeth's sister Jane Linley was living in the house as well as Betsy. Tickell dined there every night, and his three children lived there with their 'French woman' and the little boys' maid. George Edwards the butler, whom Betsy found more friendly than intelligent, goes out to wait at a Tory ball and is called a rat by his footmen. Mrs Bouverie's daughter comes up to show off her first ball dress. Mrs Crewe sits in the little drawing-room listening to the talk in the large room, or spreads her dismal feelings over the party. Dick brings bad news from the House of Commons 'in a spirit unacquainted with despondence'.

Betsy is expected to be 'a little grand' and not to go out in a hack though the carriage is seldom free to take her. She must sit up till the small hours when 'the fine people' come to an evening party – the Prince and Mrs Fitzherbert, the Duchess of Devonshire, Lord John Townshend, and the rest of that extravagant circle. Her general dislike for such assemblies evaporates when Charles Fox is there: 'The supper party was more pleasant than usual as I had an opportunity of seeing and hearing Mr Fox more at my ease: the good humour and simplicity of his manners is truly delightful.'

She had already felt this malaise when her father, years before, had taken her to a blue-stocking salon at Mrs Vesey's, where she met a crowd of literary notabilities, 'conscious that I was the only person in the room who had not some consequence in life. I cannot make my father feel the difference the world makes between a man of talents and the women of his family.' She felt it more keenly among the Whig grandees, to whose free and easy morals Mrs Sheridan failed to convert her. She avoided a ball at Devonshire House, but luckily for us went to a masquerade at Hammersmith, where her brother as usual was 'particularly attentive to me in public' and her sister-in-law 'held me fast by the hand' till she was seated among the Duchesses at the Prince of Wales's supper-table.

*   *   *

Betsy and her husband moved home several times, when Henry received various barrack postings. They had three children, of whom only Alicia survived. Henry died in 1821; Betsy was to survive him by sixteen years. In 1804 Betsy published a lively novel, *The India Voyage*; her sister Alicia went on to publish poems, several romances, and a *Life of Mrs Frances Sheridan* (her grandmother), which is still used by Sheridan's biographers.

Betsy's Journal was evidently treasured by Alicia. After her death in 1817 it passed to her son Thomas LeFanu. There are some letters written to him by Tom Moore the poet and biographer of Sheridan, which suggest that he gave Moore access to it with some misgivings. After Thomas LeFanu's death in 1845 the Journal descended in turn to his elder and younger sons: Joseph Sheridan LeFanu the Victorian novelist and William LeFanu my grandfather. My father the late T. P. LeFanu owned the letters from 1894 to 1945 and allowed many students of Sheridan's career to examine them, though refusing permission to publish more than occasional excerpts. Eighty years ago he had thoughts of editing the Journal himself and began to collect notes on the people whom Betsy mentions, but he did not pursue the project. Towards the end of his long life he proposed to me that I should edit it – 'but', he added 'wait till you have read all Boswell'.

Betsy Sheridan's Journal

Her doing so was the more inexcusable as Mrs. St. Leger expressly says she supposes me ignorant of the circumstance — I did not from your account think he had been so very ill & I can not suppose a more alarming idea, that this sort of attack naturally gives rise to. My anxieties. I must keep to myself for I see less of the family than ever except I join in the crowd which I sometimes do to avoid my own thoughts, as I am necessarily quite alone when I do them even perusing them no Friend visiting me here — I feel now unable to fill up my own time in the midst of all quiet occupations the unhappiness ideas occur & I have nothing for it but letting myself be led till this state of painful suspense is ended — I think I must have a letter tomorrow & shall then be able to determine what to do — At present I can think of our sleeping at Richmond tomorrow night after leaving Lord Palmerston's which is in that neighbourhood. But if Harry is really set out I shall not leave Town till I see him. Today we dine at Mrs. Crewe's a sort of farewell family dinner — God bless you my dear Woman — I had hoped her melancholy thoughts would win in the course of this letter — the next will I trust be freer from them but indeed this little foolish woman has made me very uneasy — adieu kindest love in Cavendish — ever most affectionately yours
R. B. Sheridan
Mrs. Sheridan always desires best love, & Dick too ——

Facsimile of part of Letter No 60. 14th and 15th June 1789.

CHAPTER I

London, September 1784 to June 1785, with a visit to Bath in April–May

---

1 : LONDON, 30TH SEPTEMBER TO 8TH OCTOBER 1784

My dear Love

My paper was so full yesterday I could not say all I wish'd. In the evening My Father and I had a great deal of conversation. He has no objection to my seeing Dick and his Wife as he is convinced I will in all act perfectly properly but for his part he never will. This was no time to urge him to it but I said enough to convince him it was a point I had much at heart, our conversation ended in perfect good humour.

After breakfast this morng. I went with my Father to see Mrs Angelo. She received me with the greatest cordiality, Ask'd why I had not brought you over and upon hearing me speak accused me of having some brogue which my Father would by no means allow. She had been to see a Balloon fill'd yesterday which took fire in the midst of their opperation and so destroy'd fifteen hundred pounds at one stroke. She then proceeded to domestic matters and has promised me every advice and assistance in her power.

I then proceeded to Devonshire St. Miss Yarker received me kindly but nothing can thaw her. Her Mother is just the same warm affectionate being she ever was. They enquired most kindly for you. Your Old Flirt is not in Town. The Old Lady still living. No one will allow that I look an hour older since I left London, and I confess every one I have met appears the same as when I left them so that when I find myself in the same spot and see the same faces I feel as if I had had a long sleep and some very strange dreams, but the strong sensation of past vexations which I felt in Ireland is entirely lost. I only want you and our Emily to be perfectly satisfied.

I should have told you that I called yesterday on Mrs Wilson for half an hour and found her with her Husband and her dear little girl. She complained of not being very well and of having been bled that day and says she cannot go to Ireland for some time so you may infer something from these circumstances. She ask'd me a thousand questions about you and our Tom and I made her happy by the good accounts I gave. I like Wilson very well. Mais pour revenir a nos Moutons, I had scarce got home when Mr and Mrs Roberts were announced. I should have told you that they had offered my Father a Bed for me the day I arrived not knowing he was prepared for me – this may be English Coldness but I think it very like Irish Cordiality. After some chat they proposed stepping into the Pantheon to see Lunardi's Balloon to which I most readily agreed. It is suspended to the Top of the Dome and really forms a most striking object. We saw Lunardi, and his poor fellow Travellers the Dog and Cat who still remained in the Gallery to receive the visits of the curious. Mr. R. told me the Diameter of the Balloon was thirty four feet but to me appear'd of much greater extent. All the World gives their shilling to see it. I hope Lunardi will make up for his disappointment in the Artillery ground.

I then went to Norfolk St. where Dick and his Wife are at present. Dick received me more affectionately than I expected, he ask'd a thousand questions about you and then immediately turned the conversation on my Father. He said he hoped now I was come that all would be made up as there was nothing he wished so much as to be on terms. If he is in earnest and I think he is I am pretty sure all will end well. We sat some time together and when summon'd to Dinner I was introduced to the Linleys. I am very Angry with the Old Man but as his Guest was obliged to be civil to him. Mrs Linley is grown older than any one I have met. She has lost all her teeth and looks a compleat Witch but in manner she remains the same. She gave us a bad dinner not to make a stranger of me and hoped I would often come and play a Pool. Jenny is with them and is grown up what she promised. Poor Maria did not seem to be remember'd among them. Dick sat by me and ask'd me a thousand questions about Ireland that made me smile as one would have supposed I had come from the farthest part of America. When dinner was over Mrs Sheridan and I went to Drury Lane. We found Mrs Tickell seated in the Box. She came up to me with the warmth of an Old Friend and I was really happy to see her. She is grown a compleat little Matron. She looks I think much older than Mrs S. and has more compleatly lost her beauty than I thought possible for so young a woman. She press'd me much to go with her to Hampton Court for a few days but I thought it too soon to leave my Father. She regrets much not having seen you when you were here and bid me assure you of her kindest wishes. Tickell soon came in and join'd very kindly in her invitation.

Dick sat behind me the whole night and often renew'd the subject of my Father. He is I think greatly alter'd, he is altogether a much larger Man than I had form'd an Idea of – has a good deal of scurvy too in his face, in his manner very kind but rather graver than I expected indeed I should rather say melancholy than grave. He complains of Charles's neglect a good deal as he wish'd much for some correspondent in Ireland who would have written to him at large on the state of that Country. Our entertainment was the "Clandestine Marriage", King appear'd for the first time these Two years – He spoke an occasional address written by Cumberland in which he compared himself to the Greenwich sailor returning again to the fleet in time of need but grew rather sublime and unintelligible towards the latter end – He was received not only with the most violent applause but three loud Huzza's. I think his Lord Ogleby one of those few performances that answers the Name it has got. I never was more pleased with anything. The House

[25]

was very full tho' the Town they say is empty. The rest of the play was well fill'd but I was not struck with any great superiority over some comedy's I have seen done in Dublin – O'Reilly pleases me as much as Parsons and I did not like Miss Pope as well as Mrs Daly. My Father sent up to me when the Play was over as I had promised to return to sup with him for I thought he deserv'd that indulgence for having so cheerfully consented to let me see Dick. We sup'd pleasantly together and parted at Twelve tho' now past One so God bless you my dear creature.

Octobre 1st – We had visit this Morning from Dr Morris. I think he has taken off ten years from his age when he took off his Wig. He enquired kindly for you and yours. I left him to dress when Mr and Mrs Wilson were introduced so that I was obliged to admit Gentlemen at my Toilet – upon gathering the Voices I found a Spanish hat was what I must bye – It is of the form of that in my picture but made of azure blue silk (the exact colour of our Poplin) trim'd with white ribbon and a plume of white feathers. They are also made of black silk and of straw in the same form – without Feathers for undress. Even silk Balloons are almost out – I have not seen a Cap since I came.

These Visitors were succeeded by Mrs Craufurd. I admitted her tho' still half dress'd. She says I am the Image of you. I think her very pretty and my Father assures me she is a very honest fellow. She made me a thousand offers of service which I may perhaps be obliged to accept, as poor Mrs Angelo is in a good deal of trouble about her Husband who was brought home to her last night with his shoulder dislocated and otherwise much bruised. He was returning to Town from Windsor his Chaise at the Inn Door and everything ready when unluckily he went back to give some direction and fell twelve feet through a Trap that the Waiters had been so unpardonable as to leave open in the passage. The bone has been set and he is now pretty easy.

At half after three enter Mrs Sheridan and Mrs Tickell. After some time they ask'd for my Father. I went down to prepare him for the Visit but he positively refused to hear of

[26]

it – I used every possible argument but he at last left the Room and said he would leave the House if I persisted in urging him to what was so very disagreable to him. I return'd a good deal vex'd to Mrs S. – and tho' I soften'd the refusal as much as possible yet I could see she was greatly hurt. I think she should not have left off seeing my Father and bringing her son as she certainly did so for a length of time after the disagreement between him and Dick. This circumstance is a very great Bar in my way. She enter'd on the subject with great warmth and from her representation you would have thought my Father a most unreasonable Man who had persecuted and distrest a most affectionate and generous son. Mrs Tickell told her with her usual honesty that of course she thought her Husband right but that all retrospect had better be laid aside and that all that should be thought of would be to bring about a cordial reconciliation but the difficulty lies here that My Father thinks he has been materially injured by Dick and that they expect to be received again into his friendship without any kind of submission or attonement. Now that Younger is dead they have again engaged King as Manager. As my Father did not decline the management when proposed to him by Mr Siddons and only waited to receive proposals which however were never made, I think any advances to a reconciliation would have come with a better grace accompanied by some solid offer of friendship. So much between ourselves. From whatever motive they seem anxious to be on terms but I do not think they have taken the right method and they even hurt my schemes as I knew anything like an intention of surprising him into compliance would only make my Father fly off. Dick spoke to me of my Father's plan and hoped he had drop'd all thought of it and said he wish'd he had some good employment to put such things out of his head. I said I wish'd so too but in the mean time as I knew of no Estate in the Family I was glad my Father had any plan that promised him a provision or at the worst kept up his spirits by the hopes of it. He said very true and immediately turn'd the conversation but not seemingly displeased. I believe the hint was drop'd to sound me but I have no idea of joining in sentiments which I wholly disapprove, and am convinced that it is possible to differ in opinion with perfect good temper.

This subject has led me from the regular train of my Narrative. The Ladies stay'd so long that at last my Father sent word he was waiting for me and they took leave not without many promises on both sides of meeting as often as possible. We then drove to our engagement at Mr Roberts. His house is delightfully situated in a place call'd Millbank fronting the Thames and a beautiful garden behind it. We met the Hendersons here. He enquired particularly for you and Emily and said he was in love with us all till his Holy Vow forbad his thinking of any Woman but one. He looks better than he did as he is not so fat but I don't think he has quite such good spirits – I am told he is very unequal in that respect. My Father and he are great Friends. We supt there and were quietly at home at twelve o'clock.

I have found your letter at my return and am sorry to find you have been engaged in so melancholy an office but considering her situation my poor Aunt's death can only be consider'd as a release from pain. Poor Bee has ever found you her real friend, give my love to her and tell her when I can snatch a minute I will write to her. I found also a Note from D'Ivernois who had called in our absence. It contained a great deal of *chagrin* and *espérance* but he did not leave his address. He wrote to inform me that Mr Du Roveray went to Ireland tomorrow and would take any parcel for me but he lives at such a distance that the information comes too late.

October 2nd – I did not tell my Father till this morning of my Aunt's death. He seem'd affected but as He writes himself I say nothing from him. I had a long visit from the Yarkers and then went out to Mrs. Angelo. Poor Angelo had me brought to his Bedside and seem'd most truly glad to see me, as there is no feaver I hope his accident will not prove of any fatal consequence tho' it is very severe on a Man of his time of life. I saw Harry's Wife and Children – they are beautifull, but I do not

[28]

think her as Handsome as I expected. I was introduced there to a Mr. Marriot whom I think you know and also saw Mrs Wyndham (the famous Miss Hartford) – I think her rather an Elegant than a pretty Woman. Poor Mrs Angelo has suffer'd greatly these two days – Kitty is employed in Nursing and the other girls are out of Town. From thence I went to Mrs Craufurd but she was out so I return'd quietly home and dined tete a tete with my Father. I have been part of the evening reading his life of Swift. The works I find are dedicated to Grattan –

3rd – I am just return'd from seeing your Old Friend Mrs Hamilton. George and Edward Morris came to pay me a visit this morning. The former is grown a sensible pleasing young Man the other a very pretty Lad – the other brothers are not now in Town. They offer'd to walk with me to de la Haye St which offer I most gladly accepted. As we were crossing the Park I met Mr and Miss Carroll and Nancy Sheridan. She was rejoiced to meet me and is to call on me tomorrow. The Hamiltons received me as usual. While I was with them Miss Woolery came in, she thought they were alone and had brought with her a Picture she had just finished, it was Charlotte looking at Werter's Urn. The Idea was taken from a print but the painting was extremely well executed. She is strikingly Elegant in her appearance and has I think more real Beauty than any Woman I have seen for some years. Yet Beautifull and accomplish'd and of an excellent family she is obliged to seek her bread and even in the endeavours she has made she meets with the most cruel opposition from Persons who do not chuse she should appear in Public. The Hamiltons almost idolise Mr Coleman for his conduct to her which was generous to the greatest degree and he has engaged her for the next Season. Mrs Hamilton desires a thousand loves to you tho' her daughter writes so often – they both spoke handsomely of D'Ivernois.

And now my dear Love in answer to your last I always delighted at every proof of affection from you and am sure you regret my absence but had I staid you never could have enjoy'd my society for even you did not know half the misery of mind I

[29]

felt in Dublin. I could in a degree suppress the appearance of that but I could not command cheerfullness. You have thank God two of the first blessings in life in the possession of your Husband and my Tom and I somehow feel that our separation will not be long. All your friends here call loudly for you so when our Boy is wean'd you must begin to pack up. My Father had I find totally forgot the Chest of things he left under the care of Mrs Guinness but he wants them now very much. I shall draw for my present quarter as my going into mourning when I had made my millinery purchases interferes with my plans of economy and I will not allow my Father to be at any expense for me tho' he forced five guineas on me which by the bye were not wholly useless as I was rather lower in Cash on my arrival than I expected. However if you wish to pay O'Rielly and Porter before January I can remit you the money immediately – the two Bills ammount to about Six guineas and a half. I shall enclose a list of my other debts which I will remit money to clear as fast as I can but as I am expected back in Spring I think I need not be in such haste as I first intended.

My Father and I dine together so I may close this day's journal. I sent Mrs Warren's papers by Thompson as I would not trust the Servant. I hear she is pretty well so I shall call there the first day I walk out.

4th – I had a Visit this morning from Tisdale. He came with a Captain Williamson who introduced him to my Father, he received him very civilly. Nancy Sheridan then call'd and I presented her to her Uncle. She speaks very highly of Carrol's behaviour to her, he brought her here and call'd for her again. Mr Bolton then came in, as the hair dresser was waiting for me I could not stay long.

I was but half dress'd when Mrs Sheridan came in. She sat near two hours with me talking of a variety of matters still very anxious to be on terms with my Father but I begin to have little hopes – he leaves me at liberty but insists in return that I should not urge him to what he is determin'd never to consent to.

We dined with the Craufurds, I like her very much. Your

Picture made part of the company for the day, The eldest girl knew it immediately and said she remember'd you very well. Mrs C. loves you very much. We are as well acquainted as if we had known each other this twelvemonth. Our party consisted of Men and the day pass'd pleasantly – they were all Scotch officers – McCleod, Ross, Bruce, &c. &c.

My Father has had a severe attack of the Rheumatism this day, I much fear he is going to be confined if so I must make home as pleasant as possible as I could not think of leaving him. Indeed he has been so very kind and attentive to me that I would not even form a wish to do so.

5th – We sent an appology this day to Mrs Morris where we were to have dined but my Father was not able to stir. The Young Men call'd in the evening and made up a party at Whist which I find I must learn as every one here plays.

Mrs Siddons made her first appearance to-night, we had taken places but I do not regret giving them up as I find she was very ill received as a Riot was expected, however they had taken care to provide friends to drown the Hiss.

I had a visit this morng. from Mrs Henderson and an invitation to a Haunch of Venison tomorrow but we were obliged to refuse. We went together to Mrs Angelo's and found him walking about, but Mrs A. appeared as low as ever. When I left the room with Kitty she told me that she had received an account of Sophy's having fallen from her Horse, that she had a very narrow escape of her life but that she was severely hurt – this they have not told the Father in his present weak state but you may suppose they are greatly shock'd.

6th – I subscribed this morning to your old friend Hunt and Halbouch – and have got the Paisan Perverti. At my return I went out to take the air with my Father who took James's powders last night and is something better. Mrs Craufurd call'd to see us and has given me a fine Cocoa Nut, I wish you had it. While she was with us Linley came to see my Father, he received him very kindly but poor L. look'd very small. He told us that Mrs Siddons behaved with great resolution and propriety last night. She address'd the Audience and has promised a full explanation of her conduct. I think Mrs Bulkeley's method the best for I do not see any right the public have to call her to an account for any thing that does not immediately concern them. Brereton has written in her justification and I hope Diggs will soon do the same as I am positively inform'd she took nothing from him.

I write to Charles tomorrow and shall anounce this Paquet to avoid mistakes as I can not think of making you pay for this paquet of nothing and can not get any other conveyance at present. As Mr Erke is always in Town it might be more convenient to send them to him, I would not enclose them under cover but direct them to him and distinguish them by two small seals – the impression a small Head. We were engaged this day to the Yarkers but for reasons aforesaid could not go. Bon soir ma toute chère.

7th – I went this morning to return a few visits with Kitty Angelo in their carriage. As I was returning I met Mrs Harvey, I knew her instantly but she did not seem to have the smallest recollection of me. She is almost as handsome as ever. I found Mrs Siddons at the hour we came in together and she enquired most particularly for you &c. Miss Kemble was with her – I think her rather on the dowdy order. Mrs Siddons' strange reception was the subject of our conversation. She seems hurt to the soul but her feelings seem more of the indignant kind than any other. The Breretons have used her shockingly – Mrs B. was mean enough to sneak off the stage and leave her to stand the insults of a malicious party tho' she knew the whole disturbance was on her account and that her husband had at least been obliged to contradict the reports that concern'd him. In the evening the Craufurds came to us in a Neighbourly way and the Morris's dropt in so we play'd whist and sup'd pleasantly together. Mrs Craufurd seems after my own heart – she loves you very much.

8th – My Father has conquer'd this vile attack so we drove out to Kensington to call on D'Ivernois. The Servant ask'd for Mr

D'Ivernois and a tall figure advanced to the Coach, it was like our Friend, My Father said he wish'd to see Mr D'Ivernois; Monsieur je m'appelle D'Ivernois, said the figure; the voice and manner of speaking were exactly his. I began to think this was some strange Impostor, when I recollected that Miss Hamilton had told me D's Brother was with him which un-ravell'd the mistery. We then walk'd some time in Kensington Gardens but saw little company there. At our return we found the real D'Ivernois had call'd on us in our absence and had promised to call again in the Evening which he accordingly did. He was *enchanté* to see me and ask'd me a thousand questions in French about you, Mr L.,[1] la belle affligée and all friends, but as my Father don't *like* speaking French I forced D. to speak English in which by the bye he is no way improved.

With respect to the Genevese establishment I find it is totally at an end. What his own private plans are is more than I can devine as he is very reserved on the subject. He hopes however not to leave this Country till he sees you. God bless you my dearest love – a thousand loves to all.

Ever yours E.S.

My Father always desires his kindest love to you and Mr L. – à demain.

2 : LONDON, 18TH OCTOBER 1784

Monday, 18th – We dined yesterday with the Hamiltons. They had engaged in the Way of Men a Mr Smith who lives with them and D'Ivernois. Smith is a very sensible companionable Man – Attorney General in Ammerica. D'Ivernois and he seem particularly intimate. I have heard nothing of D'Ivernois but what was in his praise since I came over so you need not mind Dublin Scandal about your Friends. He talk'd half the day to me of you and Mr L. and seems to remember with gratitude the civilities shewn to him in Dublin. Mrs Dorine dined with us and enquired most particularly for you. She has great remains

[1]Joseph LeFanu.

of faded Beauty but one can not now call her handsome – tho'
I do see a resemblance to Mrs Sheridan. Her conversation turn'd
on the most melancholy subjects when she talked to me, a dread
of living seem'd to be uppermost in her thoughts. What a
Wretch she has been tyed to. Miss Woolery was also with us.
She is certainly a lovely girl – My Father admires her very
much. She shew'd me more of her paintings and Miss Hamilton
tells me she understands musick and sings pleasingly. She
speaks French perfectly well and in dancing she probably is not
deficient as she was in Le Pic's hands for some time. Her
Mother and Sister are gone to the Country as London was too
expencive and she is now left solely under Mrs Hamilton's
care. She has made every attempt to be allow'd a trial at either
of the Winter Theatres but has hitherto been disappointed by
the interference (as they suppose) of a Man who in her prosperous days had proposed marriage to her but deserted her
when her Fortunes changed – this Miss H. is convinced is the
Bar that stops them. She is an interesting Creature and I
sincerely wish her success. She has lent me Hayley's Plays.

I was just interrupted by a visit of two hours from Mrs
Craufurd – she is a delightful little woman. She has brought a
huge packet from Mr Coleman which I send by this post. He
is still at Margate. I saw the enclosed Balloon print in a shop
this morning so I got it as I think it will gratify Mr L. Mrs
Craufurd who saw him rise says it is a very exact representation
and I know it is just what I saw at the Pantheon. I also enclose
you a relick of Mr Blanchard's Balloon which you may present
to the Curious. We had an account yesterday that Sheldon had
sent an express to his Wife with notices of their being safe
landed at Guilford in Surrey, the paper of today gives a different
account, I don't know which is to be depended on.

You ask me how the Women here strike me – whether from
the advantage of dress or what I know not but they appear to
me to be full as Handsome as the Irish Women and in general
have less airs (but this *entre nous*). I read my Father what you
say of his life of Swift and he seem'd much pleased. As far as I

have gone I agree with you but I have not been able to find time to get thro' it. God bless you my dear love and Tom too – Love to Mr L. and to William. I assure you he stands high in the opinion of the people here from his letters. A thousand loves to Emily, I have introduced her to my Father who would be glad to see her so when you come put her in a corner of your portmanteau but I would not be so selfish as even to wish to rob you of her.

Now that I have a little composed my scatter'd senses I recolect all the people I omitted seeing when I left Dublin but my mind was a little in the state I have heard Mr Lunardi's described to be when he landed – he was scarce able to give any rational account of himself for several minutes. I am impatient to hear the fate of our Saturday's adventurers – the Child that was to have gone up belong'd to a poor Man who had consented for a sum of money to let her try how the upper Regions would agree with her but his heart fail'd him the night before and they were forced to go without her.

Once more adieu. My Father's best love ever attends you, he is impatient for his goods I can tell you – I wish he may get good tidings of them. The Shirts will be very welcome.

3: LONDON, 31ST OCTOBER TO 1ST NOVEMBER 1784

God bless you my dear love – I scribble to you when I can but from the account I give of myself you will see I have very little time. I breakfast with my Father and we always sit some time chatting which takes up my time. And the days we dine at home I always devote the whole evening to him. On the other days dressing, visit and a little necessary attention to domestic matters scarce leaves me time to breathe. We go on as well as possible and are likely to do so. He introduces me to every one as Young Wife – asks if he is not a bold Man to venture on so Young a One. I feel a little as I used to about *little Blossom* and am plaguily afraid the people will say "no such suckling neither", some say he has made a good choice and all are kind

[35]

and civil to the greatest degree. And it certainly is a pleasant thing to find oneself caressed and attended to, especially after having in some degree experienced the contrary. I tell you all this because I know these trifles are interesting to you. I must leave you to go to prepare for my company.

I assure you Madam I have business on my hands. I went myself to Market this morning. You know Carnaby Market which is an excellent one is close to us. I have already establish'd my self as Customer to Fish Monger and Poulterer so that I have only to chuze what I wish, my Butcher calls every morning, I go sometimes however to shew that I am willing to attend to these matters. I bought a very fine sallad Lettice &c. a good dish of Purple Broccola and another of Colly flower for 18d. Does that bear any proportion to the Dublin prices of vegetables? I tell you these things as they occur to tempt you here. I am almost like those people who having told the same lie often come at last to believe it themselves – I have so often told all your friends here that you will be here in Spring that I have persuaded myself it must be so.

Novr. 1st – My dear Love I will just add a few lines and send this off. Our day passed very pleasantly yesterday. I had a visit from the Siddons and her sister this morng. All disturbance about her is over but an opinion of her being avaricious prevails very universally and has hurt her in her private Character and will I fear injure her public one. For my own part I do not think she has shown a propper sense of what she owes my Father but I have avoided making any comment to him as I am sure he feels it.

Two letters from you are just brought to me – from the 20th down to the 25th. I will answer you tomorrow but we have dined tete a tete and I am summon'd to Coffee. God bless you my best love, love to Mr L. and our dear little Boy with four teeth.

4: LONDON, 15TH NOVEMBER 1784

Yesterday I was so busy I could not write – in the morning

preparing for my company – in the evening entertaining them. Our party were Yarkers, Oddies, Hargraves, Hendersons and Mr Jodderell. While I was making tea I received yours of the 10th and grew impatient to read it. Your verses are beautifull – why can't I write? If I could I would answer them, as it is I can only thank you. I shew'd them to Anne Yarker who wept her approbation of them – I like your beating me on her shoulders about card playing on Sundays. You know it is a thing I very early learn'd to consider as perfectly indifferent in itself and with regard to your arguments about Servants I think it only holds where it appears to them that you are acting wrong, but where a thing is universal as it certainly is here you must allow they can hardly see it in that light. If I thought I did wrong I should not do it, as it is I do it with the same indifference that I would sing dance or play Chess which you know is the way in which I have spent many a Sunday Evening and I hope innocently. Not but that I entirely agree with you that those hours might be spent in a much better manner.

This morning I went with my Father to Millbank to visit Mrs Roberts. We then call'd in De la Haye St. and as the morning was fine I proposed dismissing the coach that we might walk home thro' the Park. I saw Miss Woolery who had come down for the first time. Poor girl she looks wretchedly, the Hamiltons desire a thousand loves to you.

We then proceeded to see poor Mrs Morris, she made her appearance with a large black eye her left. I think I never heard more perfect patience than she shew'd on the occasion of this accident. They had a Young Gentleman on a visit to them who happen'd to stay out after the family were gone to Bed, the Servant who sat up for him had fallen asleep and on hearing him rap in vain poor Mrs Morris got up with the intention of awakening the Servant. She was in the dark and unluckily missing a step pitch'd head foremost down the whole flight of stairs, her son Michael hearing a noise call'd to her to know what was the matter, she said nothing – crept back to her room bleeding all the time from a cut over her eye and violently bruised in the body – she wash'd away the blood as well as she could and stole to bed. In the morning they found her in a shocking way but the poor little woman could not bear the idea of disturbing any one. She is now however pretty well.

When we left her we took a turn in the Mall. George Morris came with us he enquired most kindly for you. I had the pleasure of seeing that Puppy Pitt – I can tell you he is by no means popular and your Friend[1] I believe stands a very good chance but then 'tis great pity he games so deep and loves Women so bad. We took a good walk and Morris came to the door with us. My Father wanted him to take pot luck but he was engaged so we dined tete a tete.

After dinner I had a letter from Mrs Sheridan[2] but I beleive Charles wrote it first. She envites me back to the life of *comfort* and *content* which I may *remember* they lead there – Ma foi s'il m'en souviens, il ne m'en souviens guere. We intended going to the Angelo's, but Madam was gone to the new Opera at Covent Garden. You know she never misses anything of the kind. She exists but in a crowd but she is a good hearted creature. She and the girls never cease enquiring for you, Mr L. and our Tom. God bless you my dear Love I will send this off tho' I wish I was a little more in the way of picking up London intelligence for you but I can not at present leave my good Gentleman when he is all kindness and attention to me. He had a fine letter of congratulation from Mrs Wood last night on my return and with it a fine pheasant I suppose to feast poor Prodigal. Do you know Mrs Siddons' Tea party to me has done her no service in my Father's opinion. He has said it often. You know how he hates narrowness of spirit. By the way it is a great pleasure to me that we return the civilities we receive, but you know it is his way. As to the Ladle he did not think you had made yourself a present of it but he was glad he had it to give you and only regretted he had not more.

[1]Charles Fox.
[2]Charles's wife.

Monday – After I had sent off my packet on Saterday I received a note from Mrs Craufurd to ask us for Teusday and a present of fish by way of a peace offering I suppose, as people have generally a curious way when they have been wrong. I return'd her thanks but was forced to decline her invitation as we are engaged to dine at Brathwaites to meet Lady Saville – Mother to Sir George Saville. She is a great admirer of my Father's, and when she read his dedication,[1] she shut herself up for three days to cry over it in quiet. Yesterday we dined at Barnards. I do think Mrs B. is not the match of the *elegant* Barnard – but she has many appology's for Beauty, she has I think as good a countenance as ever I saw and is perfectly good humoured and unaffected. They made a thousand enquiries about you. They have almost put me out of conceit with your Picture as they won't allow it does you any sort of justice. Our party was small – nothing very entertaining – the dinner good but in the family way – we did not sup there and I was not sorry for it.

This day we dined at Mr Vesey's. I was introduced to the old Lady and Mrs Handcock a lady who lives with them, nothing could be more polite than their whole manner to me. Our party consisted only of Lady Dartree and Mr Bingham, son to Lord Lucan – a pleasing young Man perfectly free from the present fashionable airs. But I must talk to you of Lady Dartree for she is a woman after your own heart. She is about fifty but looks younger – Elegant in her manner, lively and pleasing in conversation, with that an excellent heart and a fine understanding highly cultivated. Her affability really puts you at your ease not like that of most fine Ladies whose attentions only remind you of your inferiority – in short she gives me the idea of those characters that Richardson has some times drawn but that few people beleive really to exist – had I rank and fortune how proud I should be of the friendship of such a woman. Mrs Vesey too is a charming woman tho' so far

[1] He dedicated his *Life of Swift*, published 1784, to Sir George Saville.

[39]

advanced – (she is near fourscore). She has all that old fashioned good breeding we so much admire join'd to a fine understanding and real taste – *Agmondesham* has not her head but he is well bred and likes talents in others. Our entertainment was elegant – *Ices* &c. &c. After Tea our circle was encreased by the arrival of *Mrs Carter* – on her being announced you may suppose my whole attention was turn'd to the door. I don't beleive you saw her when you were here. She seems about sixty. She is rather fat not very striking in her appearance, dressed in a scarlet gown and peticoat, a plain undress cap and perfectly flat head – a small work bag hanging at her arm, out of which she drew some knotting as soon as she was seated – but no fuss or airs about her. She entered into the conversation with that ease which a person has who has both their thoughts and words at command, but no *toss of the head* – no *sneer* – no emphatical look – in short no affected consequence of any kind. I wished for you as one who could not only enjoy but take a share in such society. It is not the fashion of the house to sup so at ten we came home and I *was sorry* the party broke up. They have however engaged me for Friday Sevenight when we are to meet Mrs Montague.

At my return I found a half angry letter from Charles which I shall answer as soon as possible. D'Ivernois had called I find, he wrote a note then burned it, and said he would come in the morning. In the morning I had a very kind note from Mrs Sheridan to enquire how I did as I could not go with her to the Opera on Saterday. Her horse is still lame so she could not call on me. God bless you my dear love – past one o'clock and *Litteraly* a frosty morning for the weather is colder than ever – good night.

Wednesday – Our party yesterday turn'd out very well. Lady Saville is very old and tolerably deaf, but good humour'd and unaffected, very plain in her appearance and does not seem striking in her understanding. With her came her Husband Dr Moreton and a Miss Pratt. Dr Moreton is Head of the Museum, a Gigantic Man who evidently has been handsome – grand diseur de rien and at the same time as Male creature laying violent hands on a considerable share of the conversation. Miss Pratt a good humour'd Irish girl, of about 5 or 6 and thirty, related to everybody and knows every body, daughter to a particular Friend of my Father's, but came here for 6 months and has staid 14 years. Sir George left her two thousand pound in his will as a friend of his mother's. Nothing could be more civil or attentive than the whole set were to me. I am to spend a day there soon so my wish of reducing my circle to a small compass is not likely to be gratified. Miss Braithwaite I like very much. She is really a companionable sensible girl. She tells me Mrs Whyte wishes much to see me as she had heard great accounts of *me* from Mrs Aikenhead, so I find you are the person she expects to see. To prevent a disappointment I told her, like Mle de Scuderi, that it was not I, but ma Soeur qui avoit de l'esprit. I was sorry to hear that poor Mrs Aikenhead has retired to France in the utmost distress. Dance thro' her interest got a good employment in Jamaica where he is gone to settle with his wife. I forgot to answer your question about Lord Deerhurst. I think he has no remains of beauty – one eye is open, the other cover'd with a green silk patch. I must leave you to attend our readings – *Proud stomach* is come down – they are likely to prove profitable, and I have fought and conquer'd some prejudices, which however I could excuse from the scenes of life I have at times been thrown in – but I never own'd my folly to any one but you.

Thursday – I have got J. Gilpin for you, so off goes my journal. The room was much fuller last night than the first – we had above six hundred people, all really delighted. All make up to me and are very civil – it would not be so in Dublin. My father really equal to what he ever was and if possible more admired – Henderson the pleasantest creature in the world. I went with my Father that I might chuze my own party at the Room. I fixed on the Yarkers. Mrs Craufurd came with a party but she left them and came to beg a place of me which I gave her. She regretted much I could not be with them Teusday as Mrs

Gilbert &c. were with her – poor Craufurd is still held fast by the hand. I saw Mrs Fitzgerald for a moment. God bless you my love. I have not time to add more, so my dear I shall give a further account of matters in my next. My Fathers best love allways.

6: LONDON, 8TH TO 14TH MARCH 1785

Tuesday – Yesterday I did not stir out – I expected a letter from Emily in the evening but got only a vile Hibernian journal. I was uneasy but would not give way to it. I wish she had thought of supplying your place by a journal if it was only one line a day. This day I have also spent at home I was to have gone with the Brathwaites to Hendersons benefit but I have sent them an excuse. I don't suppose I have any loss as He takes a Tragedy of Cumberlands. If the Arab is not better than the Carmelite those are best off who stay away. I have been watching the post – I will try to do like Mrs Foster and picture things to myself as I wish them. So God bless you my dear love.

Wednesday – I have just received my dear Emily's letter and am as you may suppose much easier than I was. I am truly happy she is with you and among them they will soon restore my own correspondent to me for I don't like this proxy work. I will go on with my journal to you as usual. This is the last night of the course so I must go. I have promised to sit with Mrs Wilson. God bless you my dear love and a thousand thanks to your good little nurse for her letter.

Tuesday – The crowd last night was astonishing. The Room is calculated to hold a thousand people but near Eleven hundred contrived to fit in by squeezing into nooks and galleries that had never before been opened. Mrs Wilson came late so I was forced to take one of the Morrises as my Chaperon till her arrival. Mrs Yarker had as usual reserved a seat for me but there was no possibility of getting near her. Another course was announced and received with great applause, so that it is likely to prove a profitable business – whether it will advance my

Fathers great plan I do not know. I had a thousand enquiries about you – D'Ivernois – poor Mrs. Morris who had heard you had been ill from Miss Hamilton. The company was in general more select than it had been, at least there were more people of fashion. But my Father was no way delighted with the crowd as it made it impossible to keep the room as quiet as he wished. He was a good deal fatigued but not the worse for it after, tho' he has been lately very much plagued with his windy complaint, at these times he dont like going out and I dont like leaving him so we have spent the day at home. Good night my dear love.

Saterday – Yesterday evening we spent at Mr Vesey's – a sort of *conversationé* – and reading party. The company was rather numerous – Lords, Ladies, Bishops – in the Literary way there was Miss H. Moore,[1] and the famous Soame Jennings,[2] who is without exception I think the most hideous mortal I ever beheld. Miss Moore is exactly de ces figures dont on ne dit rien – her manner is I think unpretending, at least it was so last night. My Father read one or two things which seemed to give the highest delight to the company. Lady Spencer came rather late and seemed to regret having lost the reading very much, so my Father to oblige her read a passage of Milton with which she seem'd greatly pleased and from her observations show'd both taste and sense. She is pretty and has an engaging countenance and is neither vain nor impertinent in her manner. My favourite Lady Dartree was there. We had also the great fortune Miss Pulteney – Heiress to thirty thousand a year. She is not handsome but no way unpleasing in her appearance and has none of the pride of wealth about her. I was disappointed in my hope of seeing Mrs Montague.

Mr Vesey's House is by no means large but by the exquisite taste of Mrs Vesey in disposing of things the apartments appear larger than they really are. As I was a stranger to most of the company I had little pleasure from the party – conscious that I

[1]Hannah More.
[2]Soame Jenyns.

was the only person in the room who had not some consequence in life from fortune, rank or acknowledg'd abilities, I felt alone in the croud and could not wholy banish the mortifying ideas this consciousness necessarily brought with it. Yet the people were all civil and attentive to me, but I have no business among them. I never coveted the honor of sitting at great people's tables and every day I live I wish for it less. There can be no true pleasure derived even from the most delightful society unless you feel you have a right to your place in it. I cannot make my Father feel the difference the world makes between a man of talents and the women of his Family unless these are at least independent. He wishes me to be intimate with Lady Dartree, so should I were the thing practicable, but our lines are totaly different and were she even to wish it, from my confined circumstances I could not be frequently with her, on a respectable footing, with any sort of comfort or convenience. These are ideas that never seem to enter my Father's head, but I own my wish would be to spend the remainder of my days in that middling state of society where people are sufficiently raised to have their minds polish'd though not enough to look down on a person in my situation.

This morning I call'd on the Yarkers, as Miss Y— had been ill. I sat a long time with them and they made a thousand enquiries about you and desired their kindest love. I then came home and spent the remainder of the day with my Father.

Monday – I have nothing to add but the warmest wishes for your health being restored and that I may soon have the good news under your own hand. My Father was ill yesterday and we spent the day at home. He sent for Dr Morriss and is I think better today – this day we spent at home. I have a thousand tickets lying before me which I must number and sign at full length for my Father, so I must leave you – Mrs Yarker told me the Arab was detestable.

I open my letter to tell you I have just received your little note of the 7th and my kind Emily's long letter both which have

[44]

made me happy. Do pray take Bark I am sure it will be of the greatest service to you.

7: BATH, 25TH APRIL TO 3RD MAY 1785

Monday – I this day received yours from the 15th to the 24th. I thank you for your Ballads and your Fancy Ball and mascarade intelligence, some of the songs are very well and I dont suspect Scot of having written them. Mary Walker was I suppose truly happy. But as Charles once told her she would be handsome with a mask on, I do not doubt that she met admiration sufficient to justify a little vanity and she is bless'd with a sufficient portion to keep up her spirits and make her go very comfortably thro' life. Poor Lady Landaff I pity, mais aussi qu'alloit elle faire dans cette maudite Galere. For what woman in her senses would unnecessarily put herself in the power of a perfect stranger? But I won't finish answering your letter without scolding you: So Ma'am I am to look out for a young Batchelor here – and Harry *says nothing* about coming home. I see how it is, I am thrown off and you are keeping him for someone else, but to be even with you I am determined not to accept of one of the numerous offers which I shall certainly meet with here. My father is mending but still does not stir out but to take the air. God bless you my dear Love.

Teusday – Still the same old life. – Airing – home and cards, not very enchanting but to say the truth I am not in spirits to enjoy any other. I was truly alarmed about my Father and with reason, and the effort I made at the time to support my spirits, unassisted by any comfort but what I could draw from my own reflections has left my mind as tired, as a person would feel their body after any extraordinary fatigue. The Fletchers have been as attentive as possible. She has made me jellies &c. &c. and Fletcher who is market man would have thought Ortalons a cheap purchase if my Father's appetite would have allow'd him to eat them. We had a letter today from poor Thompson who is in fear of losing his employment from a change that is made in the office he is in – the business it seems is to be removed to the treasury. He wrote to beg my Father to apply to Mr Beaufoy who has great influence with Pitt. My Father has written in the strongest terms so I hope the poor Fellow's fears will prove groundless. He has the strongest recommendations from all the Commissioners of the Stamp Office.

Friday – Yesterday as usual, but I think My Father visibly mending, his complexion is much clearer and his appetite much better. While we were on the Downs Miss Brook call'd so after dinner I went and sat an hour with her. I like her more each time I see her and regret her society more than all the amusements of Bath put together. Among other things she told me she had seen Mademoiselle D'Eon at Dijon and was delighted with her. She says *que c'est bien triste pour un Capitaine de Dragon de se trouver reduite à la Cornette*. I think so too – for with her spirit and understanding what an awkward situation is she reduced to. I have been reading her memoires and all the letters that passed relative to that shabby business of the Comte de Guerchy and to all the shabby treatment she received from the French Ministers. I don't know whether you have ever met the work but if you have not you will be pleased with it. There is such spirit and elevation of soul in all she writes, so superior to the fauning Courtiers and Secretaries one sees and hears of that she makes all her opressors sink into nothing. This instance alone I think a strong argument against Charles's favorite doctrine of Male and Female souls.

Tuesday, May 3rd – I have been so ill with a severe cold I have not been able to write for some days. The Maid of the House watch'd her opportunity to wash my room one evening I went to walk and it was quite wet when I went to bed as she did not light a fire or take any precaution to dry it – I have been out however constantly to take the air tho' scarce able to hold my head up. My Father is still mending but we cannot go into public.

I this day received a letter from Thompson to let me know that his *good friends* Mr R. Sheridan and Mr Beaufoy had secured him in his employment. I received yours of the 25th, and Maria's history last night and shall answer them to-morrow. God bless you my dear Love. I am just return'd from airing and have scarce time to dress for dinner.

8: BATH, 4TH TO 6TH MAY 1785

Wednesday – I sent off my journal in a sort of hurry yesterday as I was afraid you would be uneasy if you were longer without hearing from me. I have got quite well again and my Father is getting on and he allows himself that he is rather better. What is your plan for this Summer? – I wish for money every day, for certainly it could procure me the highest gratification I can taste in this world – the society of the few I truly love. How strangely Charles was wanting to himself in the neglect with which he suffer'd me to be treated. On looking back I am even more struck than I was at the time. My present situation is in those respects so very different that tho' as you will conceive I have many sacrifices to make yet poverty staring me in the face on the one hand and Charles on his knees to me on the other would not prevail on me to return to the situation I have left.

I met Miss Brooke on my return from airing and fix'd to spend part of the Evening with her. Her Father was with her – I don't know whether you have much recollection of him but I think him a disagreable Animal and unfortunately for Miss Brooke that is the general opinion – If the character of Old Vinaigre had not already appeared he would certainly suggest the idea of it – luckily he grew tired of our conversation and left us to ourselves, so I sat on chatting and listening to her Harpe much beyond the time I had intended giving her. She gave me leave to copy the enclosed for you. It is a letter Beaumarchais wrote to the Duc d'Aumont in answer to his application for his *loge grillé* for a lady who was too modest to make her public appearance at Figaro – There is more spirit and freedom in the stile than one would expect from a *particulier* to a French Duke.

Friday – Yesterday I received yours from the 27th to the 29th,

[47]

and am truly sorry to find how severely you have suffer'd from this vile easterly wind – 'till it changes there is no depending on a days comfort. I pity Parvisol from my soul but I can not see why the infamy of his relation should break off his intended marriage. The lady I should think must have very little attachment as surely his good character and conduct would more than ballance the wickedness of people who tho' related were little connected with him. This is pushing the ideas of honor to a degree of refinement equal to that of french nobility.

With yours came a letter from Grattan to My Father and another from Charles – that of the former was very grateful, very civil and written I beleive in his best manner but evidently a little labor'd. Charles very sentimental, *Surface'sh* &c. &c. – he presses my Father much to come over to a little Farm he has purchased with part of his *Wife's Fortunes*, and dwells much on the delight he should have in seeing him by his *fireside* – and introducing to him a *charming* daughter disposed to love and reverence him, and a dear little grandson who already *lisps* some words – lisp he must, for by your account he has no teeth. Can anything be more sickening. I confess there is scarce any emetick more powerful to my stomach than an affectation of sensibility where I know the heart to be truly selfish, perhaps my having been so completely *surfeited* with unmeaning professions may make me feel the disgust to every thing of the kind more strongly. However I do not apprehend that my Father will trouble him with his company. It is the last thing I should wish. If I am ever Mistress of the smallest independence – where you live will I live. And as my ideas of a competence are truly moderate I think I may reasonably indulge in the prospect of our spending many happy hours together.

I think my Father better but he is not satisfied of the matter himself. The Bath waters are certainly slow in their operation but he probably would be worse without them. I beleive he is tired of the place and wishes on that account to change the scene and would therefore persuade himself that some other water might be of more use to him. He seems to have a strong inclination to visit Spa – which I found out by his great concern at the fire that happen'd there, but Hutchinson is for his remaining here by all means, so that I suppose when we leave this a trip to Tunbridge will be the utmost of our travels this summer.

9: LONDON, 1ST TO 4TH JUNE 1785

Wednesday – Yesterday we had a visit from Luke Yarker who is come to Town for a few days, he caught us just going to visit them so we all went together. He wish'd to prevail on his sister to go to the Abbey[1] tomorrow. She was rather doubtful but at last it is fix'd that we both go with him and that I accept my Ticket from him. My Father had intended giving me one but I found I must offend the whole family if I refuse their offer.

In the Evening I had a very long visit from Mrs Sheridan. It was before her dinner hour and rather an awkward one but I have given orders never to be denied to her. She enquired kindly for you but did not seem well, she complained much of her head but indeed the life she leads would kill a horse, but she says one must do as other people do. They have given up Tunbridge on account of our going. I made one more effort with my Father but as unsuccessfully as ever. I am now convinced no human power can change his heart in that respect. I pray to God to do it as I think for his own sake it would be much better he could think and feel differently towards his Son, but I believe I must entirely drop a subject that only agitates his mind without producing any advantage to the people I wish to serve.

This day I have been kept at home waiting for Mr Marshall that my head may be beautiful tomorrow but I begin to dispair of him. Miss Hamilton has requested I would hear Miss Woolery read over Lady Russel which she is to perform tomorrow so I have appointed them to call on me but my Father will not see them. God bless you my love.

[1]For the Handel Commemoration.

Miss Woolery has just left me. I think she will be pleasing and interesting in the part. I wish the poor girl could get an engagement somewhere – with regard to Drury Lane, the whole system is not to advance a shilling that can be saved tho' it might be ever so much to their advantage. I spoke of her to Mrs Sheridan – she says their only objection is they do not want her, the fact is they have no one but that shock Miss Kemble to fill the cast she wishes to be in and the Town only suffer her on her sister's account. Mrs S. said she had heard her Mother[1] speaking very highly of Miss Woolery's appearance and that she seem'd much to wish she should be engaged, so perhaps something may turn out.

Friday – I meant yesterday to have given an account of my entertainment but could not leave my Father 'till bed time when to say the truth I was too sleepy to hold a pen. A little before nine Luke Yarker and his sister call'd for me as we thought to have our choice of places by going at that hour. However we found the middle Aisle entirely full and a considerable part of the others, but we got very good places. At twelve the performance began and never was I more truly delighted. The beginning of the Te deum was so truly great that my whole frame thrill'd and the tears ran down my cheeks in spite of me. I would have given any thing to have been behind a Pillar to have cried in comfort – but I was forced to struggle and almost choak to behave decently. I know you do not like that stile of musick in general but I am sure you would have join'd me yesterday. I thought it the only homage worthy of the Devine being which I had ever heard offer'd up. The number of performers did not by any means produce a too powerful sound. An Oratorio in the Round Church has appear'd to me infinitely louder. All was one compleat full sound the most perfect than can be conceived. The single songs appear'd to disadvantage I think after this glorious Band. Madame Mara was the only singer of real merit – her voice is uncommonly fine perhaps beyond Mrs Sheridan's, but that

[1]Mrs Linley.

something Angelic which was in the sound of hers is wanting as well as that beauty and expression which necessarily gave such additional charms to our sister's singing. Norris, Reinhold &c. you know, Fischer was almost beyond himself. At the Dead March in Saul a Second suffocation seised me. Indeed I had scarcely an idea of the power of instrumental music before.

I wish'd you with me for we suffer'd nothing from heat or croud from the amasing height of the building and the regularity with which every thing was conducted. The King, Queen, and the Three Princesses with two of the younger childred occupied two Boxes fronting the Orchestra. The Duchess of Devonshire and all the women of Fashion in a gallery near them. The Bishops in a seat adorn'd with Purple and our Bath Dr Cleaver so near as almost to rank among them. The Band which consisted of six hundred performers entirely fill'd a scaffolding that was raised almost to the Ceiling. The whole place was boarded and the side seats raised but not entirely to conceal the monuments, which added rather to the dignity and solemnity of the Scene.

With regard to the company the Women appeared to disadvantage as being forbid Hats and Feathers they had almost uniformly put on the most disfiguring head-dress I ever saw – A Mob of a most immense size, simply *illustrated* with blue or yellow ribbons – this over friz'd Heads and sallow complexions had a very bad effect – a few with fair skins and clear brown hair bore the disguise tollerably.

There was between 2 and 3 thousand people there – Crouds of clergymen. In the way of acquaintance I met some of our Bath gentlemen, D'Ivernois, and Purcell who sat just behind me. The whole performance was over at four and we got out without trouble or confusion. Mrs Yarker for fear the children should be famish'd had provided each of us with a paper of sweetmeats and another of cakes. My Father has consented to dine there to day so I must leave you to dress, so God bless you my dear Woman.

CHAPTER 2

Tunbridge Wells, June to October 1785

10: TUNBRIDGE WELLS, 12TH TO 14TH JUNE 1785

Sunday – After I had sent off my letter yesterday, I walk'd out with my Father to a Grove that is one of the most charming circumstances of this Place. It consists of Venerable Oaks, Beach and Elm, all of such a size as to form a compleat shade at noon on the warmest days. It is about a quarter of a mile round and about 2 minutes walk from our House. This delightful walk was bequeath'd to the wells many years ago, by some benevolent good minded soul whose name I have not been able to learn; It is so settled that a tree can never be cut down, the Corporation are Trustees to the Legacy and take excellent care to keep it in order and supply it with a number of benches for those who chuze to rest there, but this sweet spot is I am told quite deserted, no one walks but on the Pantiles.

Our young Man is I find only a Bird of passage so the Lady will be our only dinner companion probably for some time. She proposes walks &c. with me but it must not be. She thinks it necessary to be very wise with us, talks of books which probably she dont understand, and that in vulgar language. We have beside a number of lodgers in the House who do not board – six in one family, 5 of them Ladies, some young and some old. We curtesey when we meet, say good morrow and so on – pour cela tant qu'il vous plaira. Good night my dear Love.

Monday – This morning I observed at the Top of Hill that is facing our House a Grove which I concluded would afford both shade and a pleasing prospect. So I mounted and was amply rewarded for my pains. One can not conceive any thing more pleasing than the appearance of Tunbridge from that spot. Tho' a large village we have no streets here but each House lies separate and has a garden and often a field or two belonging to it. They are situated either immediate close to the Pantiles which to Invalides may be a circumstance of consequence or dispers'd on the surrounding Hills, which are call'd Mount-pleasant, Mount Sion, and Mount Ephraim. This is a smaller grove than that I saw yesterday but still is very pleasant, it joins the race ground where my Father was Riding while I walk'd. He mends visibly since we arrived. Both the Waters and the Bark which was prescribed for him in London agree perfectly with him, so that by the time the amusements begin I expect we shall partake of whatever is going.

This day our Fellow Lodgers (having eyed us and taken a little time to overcome the aversion 'tis said an Englishman feels to a stranger) have made great advances to us. The old gentleman, a Mr Hallet has paid my Father a visit, and the Ladies have all made civil speeches to me.

I am just return'd from a strole on the Pantiles where my Father met a few of his old acquaintance and I saw Mr Cumberland, supported by two daughters. He is almost a constant Resident here.

Teusday – I have been just returning the visits of my Neighbours – Mrs and two Miss Hallets, and Mrs and Miss Bright, all one family it seems. They are people of fortune but not fine Ladies which is the sort of society I like. They seem rational and civil and will do very well to prevent a forsaken feel on the walk or in the Rooms. As to my fellow boarder, I do not think she has a right to my acquaintance as I am so far from knowing who she is that I have not yet learn'd her name. I feel tempted to answer her invitations to walking with some of Barne's song – 'I know not your Name, Nor from whence you came, therefore *good Woman* I'd not go with thee'.

I have call'd since at the post office and found yours of the

5th. I think Kemble is in Clover among you all. What says the Gentle Patty? If she ever felt a preference I am sure it was for him. I think it would be a good match. So Miss J. Whitingham has hopes of being Lady Tremblestone? What a dear Bought title – Yet I am told she neither wants understanding nor rectitude of heart. Mrs Stratton was boring me to get my Father to read a play written by a friend of hers but he begs to be excused. You are a good Creature to talk as you do of plans for next Summer. Now my Father is getting well we must realize them one way or other.

As to Harry I am sure He ought to be much obliged to you for saving him all the plague and trouble of chuzing for himself in such a trifling business as matrimony and as continuing a Batchelor will now be attended with some expence, of course all those who have hitherto preserved their liberties, will be much inconvenienced at first by the necessity of looking out for an agreable companion. But I must tell you a secret which is that I fear this part of our plan must not be too much insisted on. I was told in London of a Lady who loved him and whom he loved, so you see you are not quite in his confidence. I have written a few lines to Maria which will keep her quiet these six months to come.

I forgot to mention to you that the Memoires of D'Eon I got at Bath was not the pamphlet we saw in London but a very large Volume containing a great variety of letters to different people.

11: TUNBRIDGE WELLS, 15TH TO 20TH JUNE 1785

Wednesday – After dinner we had an invitation from the Hallets &c. to tea. We found with them a very long young Clergyman who was not otherwise Beauish in his appearance than wearing two watches, however I found out he was quite the Ladies man, attended us in our walk and seem'd perfectly conversant in hairdressers fashions &c. We went to look at two Houses in the neighbourhood that command the prettiest prospect imaginable. The girls are all very good humour'd and pleasing in their

[54]

manners and the old people comme de raison let them enjoy life while they can.

I am more pleased with this place every day so I have been thinking that if any thing should prevent the Spa expedition we must make a party to spend the next summer here together – to tempt you I'll tell you our life. Rise at seven go down in a Habit to the Wells, walk on the pantiles, saunter into the library, look at the shops, say good morning to your acquaintance, come home, breakfast in a pleasant room – pretty garden before the door – Hills and Groves at a little distance. After breakfast go to my room – don't chuze walking in the heat of the day. Write, read, work a little – new dress my hair and clean shirt – all the toilet that is necessary here except on Ball nights or very particular occasions – very convenient this for Ladys who like me have no maids to give them any assistance in a female dress. At four come down to dinner, a tolerable society, very good dinner – everything well dress'd and provided without trouble – one of my favourite luxuries (you pay for board 16 shillings a week and ten shillings a room). After dinner chat a little, then walk in the garden either alone or with some of the Ladies, return to my parlour, drink coffee with my Father and then either walk with him or any party I chuze to form for the remainder of the Evening. At nine supper is ready but we seldom go in. There is nothing particularly delightful in the party and you know I don't eat supper so we have a biscuit and wine by ourselves and chat or sometimes play a little piquet to amuse my father till Eleven. When the season commences we are to have Balls, tea drinking &c. – so you see one may pass a little time here very well.

Thursday – This morning I walk'd down to the spring with Miss Hallet. I find them a very pleasing set of young women – perfectly civil and unaffected. We met on the walk an old General Robertson my Father had introduced me to who has offer'd me a very safe pleasant horse whenever I chuze to ride so I have gained another source of amusement. We rambled among the shops and I chose a few little toys which I will get

Mrs Clarke to take with her as she was so kind as to make me the offer when I saw her in London. Made one more unsuccessful attempt to get Mrs Bellamy's memoires. At Bath the Booksellers said they were sixty deep on their list before we had a chance and here I find I am at least ten too late in my application so that it will be like reading an old newspaper by the time I get it.

This evening we envited the Hallets and Brights to tea with us. The old ones play'd a quiet party of Whist while the young ones walk'd. I rather encourage this acquaintance as my Father seems to like them and it will enable him sometimes to have his party without confining me. Goodnight.

Friday – A most ruefull bad day – not able even to walk to the spring. Well good fires and our books will make it pass very well. This evening there is a little tea drinking to which the Ladies press'd me much to accompany them, but to say the truth I do not think any pleasure I should find there worth the trouble so I stay at home. I do not intend going to the Rooms if I can help it till Tyson arrives and then the company may make them in some degree amusing. I have left my Father very busy reading the Mirror with which he seems much pleased. We have not yet got the Volume in which yours is contain'd, but we must soon as my Father seems to have a great wish to see it.

Sunday – Yesterday my dear love I received yours from the 6th to the 9th. I was preparing to answer it and send off my packet when I found no post goes out on that day so I put by my paper and went out to walk to my old favorite the Grove. As I pass'd thro' a little gate open'd by a poor little old Man I told him I had no halfpence and would remember him another time – 'God bless you Ma'am,' said he, 'but I shan't know you again for I am blind' – tho' I had frequently passed that way this circumstance had never struck me, and indeed I found nothing particular in the appearance of his eyes. I asked how long he had lost his sight – 'about a year Ma'am, 'tis no wonder for I am very old, fourscore and two. I had a wife one year younger than myself and we lived happy together fifty years, about this time 2 years in the month of June we went to dine with a friend on a holyday, at dinner as my wife was eating, a bit went the wrong way and she was choak'd. I had her alive and hearty by my side and dead in my arms, in the space of four minutes.' I repeat the old man's words but I cannot give you an idea of the quiet but affecting manner in which he told his story. I went on to the Grove but soon left it. I could not conjure up my usual pleasant dreams, the idea of the poor little old man met me at every turn, so I came home and sat with my Father who had just got a volume of Mrs Bellamy – her whole story of the Play acted at Hamptonwick, and that of Mrs Furnival stealing the dress are totally the fabrication of her own brain – various other lyes he detects almost in every page, yet her sincerity is her chief virtue by her own account.

I have written to Mrs Sheridan,[1] was not that *proper*? A propos your approbation of my letters makes me smile and apply Molière's words, J'ecris donc de la prose sans le savoir. I certainly have the merit of not aiming at wit, therefore I do not miss, my whole idea is to amuse when I can with any anecdote, scene, or character that may fall in my way, and at all times to prove my regard by punctuality to our agreement, whether I am supplied with entertaining materials, or not. But as I scribble a great deal I am forced to write the first word that occurs, so that of course I must write pretty nearly as I should speak, and as I am not famous for much deliberation on that occasion I fear it requires all the partiality of a real friend to find out much merit in my Epistles, but I am pleased with that partiality and will go on and prosper.

Monday, 20 June – I am just returned from a walk with my Father. He has introduced me to a Dr Millman, a Physician, a very sensible Man and skilfull in his profession, his wife I was also introduced to, she is a pleasing young woman. My long Clergyman, Mr Egerton keeps up his acquaintance with me, and from the number of Persons my Father knows here I find I shall be in no want of acquaintances.

[1]Charles's wife.

I called at the toyshop and desired my purchases to be properly pack'd and tomorrow I shall forward them to Mrs Clarke – there is a box for you to put your netting in while you work it and to keep it in when you are idle, with lock and key – a little writing box for Madam Emily as may be she has not allways pen and ink at hand which makes her seem to forget her friends – a shaving box for Mr Lefanu which he must have the ingenuity to put in right order so as to be glass and box and all – a little case for William which holds pens, ink, sand and wafers, and serves as a ruler, you must find out four screws for him – and lastly there is a little pincushion which you will give Bee with my love. I was tempted to send a few more trifling toys but found it necessary to enlarge the Box that contains them and I was unwilling to trespass too much on Mrs Clarke's good nature. I hope you will like my taste. God bless you my dear love. My Father always desires his kindest love.

Let us know what Grattan does. Dick is a very warm friend to the Irish, Mrs S. cannot conceive the violent attachment he has to that country, but from her I found he acts on this occasion from his own feelings, totally independent of any wish his party may have to harrass the Minister.

12 : TUNBRIDGE WELLS, 5TH JULY 1785

I am not surprised you do not find Kemble improved, but I chose to leave the discovery to your own sagacity. In London I thought him spoil'd.

Now for the Article of fashions. I like your habit very much. I hope you wear no powder, all who have fine hair go without and if you have not quite enough 'tis but buying a few curls. We wear no belts over our Coats I have seen no such things but on great Coats – My Habit is what they call *Pitch* coulour – a sort of blackish green not beautiful but the most *stilish* now worn. Dark blues are very general – indeed all dark coulours are fashionable. cambrick frills and white waistcoats. Rather large yellow buttons. The most fashionable Hat a large black beaver with gold Band – but in that article you are perfectly at liberty – mine is a black Silk Spanish Hat with feathers.

Washing gowns of all kinds are the ton. Dark dutch Chintzes are very much worn, and now I think of it I must tell you I never had a gown so admired as my Irish Lawn. It has been wash'd three times and appears now if any thing better than when new, so tell Mr Porter if you think of it. It is always taken for a dutch Chintz but I take care to publish its country. As a Dress gown I have brought down a Robe à la Turque – violet coulour – the peticoat and vest white – Tiffany,[1] guaze and pale yellow Ribbons – with that a sash and buckle under the Robe. Guaze gowns and clear muslin gowns are much worn in full dress.

The undress Hats are straw, chip or Cellbridge or Cane, of the dimensions pretty nearly of your round tea table,[2] two rows of narrow ribbon or one of broad round the crown and three or four yards pinn'd loosely at the back. I have got a Celbridge for the Honour of Ireland, these are for walks or Church, as a more dressy one I brought from London a white Persian Hat – Tiffany quilt'd on it and bound with pale pink ribbon – at the edge a fine Black lace quilt'd thick to hang down, and still at the edge pale pink ribbon quilt'd which turns back, round the crown pink ribbon and black lace – it bends down a little behind and is worn with or without a plume of feathers. I have one for mine of dark sage, pink and white feathers – this is for the Rooms or any dress. Something of that kind is pretty general. I forgot to mention four or five yards of ribbon to hang at the back of the hat. Whether full dress Hats for balls will be worn I can not yet tell – the full dress caps are turbans with wreaths of flowers and feathers. Hats tied under the chin, beefeaters etc are not worn by fashionable people. Muslin Cloaks are very much worn – dress cloaks to go round the waist and fall behind like a scarf – pale pink and straw coulour and pale blue seem rather prevailing coulours. I will send this off on account of the important intelligence it contains.

[1]Tiffany – gauzy silk or muslin.
[2]The editor still has this table – 29½ inches across.

Thursday – I dispatch'd my scrawl yesterday in a sort of hurry. This Morn we ask'd the Leighs to Breakfast with us. I purposely did not envite them in an Evening as I think it no compliment to envite people to spend their time in a duller way than they would if left to themselves. Mrs Leigh is what one calls a pretty sort of woman, very civil and a good deal of the old Irish gentleness of manners.

At dinner a trifling circumstance occurr'd that reminded me of what we have often observed together of the want of that delicacy in most people that prevents their entering into the feelings of others. From being one of the first Ladys that came here it falls to my lot to sit at the head of the Table. I had given orders to the servants never to place a large joint of meat before me, not from Laziness as you know I am no away averse to carving but that I do not think a sirloin of Beef or saddle of Mutton a pleasant bouquet in the month of July – however this day a loin of Veal was placed before me. I perceived all the Gentlemen were out but Captain (*Graham*) *Gream* (that is the right way to spell his name). My Father was going to order the dishes to be changed when I gave him a look which stop'd him, but one of the Ladies immediately call'd – Lord, Miss Sheridan why dont you send that dish down to Captain Gream? The Poor Fellow look'd distress'd – said he wish'd he *could* save Miss Sheridan the trouble – I never felt more vex'd.

I have just been reading Hackman's letters – considering them as genuin they greatly add to the compassion I always felt for that unfortunate Man. What a dreadful lesson for those who think a criminal attachment can ever be indulged with safety – for such his appear'd even to himself so long as Miss Ray continued with Lord Sandwich, and more particularly so from the obligations she lay under to him. He was in Ireland in the year '76.

Friday – This Morning Lady Anstruther gave a breakfast to which we were invited. Our party was not large as it seems a real matter of difficulty to collect any number of people together. Lady Anstruther is a true scotch Woman, civil rational and unaffected and speaks the *scotch dialect* with great purity. Miss Anstruther as I before mention'd Elegant, fashionable in her appearance, but nothing of that *provenance* in her manner that caught me so much in Miss Brook. The Old General introduced me to his Lady, a fashionable woman and well bred. She had a young lady with her whose name I could not learn but I found her the least distant or formal of the party. We had also Lady Elizabeth York one of the Lady Lindsays. She is reckon'd a beauty, but I think her very much inferior to Lady Margaret Fordyce.

We broke up early and some of the party went to see a Giant who is here but I have seen sights enough so I went to walk in the grove with one of the Miss Mallets whom I call'd on. I then went to the post office where I found yours of the 2nd I am happy to find your torment[1] is going or gone as you do not mention it. I am sorry you have no Irish politics for me as my Father is deeply interested in whatever relates to his Hero Grattan – I think I see Mary smiling.

I wish I could send you some of my flowers I have so much fruit and flowers here as if I had the best garden of my own. Those articles are very plenty here and my Father you know is the reverse of shabby in all those respects.

Well but we are positively to meet next summer, that is you come to us for I fear my Father will hardly be tempted to visit Ireland – so there must be no encrease of Family. My Tom will be a great boy by that time. For his sake I feel a particular regard for young gentlemen who reckon by months – this morning I met three fine children of Dr Milman's in the Grove – one little fellow of eight months old caught my attention by a resemblance as I thought to my dear little Boy, while I was looking at him he laid violent hands on my nosegay, which I most willingly gave him to the great delight of the Nurse, who attributed my apparent fondness for the child to

[1]Toothache.

[61]

his merit when in fact my feelings really refer'd to my nephew.

Miss Belsey has taken a particular fancy to every article of dress she has seen me wear and frequently apply's for patterns, this I most readily comply with. Last night she was examining my dress cloak and ask'd whether I thought it fit to *dance* in – I told her I could not give her information on that head as that amusement made no part of my plan for the Summer. Can you blame me for chuzing rather to resign the very youthful pursuits rather before my time, in preference to the ridicule which it is impossible an *old girl* can escape. Now I am on that topic I am struck with a great difference in the treatment of single women here and in Ireland. It seems as in France, to be *un état*, no ridiculous jokes on *Old Maids*, no anticipation of young ones becoming so. No Man here thinks of marrying without money and as tolerable fortunes are so much more general than in Ireland a Man finds little difficulty in uniting interest and liking. Now as the Men in Ireland who have the means of supporting a wife are very ready to overlook the want of money in a Woman who pleases them, It seems as if a girl was either totally without merit, or foolishly ambitious, who remains upon hands, as they phraze it, and so I account for the disregard generally shewn there to Maiden Ladies, and as slights displease, their tempers gradually sour 'till at length, in her own form, up starts a Miss Ellard etc. My addressing all this to you reminds me of Cambell's letter to my Father about the great rains in Cork, not much to the purpose.

14: TUNBRIDGE WELLS, 3RD TO 8TH AUGUST 1785

Wednesday – This is a most dreary rainy day – no Ray of light but the absence of Miss Belsey – too bad even to venture out in a Carriage. Yesterday we had new Ladies – Quakers – one about six foot high large in proportion – the other between three and four and thin in proportion. They quietly took their seats beside each other at the foot of the table and I would not have met your eyes for a hundred pounds, indeed it was a universal effort to refrain from laughing.

Thursday – My Father had not dined below for a day or two and yesterday for the first time he beheld our Quaker guests. As his aversion to frightful Women about equals that of Mr votre Beau Père he made his escape to the Top of the table at the expence of Miss Farley whose seat he seized on – however to justify his dislike these women are shockingly vulgar. This Day he again saw them and his aversion seems to encrease.

Friday night – Nothing but alterations and revolutions, my Father's dislike to our primitive Christians has risen to such a height that he declared to me he could not digest his dinner in such company and so we withdrew from the boarding table. I am not glad of it as a little society was better than none but to say the truth those Women are too much in the Cook Maid stile.

Sunday night – Yesterday our desertion from the table spread a general spirit of revolt. Mr Onslow declared off, Mr Dashwood said he would look for other lodgings and poor Hilliard did not chuze to remain Page au Vielles. Mrs Dale and her little friend have left us this week. Mrs Hodges allarm'd at the impending ruin promised to dismiss the objectionable part of her company and all remain'd pretty quiet. It is rather provoking to have our party so compleatly knock'd up just as we promised ourselves some comfort from the absence of Mr Knightly and my eternal torment Miss Belsey. Onslow is one of the best natured beings in the world – A Man of Family and who was many years in the Army. Dashwood is very well and Hilliard just one of those young Men that in your *wicked* days you would have found pleasure in turning his head – he seems not more than one or two and twenty.

This Evening We were again at a public Tea drinking and I was introduced to new female acquaintances – Mrs Bagshaw and her daughter. They are Irish. The Girl very Elegant in her appearance and I am told a remarkable fine dancer, the Mother good humour'd and Civil but talks nineteen to the dozen, Rouges highly and dresses rather younger than her daughter.

We have few Beauty's here – A Miss Drummond is the only one who in my opinion merits the title. She is really a most lovely woman. Fairer almost than any thing I have seen yet her countenance animated but perfectly modest and free from affectation. My Father dined out for the first time and I eat Chicken all alone, for Mrs Dale whom I meant to have ask'd was better engaged by a visit from her Husband. God bless you my Love it is late.

Monday – Within these few days I got the last Volume of Bellamy. I wonder that she who is so fond of quotations from her favorite Shakespeare did not think of a very applicable passage to the description She gives of her intention of drowning herself – or rather letting the river come over her. Certainly the Grave-digger's reasoning about Ophelia might have come in there with a very good grace.

I attempted too to read *Lady Barton* and was I own astonish'd to see comme bien il faut peu de merite et d'esprit pour charmer the world in general – and this very moderate production is introduced with a preface more replete with vanity and self consequence than would be pardonable in the first genius of the age. I could not resist the temptation of pointing this out to my Father, as Madam Frances is one of the people of the world who had very undeservedly obtain'd his good opinion, but he begins now to see her such as she really is.

I shall get Heron's letters if I can but our library here is by no means well furnish'd, and I am told the good gentleman who owns it scorns to admit any intruders into his collection – The same Volumes allowing for losses having occupied his shelves these twenty years.

15 : TUNBRIDGE WELLS, 19TH AUGUST 1785

Tomorrow no post leaves this so I write an Extra, to let you know that my Father is at last thank God fairly in the Gout – And has received the congratulations of Dr Millman on the occasion. The fact is that all his Phisicians have wish'd for this event but seem'd fearfull that he had not strength enough to throw off his disorders in that way. You may suppose this is a hundred pounds weight off my mind as nothing is so dreadful as these undermining complaints, which assuming a variety of allarming forms keep one in perpetual apprehension of the worst that can happen. In the midst of his friends' congratulations the good Gentleman is in great pain and totally without the use of his right hand which is intolerably swell'd and wrap'd up in flannel. If you are well and have leisure I should wish you to write him a line as I know it will please him. Your Parlimentary intelligence made me a Woman of consequence, as I communicated the first accounts of the house having met and adjourn'd, a subject of great anxiety here.

At dinner my usual ten Gentlemen – Hilliard has got next to me and carves which is a comfort to me. The Americans are genteel pleasing young Men; two of them (Brothers) fought under Washington, and speak with such feeling and enthusiasm on the subject of the troubles of their country that one grows unavoidably interested. My friend Onslow not having an idea in his head, takes care compleatly to cut across the conversation with unmeaning stories and observations. Is it not provoking that one booby should have power to disturb one's comfort and even prevent one's getting information? And yet there is no authority from Law to gag such people – My Father and Hilliard have plan'd to make Mr Onslow (who is fond of introducing fines) propose in full assembly, a fine on any person interrupting another. If their plan succeeds he will of course be silenced – as his whole conversation consists of interruptions and he is most comfortably unconscious of his want of powers of entertaining.

Before tea I took a long walk, Hilliard overtook and join'd me, and when we return'd I brought him up to tea with my Father – I thought a third person better than the tete a tete. H— does not play piquet but after a time we did and he took a lesson as he is really anxious to be in my Father's company and would at any time give him his time or attention.

[65]

Teusday – This day I receiv'd yours of the 17th – I wonder at Charles's impudence in going to tell you of his expectations from government – he has already more than he deserves, and how dare he talk of soliciting more for himself while his debts to us remain unpaid. Indeed my dear love I am beyond all bounds and were I to speak one quarter of what I feel I fear my expressions would be infintely stronger than I should wish at any time to use. I feel to that Man as Palmira when Mahomet appears to her in his true coulours – 'See here – the friend I trusted', I can not to be sure add 'the God that I adored'.

Last night my Father was looking at a watch Charles exchanged with him on his going to Sweden, and observing that the gilding was worn away, 'Just such', said he, 'was the exchange we made in friendship; for my pure gold he return'd me base and worthless metal.' Poor Man he affects me when he talks so, as I am certain he has felt what it is to have a thankless child in the utmost severity, and yet he perseveres in putting away some comforts he might enjoy.

Today the Prince is here again and was at the Ball, some of our Gentlemen staid at home to make our whist party which my Father now seems to enjoy. In the morning he rode out and I took a long walk with Hilliard, he has done me a kindness by giving up his room to me which was not only better than mine but in a more pleasing situation as I was the only woman on the floor I slept on and my room surrounded by the apartments of the gentlemen so that I could not stir without being heard and some times seen. When I took possession of my new appartments I found two pots full of very fine flowers left for my use. After dinner he came up after me and press'd my acceptance of a very elegant lady's purse which he said he had won at a raffle, however I thought it best to decline his present, and as he has a Mother and Sisters of whom he is very fond, and always sending them presents, he may dispose of it in that way. If I was with Charles he would think it absolutely necessary that I should shut the door in his face or stand accused of villainous designs upon his heart, but luckily my Father thinks it very possible a Young man may find pleasure in shewing good nature and attention to a woman without any particular design.

Wednesday – The Prince has continued here – breakfasted at the Rocks and on his account there was a Ball again tonight, and some of his train chuzing he should have a Supper at a small expence sent round to all the Gentlemen to propose their joining in a subscription for the purpose, not one of our party subscribed which I was glad of as I think it is a most shabby peice of business, for if the Prince was not of that famille bourgoise he would have taken this opportunity of paying some compliment to the company.

This day my Father received the pamphlet and Mr L—'s note and returns many thanks, he seem'd pleased with it. I had only time to skim it over as he wish'd to send it to Lord Cremorne (late Dartree) – he returns you many thanks for sending it. Lady Cremorne has been here these two or three days but I have not seen her, nor do I expect to form an acquaintance as I had hoped, as my Father still does not go out, except for exercise. Good night my dearest Woman.

17: TUNBRIDGE WELLS, 26TH TO 28TH AUGUST 1785

Saterday – This morning died my Lord Sackville in the 71st year of his age. I think I told you he has a house in this neighbourhood where he has been ill some time, but his disorder was not apprehended to be dangerous, 'till he chose to indulge in eating a pine Apple and drinking Champaigne expressly against the advice of his Phisician – his complaint was in his bowels, and this imprudence it is supposed has hasten'd his end. As a Public character his loss does not seem to be much regarded, but I am told that nothing can exceed the greif of his poor Neighbours and Tenants. Mrs Herbert[1] has been with him for some time.

[1]His daughter Elizabeth, Mrs Herbert of Muckross.

This day we have spent alone as my Father was too much plagued with wind to like a party. His Friend and favorite Mr Erskine has been confined with abscesses that have form'd in his cheek and throat ever since the morning he arrived. Mr Hunter is here attending him, and his Lady who is in my Father's opinion the finest Woman here and I am pretty much of the same opinion. She has one of those countenances that I like, spirited good humour'd and free from affectation, at the same time that she possesses a considerable share of *real* beauty as our Sister calls it – good night my dear Love.

Monday 28th – Yesterday my dear Love I received yours of the 22nd and am heartily glad to find you are again at Annefield as I am sure you will lay in a stock of health for the Winter. You are never a fool in talking to me of Tom, you know he is my Boy as well as yours.

This day we had an accidental Guest at dinner, the Widow of a Governor Paterson. She had come here with her two Boys to dine with Mrs Hunter who happen'd to be gone out, so having formerly lodged with Mrs Hodges she proposed joining our party in preference to dining at an Inn. She seems not to want sense, chats freely on any subject, but has that masculine manner which military Ladies are apt to acquire. After dinner she mention'd her business in this country was to visit her Sons who were at School at Tunbridge, but to my utter astonishment She spoke of the Master in the most disrespectful tones and encouraged her Son to turn him into ridicule, tho at the same time she declared she meant to leave them with him 'till they were fit for the university – What can one expect from beings brought up with such extraordinary notions? Yet this is the present system of education. Every one ranting at schools and schoolmasters yet still sacrificing so many years of their childrens life to them.

The Dashwoods had been absent and return'd this day. The Handsome one is a very pleasant good humour'd creature. He does not appear to be above 25 and yet I find he has been some time Captain of one of the West India Packets, he has all that honesty and good humour that distinguishes Sea men and at the same time is perfectly civil in his manners, the other is an inoffensive being but I think a Coxcomb. This day we have again spent at home. Our Weather has been something better so that my Father gets his rides which are of use to him but I can not say he has received benefit from the Waters – he talks now positively of the Spa expedition for next year so remember. He lent *the Pamphlet* to Lord Cremorne who says it is without exception the *best* he ever read, he then lent it to Dr Millman who beg'd leave to lend it to Lord Mansfield and all approve of it but the secret is kep't – how poor a use has the author made of the Talents God has given him – But talents alone will neither form a loveable or respectable character.

18: TUNBRIDGE WELLS, 16TH AND 17TH SEPTEMBER
1785

Friday – I have just now been answering a letter I received from Thompson about our Lodgings. It is not quite fixed we shall be there but I hope it will be so. I have written to let him know we shall be in Town in three weeks but if the weather is tollerable I do not think we shall go sooner than a month. I can not say I am in the least hurry to visit London. Dick and his Wife are I find gone into Cheshire on a visit to Lord Derby. This morning I took a long walk with the Yarkers. We met Hilliard who said his departure was put off for a day on account of some intelligence he had got of a bank note he contrived to drop yesterday and which he found had been changed at the coffee House here tho' he had it cried and advertised – on my return home I found the purse he had before offer'd me, on my dressing table which he had left on the idea of setting off immediately, so all things consider'd I thought it foolish to mortify him with a refusal of such a trifle, so I keep it. He has been all day in pursuit of the finder of his note so we have seen nothing of him. I met Lady Anne Lindsay today but so *bedevil'd* by dress I should not of known her; in order to give you some idea of

[69]

what liberty a *Beauty* thinks she may take with her person I shall describe her to you – a thick muslin round-ear'd cap close to the face – no hair to be seen – a Hat of chip, alternate black and white circles, lined with black and put on in that style which has lately been distinguished by the appellation the Gypsey fashion but which formerly was confined to those elderly Ladies who mounted on shabby palfreys used to jog to market and sell eggs – a black and white spotted cotton petticoat – over that a black cloth great Coat and a thick muslin neck handkerchief compleated this ellegant accoutrement.

Saterday – H— has found the Gentleman who changed his note. He had received it, it seems, in change of a larger note from a shop keeper on the Walks, who can not be brought to own she found the note but pretends she took it and changed for a Lady's Maid whom she pretends she knew yet can not any way particularise her. H— has employ'd the Crier to desire this imaginary being to make her appearance but I beleive he wont get much information. The Gentleman insists on paying him the money and he wont accept it so this silly affair detains him a few days longer. Mrs Yarker brought us all home to breakfast with her and when the Gentlemen rode out we Ladies took a long walk – they always desire a thousand kind loves to you. At dinner we had a new comer and Captain of a Man of War of the name of Cummings – between Six and seven feet high and large in proportion, au reste seemingly good humour'd and polite. Between dinner and tea we took our usual walk and play'd whist. In the morning I had a visit from Lady Cremorne who said she did not know of my being here 'till yesterday or she would have come sooner. God bless you and good night my dear Love.

19: TUNBRIDGE WELLS, 20TH TO 23RD SEPTEMBER
1785

Teusday – I this moment have received yours – How much I wish myself among you with your Piper and with what spirits

[70]

would I have join'd in your dance. The School-master I
mention'd is Vicesimus Knox. He is reckon'd a man of Learn-
ing and some Cleverness, but married to a strange Woman who
probably gives cause for the complaints of the Parents. I am
told she is ugly, illiterate, absurd and ridiculous in the highest
degree, but professes to adore her husband and by that means
governs him compleatly and scarce allows him any comfort in
life. I am sorry you are not in the Play at Sir James Tynte's as
you delight in the amusement and really excell in it but I
should not have been satisfied if you had not by some means got
possession of a capital Part. Yesterday evening we walk'd out
and met some of Mrs Hasting's train just arrived – a parcel of
black boys and other foreign comodities. They are to occupy
the House the Duke of Leeds has hitherto had. This morning
I walk'd with the Yarkers to the Pantiles and after breakfast
went with them to the Grove, where I was join'd by my old
friend General Robertson, among other things he told me I was
treading poetic ground, for it was in that Grove that Mr
Cumberland composed *the Carmellite*. I own I thought myself
fortunate when I reflected on the many solitary walks I have
taken there, that the same Muse had never thought of inspiring
me. R— added that it had been remark'd as a lucky circumstance that Cumberland's tragedy's and comedies succeed each
other for were they to come together they would certainly produce a very bad farce.

Thursday 22nd – I have been unusually sunk for some days
by my Father who has taken it into his head to get into some of
his after supper conversations with me which never fails to send
his hearer weeping to her bed. Last night he was unusually
violent – Charles's conduct is the sorest part in his heart and
dreadful as these scenes are to me yet I sometimes think this
vent may be an ease to his mind and therefore tho' I endeavour
to the utmost of my power to soften matters yet I think it in-
cumbent on me to listen. Among other things in speaking of
both his Sons having shut him out from all means of support,
he said he could not have *subsisted* but for the money the readings

[71]

produced last year. If so what is to be done for I much fear from his state of health all future hopes of that proving a resource must be given over. His only hopes seem now the Accademy. Yet supposing all difficulties removed (which is more than I dare hope) how can he, confessedly beginning to labour under the infirmities of age, attempt so laborious an undertaking. He was never so explicit to me with respect to his circumstances as last night, but I have been thinking very seriously of the subject to see if there was any elligible and practicable method of mending matters. I wish to consult you on the result of reflection which is this: You know many years have pass'd over my head since we talk'd of opening a school in Dublin. The variety of causes that made me then see the plan in a dissagreable point of view no longer exist. The prospects I then thought I saw before me are closed; the youthful vanity or gaiety that made me shrink from the situation is I think pretty well over, and I could now very contentedly enter into any sober rational way of life that would produce the comforts of life to my Father and independance to myself. Had Charles behaved with common honesty to us, in giving up to us a hundred a year each, of his large income, when he found he could not procure for us what he had solemnly bound himself to obtain for us, it would in a great measure enable me to give my Father my company at my own expence but as it is, in my present situation I find it impossible to spend less than I do, when I include under the article of cloaths every incidental expence that to keep up the appearance of a Gentlewoman in the most moderate manner is necessary here – I say here, because poor Gentlewomen are not so common as in Ireland.

Mrs Dexter speaks in raptures of the pleasure your visit has afforded her, but She says the Goths in her neighbourhood had the impudence to think of your playing second to that Automaton Mrs Kennan – you never mention'd the circumstance or I should have exclaim'd 'Fire and fagot for the Witch' long since. The Yarkers drank tea and play'd a sober rubber of whist with us. This morning I have not been able to stir out, the weather is shocking to a degree, stormy, raining, true hanging weather, so I have been busy doing some little jobs that are very necessary but that one is apt to neglect, when the 'fair day invites the world abroad' – God bless you my dear love. The clock says it is time to dress.

Friday – Yesterday at dinner I was agreably surprised by the arrival of Mrs Gillies who has return'd for the remainder of the Season. She tells me St Leger and Anne Angelo are gone to France for a time as it is convenient from motives of oeconomy – hang this vile money. So my dear Harry stays still abroad and I had fed myself with the hopes of his sometimes enlivening our domestic circle next winter as my Father is really partial to him and there are so very few Whose intimacy he encourages. I think you must lay your commands on him to return.

20: TUNBRIDGE WELLS, 1ST TO 6TH OCTOBER 1785

Saterday Oct: ᵉ 1st – Thursday I left you to attend our Michaelmas Goose: The party were in good humour and Dr Greaves to celebrate the day insisted on spending some money, which he said he had won at cards the night before, in Claret for the benefit of the party. Good wine you know puts men in spirits and my Father who was begining to think the Dr a Coxcomb found out he was a good natured fellow and ask'd him with the rest of the Table to tea and cards in the Evening. Last night we had a Ball – The last at which Mr Tyson is to officiate, so we may now consider the *Season* as closed. I had promised the Yarkers to go to one more Ball so I accompanied them last night, but if the dread of heat and crouds had made me shun them before I now suffer'd from the contrary inconvenience for never was any thing colder than we found the rooms on our first entrance – Sir Richard Rycroft introduced his son to me as a Partner so I forgot my former resolution and danced away 'till I got well warm'd – my Partner was a very pretty young man, modest and unaffected. I was glad to find I could conquer the blue devils, but the fact is my mind has been a good deal

[73]

easier of late on my Father's account than it was for many months.

In the way of *wonderful* People there were only Mr and Mrs Hastings. She as plain in her dress and appearance as possible. One looks in vain for any trace of that beauty that could have induced Hastings to purchase her of her former husband. As to him if a Painter wish'd for a model by which he was to give an exact representation of *Care* he could not have a more perfect one. Lady Margaret Fordyce was by much the most beautiful Woman in the room. She and Lady Anne drive about in a carriage with both their Cyphers on it, so that poor Fordyce seems quite out of the question, I have not been able to learn even where he is. Lady Cremorne yesterday left a card to take leave, so you see we have been very fashionably acquainted – indeed she could not invite me to her House as her children had the chin-cough[1] of which my Father is very much afraid. But at all events I can not say I wish for the acquaintance of people of rank. The fable of the Iron and the earthen pot always occurs to me and is fully verified in the plague, expence and mortifications that attend an intercourse between people of great disparity of fortune and more particularly between Women – à propos to Women our present set are as tiresome, as exacting, as prating, as observing, and as illnatured as one could wish. This morning they had engaged the Yarkers to go to the Rocks and kindly intended leaving me out of the question, (tho' I have paid them every possible civility) however my Friend Anne call'd for me and I join'd them with the most provoking unconsciousness of their very impolite behaviour. The morning was uncommonly fine and the country beautifull so that I really enjoy'd my walk very much – but it is a pretty long one and we were all tollerably tired. In the way of Episode I should have told you that the Ladies eat cakes and milk at a little cottage that is inhabited by a poor Woman who supplies tea and breakfasts to company who chuse to indulge in a rural repast at the Rocks. I knew the Prince of Wales had break-

[1]Whooping-cough.

[74]

fasted there in one of his excursions to Tunbridge, I ask'd the Woman what he had given, She told me – *nothing*. The breakfast was paid for by Mr Bridgeman, but She was obliged to pay ten shillings for *Waiters* and She said that was the *first* party that had not left some thing for waiters as it is known She must hire them for the occasion; I am sadly afraid our Prince takes after the dear Father as to generosity of character.

Wednesday – I should wish to write every day but for every reason I think it best not to do so while my mind is under actual agitation from any unpleasant circumstance, this was the case yesterday. Monday my Father entirely of his own head chose to renew the hateful subject of his Displeasure to his Sons – I said little, hoping he would drop it – however I was not to get off so, As I found I had given offence in a point where I thought my conduct had been delicately cautious. He reproach'd me with having endeavour'd to persuade him to see Mrs Sheridan – A circumstance that happen'd *twelve months* ago, and an attempt which I never offer'd to renew – and declared himself much *displeased* with my conduct in not having join'd his resentment to Richard instead of proposing a reconciliation – so unexpected an attack and so strange a return for my constant attention and sacrifice of every wish since I came over I own cut me to the Soul. I said nothing to irritate him but he must have seen he had hurt me very severely. He then went into his usual complaint of ill conduct of both his Sons and even hints as if he may be driven to appeal to the world if they persevere in denying their assistance to his favorite plan. I should wish to know from you if you think a hint of this might not allarm Charles so as to make him do thro' fear, what neither gratitude, affection, or indeed common honesty have not been able to urge him to. I should wish if possible to be of service but I have such characters to deal with that I am fearful of taking any step lest with the best intentions in the world I might unfortunately only do mischief. After such a Scene you may suppose I did not pass a pleasant night, and tho' I endeavour to reconcile my mind to these things, Yet agitation always affects

[75]

my health. I got up wretchedly ill. We had promised the Yarkers to breakfast with them – My Father all good humour to me but 'break my heart and give me a please' will not do, however I held up pretty well while we were together, and then came home and cooled myself with pennyRoyal water.

Thursday Night – I shall execute your commission with regard to the writing Box. I put into a raffle for one this morning so if fortune favours me you shall have it from this, if not I shall delay the purchase 'till I go to Town as I find they are cheifly made there and sold much more reasonable than what the Gentry on the Pantiles chuse to charge us.

CHAPTER 3

London and Bath, 1786

Saterday – You see I have not learn'd to copy a Friend of ours in making several dates to a letter that is in fact written at one time. Since Wednesday it has been out of my power to write as you will see by the history of these last four days. I mention'd in my last that I meant on Wednesday to see 'The Heiress' but according to my usual luck George took it into his head to change our entertainment to 'The Country Girl' and 'The Romp'. As I had engaged Mrs M— I did not chuze to put off going and She call'd on me, as I thought in very good time; however when we got to the House We found ourselves in such a Croud as I never before encounter'd. We had a young Gentleman with us (a Mr Morris) but he could give us no assistance. After we had nearly reach'd the Box Office a cry of Pick-pocket raised a general confusion and those at the top of the Stairs were forcibly push'd down by the pursuers of said Gentleman. At this instant I saw a door open into a sort of lobby, into which I made Mrs M— enter but found it impossible to accompany her and was by the Croud brought Back to the Street. What made the croud so intollerable was that I firmly beleive three parts of it were pick-pockets, for the Constables Bawl'd themselves Hoarse in telling them the house was full without making the least difference in the number. Again the Torrent push'd me up to the spot where I had left Mrs Morris where we had the pleasure of cooling our heels for half an hour, during which time we heard various lamentations about purses etc that had been convey'd away. At length we got admittance but the fright and additional cold I had got made me pay dear for an evening's amusement. In the croud I had once been edged close to two immense Men one of whom spoke to me very civilly and did what he could to assist me, on coming to our seats I saw them next Box to me and discover'd my corpulent neighbours to be no other than Charles Fox and his Brother. If I had known that circumstance at the time it would have comforted me for a little additional suffocation.

With regard to the Play I do not like it. But I was pleased with Mrs Jordan's performance and really for the third time was entertain'd with her 'Romp'. Mrs Morris was delighted as She had never seen her. I sat on the King's side so could not see his face but I am told he was much pleased. We were join'd at the House by Charles and Edward Morris. They had with them young Sturgeon. He is a very different being from what he promised as a Boy: as I think he is not only very plain, but has assez l'air mauvais Garçon. I enquired for his Father and Lady Harriet, but as you may suppose he had no recollection of me. I saw Mrs Sheridan in her Box, they came to Town last Monday and Dick talks stoutly of assisting my Father – God send he may not again dissappoint him.

Well Thursday I got up by no means the better for my expedition. I call'd on the Yarkers who seem more affected than one would expect from the death of the Old Lady. She was in her ninety fourth year, but it seems what distress'd them was her having suffer'd a great deal before her death. On my return home I found my cold much worse. I sat up at dinner and in the Evening Angelo came and play'd picquet with my Father, but I was forced at last to go to bed. Yesterday I lay in bed most part of the day. This day I am much better and mean soon to be quite well.

Sunday – Yesterday my dear Love I received yours of the 17th enclosing two pair of gloves and Maria Walker – ridiculous as that figure appears to you I assure you it does not exceed the appearance our Tunbridge Belles made last Summer. However you may tell her as a friend gradually to reduce her Stuffing as Rumps are quite out in France and are decreasing here but can not be quite given up 'till the weather grows warmer. The hankerchiefs are not so much puff'd out and there is now a very pretty sort of hankercheif much worn open at the neck and exactly made and trim'd like a Boy's shirt. Hats are going out – Caps of all sorts cheifly of the hood form. The hair loose – curls without pins and the touppee as if it was curled and a comb run thro' it. Aprons very general, cheifly trick'd. Most fashionable collours dark green – pale straw coulour – and a very bright Purple. Maria put all these fashions in my head.

Thursday I received a long letter from Charles still urging me to prevail on *my Father* to pay him a visit. Note that I have never been directly or indirectly envited to go to his House. But *of course* he expects me; and if I go *of course*, *of course* I must take up with such accomodation as I can find. I am a little too well acquainted with the Map of the Country to commit such a Blunder. If my Father does go to Ireland we shall have a home of our own. He tells me that Miss Woolery is a prodigious favorite with his Wife, that he was ask'd to speak to the Duke and Mr Orde about a subscription that is to be put on foot to raise a fund to purchase an anuity for Miss Woolery to take her off the Stage – have your heard any thing of such a Plan?

Monday Morn – Yesterday we spent as usual quite alone. But I think my Father is getting better and I hope he will in time return to society. I have just written a few lines to Dick and enclosed a list of the Names my Father has already received. I own I am sometimes allarm'd to find myself an acting Person between my Father and him as should a dissappointment ensue the whole weight of uneasiness, tho' not of blame, will I know fall on me and I confess my spirits are not good enough to hold up, totally unsupported by one pleasurable circumstance against perpetual domestic disquiet.

I have been in one perpetual hurry this week; partly owing to the loss of my Servant, as the one I have taken is almost a fool, but one has no choice when one only wants one for a short time. Thursday I made my Father take me to Miss Quin's lodgings where I found her and Mrs Monk surrounded by visitors who seem'd to think little attention due to a person who came in a Hackney Coach, but Miss Quin with politeness that always attends a real elegance of mind by her manner more than compensated for the airs of her company. They all went out in a party at length, and she and I remained a short time alone. My Father then call'd for me and we went to see Gainsbourough's pictures – there is an admirable one of Mrs Siddons, but I am not delighted with that of Mrs Sheridan tho' he has alter'd the idea of making her a Peasant, which to me never appear'd judicious. Friday morng. I went to Dick's and engaged Mrs Sheridan to give me her Box at Drury Lane for Monday for Miss Quin who express'd a great wish to see Mrs Jordan. I have also her promise for tickets or her Box at the Opera for her some night.

Teusday – Sunday was interrupted by a visit from Mrs S: who call'd with Tom to see my Father, who was all smiles and good humour with them, but she could not let me have the Box for Monday as Linley, *od* rot *un*, had scruples about using it at benefit night. She offer'd me the Box for the Opera for this Evening but Miss Quin I knew was engaged so I accepted of tickets for her for Saterday next.

What you say respecting the fuel required by the mind no one feels more strongly than I do: mine is not only starved, but to use your own figure, overwhelm'd with Slack and choack'd with smoke.

Yesterday Morning by my *Father's desire* I call'd to engage Mrs Sheridan for some Evening to meet Mrs Cologan etc., at two I went and found her and Dick at breakfast, She crying at parting with Tom whom they have sent to the Country with

Doctor Parr, who takes only four Boys – and is reckon'd a very clever Man, and Dick very dull from not being well and fancying himself worse. When I told my business he seem'd pleased and desired her to put off all other engagements to come to us, but that not being necessary we fix'd on Sunday when She was disengaged, and I ask'd them to dine and the rest are to come in the Evening as I am so situated as to make it impossible to see company from the absolute want of Linnen, *plate*, and *plates*, etc. etc. and Cook. My Father had made no mention of Dick, but I certainly would not *now* ask her without him. We had some talk about my Father's plan and he promises to procure the names but does not seem to think it will be to any effect however as you may suppose I urged him to do that.

At My return I found Mrs Wilson and Alicia waiting for me. She had written me a note to fix yesterday for dining with me and to bring Alicia as we were to visit the fine things in the Pantheon – we first saw the immense *Fish* Balloon which *is* to do wonders. Three Eagles are *Harness'd* to it in order to serve as *Horses* in the Air and are so train'd as to be under the perfect command of the Person in the Car. We then visited the floating figures which are really curious. I enclose you a representation of the Persons which is most beautifully coulour'd and finely form'd. It must have a most curious effect in the air. Mrs Wilson did not stay late as you may suppose but I will endeavour to see her often while she stays. After Supper my Father was beginning in the old strain about Dick which I thought ill-timed considering what he had made me do in the morning. So I changed the conversation, by reading to him what you say of Orde in yours of the thirteenth which I received yesterday. He ponder'd on it some time and then said that since Orde had *received* his Plan from Charles and now seem'd going upon quite another idea there was little reason to expect success were he now to attempt what his own time of life makes him consider as a troublesome undertaking even here, where he expects so much more assistance. The truth is I beleive he wishes now for quiet more than any thing else. I am glad you are preparing

Our Tom for inoculation – he has it the best age I am told, and will I am sure have it lightly. I let you be a little anxious and but little as thank God in a healthy child and with proper care that disorder is now almost less than a common cold. London April 18th.

23 : BATH, 8TH TO 10TH MAY 1786

Monday – Here am I sitting with my head becurl'd and be-feather'd to Meet Mrs Ross at the Ball this Evening. She has visited me but I have not yet seen, but from my Father's account of her I think I shall like her – She is Daughter of Lady Charlemont and Mr Adderly, but entirely free from imper-tinence of every kind. I have promised to dance this Evening as my Father says he don't understand my turning Old Woman; and our young Oxonian Mr Drake is to have the honor of my hand. I do as I am bid on this occasion but to say the truth I am surprised to find how very indifferent I am grown to those sort of amusements, but in my present situation I think it a duty to struggle with that indifference, as it would exclude me from the society I must mix with, and indulging my feelings will not restore me to that I have lost.

Teusday – Our Ball was what they call a bad one, but to me quite full enough; several Ladies exhibited in minuets tho' the Men have so great an aversion to them that only one Gentle-man except the Masters of the Ceremonies of both Rooms danced with them – Tyson is promoter to the upper Rooms and a Mr King, a very genteel fashionable looking young Man officiates at the lower. I danced the whole evening and was better pleased with it than I expected. Mrs Ross I like very much, She is perfectly well bred and unaffected and has made me offers of civility of every kind. We have two cards of invita-tion from her, one for Friday but I must keep to my engage-ment with Mrs Paterson to go to the Ball at the lower Rooms. My Father has insisted on subscribing for me to the Cotillon Balls which are on Thursdays so I am fairly in for a round of hurry.

This Day our Table was unpleasantly Crouded – two new boarders – a Mr Kennot of Yorkshire; between six and seven foot high and the exact counterpart of your friend Mr Clarke's face at the top of this Gigantic figure; A Mr Hayes another Giant, a Clergyman. And our *fine Man* had taken into his head to invite five of his companions as great Beaux as himself, so I made my escape as soon as possible. Young Drake and Mr Harrison are going soon and then we get into Fletcher's House which will be more comfortable than our present situation. From what my Father says I believe our travels are ended for this Summer and I am not sorry for it. He finds himself at home here and the Waters are allow'd on all hands to be most beneficial in warm weather. He was with us at the Ball quite a Beau and so improved in his looks that Tyson came up with real cordiality to congratulate me on the alteration that has taken place in him since we were at Tunbridge. I saw your Old admirer Lord Nugent looking as well as ever – Lord Buckingam is also here, but has no recollection of the good Ducks and Onions he used to devour in Kings Mead St.

Wednesday Morng. – My dear love I have had a conversation with my Father this morning which I am impatient to communicate to you. I think it opens at least a prospect of our meeting. He had been considering it seems of the alteration in the system of education in Ireland proposed by Mr Orde. He wishes you to enquire of Charles what Mr Orde's ideas on the subject are and what his opinion of the Plan he sent over may be, which he supposes by this time he has read. That is to be consider'd as mere general outline, but if approved by Mr Orde he says he will readily make such alterations, or in fact form a new plan, such as may be suited to the times and to the intention of the Secretary and will entirely devote himself to that object as Ireland was originally the place he thought of, had he not been so shamefully deserted as he was when he made the attempt. This appears to you new language from my Father after his positive refusal of last Winter to think on the subject. I solve this apparent inconsistency by the great amendment

[83]

that has taken place both in his health and spirits; he then thought his time would have been short indeed, but now thank God he may reasonably look forward to years of health and strength. I need not urge you on the Subject. I think Charles will not recede from what was originally his own proposal. Oh! my dear Woman how does this little gleam of hope enliven my present scenes! I never gave it quite up, even tho' all rational grounds were lost, but surely now I may indulge it. I am commissioned by my Father himself to speak to you on this subject and he will now be all impatience till your answer arrives. The Post is just going out so I will send this off.

24: BATH, 1ST JUNE 1786

I sent you a few lines teusday [23rd May] meerly that you might not think us lost. At present I am more myself and so devote my first hour to you, as to my little bit of journal I have put up so carefully that I can not find it but I will give the best account of myself I can. Wednesday I drank tea with Mrs Kearney and met there our Old friend Miss Stopford that was with her good Gentleman. She is just the same being you remember her and in vindication of any apparent neglect I find they have liv'd wholly in the North where his living is since her marriage. I liked Mrs J. Kearney less upon a review. There is a great deal too much wisdomation about her – I ask'd them all to tea the Next Evening but the Elder Dr Kearney and his Lady were on the wing for London (where he goes purposely that She may hear the musick at the Abbey) and the others were engaged.

Thursday Morng. – I went with the Patersons to breakfast at Spring Gardens – no dancing and wretched musick but the morning was fine and we were inclined to be pleased so it went off very well, we then saunter'd about Pump Room, Libraries etc – in short spent a true Bath Morning, I should not chuze to spend many such. Friday Evening My Father chose to return a visit Dr Kearney had paid him and had a conversationé there of an hour and then went to the Crecent fields which is the present Mall of Bath and I think the pleasantest I ever was in as one is litterally walking in the fields with a most beautiful prospect all around at the same time that you meet all the company that is now here. There is something whimsical yet pleasing in seeing a number of well dress'd people walking in the same fields where Cows and Horses are grazing as quietly as if no such intruders came among them. We were join'd by Miss White who seems determin'd to Rival Miss Brooke with my Father and to supply her place in my good graces, but it won't do. She is sensible etc, but there is a degree of affectation about her that, when compared with the elegant manners of the other, whose pretentions were so much superior, will not allow of our being guilty of the slightest degree of inconstancy – as a chatting acquaintance she does very well.

Saterday – Our Weather grown very warm, but in our present Lodging we do not suffer from heat as our Rooms are large airy and never visited by the Sun – in the Evening I walk'd with Mrs Paterson to a new Walk which has been made by Belvidere, Shelter'd to the North by an immense Hill where they purpose building the New Crescent, and on the other side commands the most beautiful prospect immaginable, we then adjourn'd to the Crecent Fields to see the World and I again tired myself.

Sunday I went with the same Lady to the Octogan Chapel and afterwards like a fool let myself be dragg'd to the Pump Room, Parades etc in the heat of the day. I sat down to dinner wretchedly ill and unluckily in the Evening I had engaged the Kearney's and Mrs P. so that I suffer'd most terribly. Mrs Paterson who saw I was really ill took compassion on me and broke up the party early when I was put to bed in dreadful pain – and pretty smart feaver, which continued 'till yesterday [Wednesday, 31st May] – by my usual mode of keeping quiet and starving I have got pretty well again. My Father was for dosing me with James's powders but as my disorder arose entirely from fatigue, I can not think such violent medicines necessary or indeed safe.

[85]

You give an account of every thing relative to your Evening
in Shaw's Court except the performance, which I construe into
dissapprobation as perhaps you think censure would be a
breach of hospitality as you were their Guest. I am sure Lady
Glarawley spoke as she thought and as they all thought but you
can not expect that those who were already in possession of
rank and reputation in the company should look with a very
gracious Eye on one who comes to carry off what of course they
value. They certainly must wish you to keep out of their circle
since you only come their to make their want of merit con-
spicuous, but I who am out of the scrape do most sincerely wish
you may study and perform the Part of Lady Randolph[1] in
which I think you peculiarly excell.

I mention'd to my Father what you say of Orde and as his
quiting Ireland seem'd to throw a damp on his views I was the
more particular in placing things in the most favorable light;
if Charles is in earnest he will now write to my Father himself
on the Subject as certainly before he had but too much reason
to think his invitations could not be attended to – but still I
mean that we are to have a home – No Castles. You see my dear
Woman I indulge the hope of seeing you on the most distant
prospect, but I have lately discover'd hope to be a real blessing
and enstead of excluding it as formerly from the fear of dissappointment, I have thrown open my heart for its reception and
reap this benefit of snatching some days, which I must pass, from
dissagreeable reflections; I have been just reading an Essay on
Sensibility in which this idea is extended in such a manner as
to make it clear that a mind not suffer'd to despond, can not
even in this world be compleatly wretched, as steadfast hope
and belief in our future state will support and even leave the
mind open to many enjoyments – Those of benevolence in be-
holding an amiable disposition, a good action, or the wellfare
of those we love. It is part of a little volume of poems and
Essays written by Miss Bowdler, who died some time since after
lingering ten years in a State of continued ill health which

[1]In Home's tragedy *Douglas*.

deprived her of every worldly enjoyment. This little work was written to amuse her Solitary hours, and independent of the book having real merit one reads it with double satisfaction from being inform'd that the Author really possess'd and practiced every virtue that She recommends. Her zealous yet unaffected praises of the powers of religion are truly interesting when we consider that She had in herself experienced how greatly it may contribute to actual comfort, since it inabled her chearfully to bear one of the hardest lots assign'd to any mortal. After her death Her friends had a few copies struck off to distribute among those who knew and valued her – by a chance one of these volumes fell into the Queen's hands, who being inform'd that the work had not been publish'd, sent to beg a couple of them for her Daughters, adding that as a Mother She was more anxious they should Study that book than any of the kind She had ever met with. You may suppose her request was complied with; This anecdote I had from Paterson who is particularly intimate with the family. Mrs Fletcher lent me the book. I don't know whether I ever mention'd to you that She was formerly Companion to the late Lady Denbigh, and by that means known to the Bowdler family and respected by them. I should tell you she was very kind and attentive to me while I was ill. My Father is as usual gone to take his ride but always desires his kindest love. His wine is still at Bristol but as it is landed it will soon be here; the Captain charges no duty but makes a demand of a guinea and a half for getting it out *duty free*. These fellows are all Rogues, however my Father is delighted at the idea of getting good Port on any terms. I believe I have not a little contributed to making him drink wine enstead of Spirits of which he now takes but little. God bless you my dear Love, I will send this off and then fall into my old track of the weekly journal. Bath June 1st.

25: BATH, 28TH TO 30TH JUNE 1786

Wednesday – Yesterday my dear love when I had sent my letter

I went to leave my Card at Mrs Kearney's – as I was returning I met Miss Whyte riding a very handsome Horse of her own, and I envied her as I have almost wore out my feet in order to relieve my head – riding would be real use to me but for various reasons I can not think of it – à propos to that my Father's horse is fallen lame and he must lose his usual exercise for a time which I am sorry for as it was of consequence to his health. He seems thoughtful at times but still has not said one word of Charles's letter. This day after dinner the Dr and Bogle contrived to pay me visits one with a bouquet and the other to shew me some very good prints and to lend me a periodical paper printed at Edinburgh call'd the Lounger. It seems to have merit and is I beleive by the same set who publish'd the Mirror.

Thursday – The day has turn'd out Stormy rainy etc and my Father ask'd the Fletchers to tea and cards. At dinner Bogle ask'd us to be with him as he had ask'd a gentleman and we might play whist. My Father pleaded engagement but however ask'd him and his companion to come to us so as there are enough without me I shall work and perhaps read a few of the Loungers which I like better than the green cloth. To avoid unpleasantness I think now satisfies my ambition in the way of amusement. I will endeavour to get Cowper's Poems but I must enjoy them alone as my Father will not allow we have Poets or Painters or musicians at present, this sort of solitary pleasure is like sitting down to a feast alone, when certainly the humblest fare will give more satisfaction if we partook of it with a social, friendly being.

I have at length seen Charles's letter – it is I think so far satisfactory that if my Father has indeed the Plan of Education at heart as much as I think he has he will certainly visit Ireland and that soon but he has said nothing to me on the Subject. Time and a little patience will probably let us know more of the matter.

Friday Eveng – I am just return'd from a curious walk and as my Father is not yet come home I must give you an account of

[88]

our expedition. Mrs Paterson, her daughter, and Miss Handcock call'd on me and they proposed visiting Thicknesse's
Hermitage. It is a retired spot near this and laid out in the most
whimsical stile: it gives I believe a just idea of the owner whose
travels perhaps you have read. After wandering for a time in
some shady paths we reach'd a kind of rude Cave where it
seems Mr Thickness chose to bury his Daughter a fine girl of
eighteen who died last year of consumption – Il Pensoroso at
the top first draws your attention – Beneath that is placed a
small Urn. The Entrance of the Grotto is overgrown with Ivy
and the sides adorn'd with Shells – in a small niche there is a
little Female figure and over it an Inscription taken from Pope's
Lines on the Death of an Unfortunate Young Lady 'What tho'
no Sacred Earth allow thee room, etc etc' but as Miss Thickness did not destroy herself I can not say I thought the selection
judicious. This strange scene is immediately under the House
and we saw Thickness and a party of ladies walking past with as
much unconcern as they look on any other garden ornament.
We proceeded in our tour and came to another little monument
with an inscription to the Memory of poor Chatterton – you
will say indeed qu'il y avoit semmé des Tombeaux – and you
will suppose our ideas were taking a serious turn when in
another path the words il Pensoroso again attracted our
notice. We approach'd a little building that Had the appearance of a monument with an extraordinary looking skull and
of a small size at the top of it. The inscription inform'd us that
there lay the remains of Jacko, a favorite Monkey who had
travell'd thro France and Italy with him and whose good
qualities he ranks above those we ascribe to Dogs whom in this
elegant composition he stiles the 'Sons of Bitches'. This scene
quite got the better of Mrs Paterson's gravity and the young
Ladies caught the laugh – as Thickness was still in sight I was
fearfull of giving offence and scolded and remonstrated in vain.
I was as badly off as I have sometimes been in your company
when Miss Cadeen or Miss Toole have suddenly saluted us in
the Green, so finding all attempts to bring them to order were

in vain I escaped into the nearest field to avoid being included in the censure I thought they would meet for a conduct so contrary to all ideas of sentiment, and at the same time to indulge a good laugh which I had suppress'd with great difficulty. Tis now past nine and my Father not yet return'd, we have no cards tonight.

26: BATH, IST TO 7TH JULY 1786

Saterday – I sent off my letters yesterday as I did not recollect this was Post day to Ireland. My Father's wine is at length arrived and is excellent – he has got Pint bottles for himself and has laid in a store of *Englisa* Port for me and *hobnobs*, so much does he think what you have sent him superior not only in taste but as a point of health. While there remain'd any uncertainty about it I did not chuze to say any thing about it but I find Captain Tripe is not the most punctual Man in the world in these matters. I mention this only as a guard to Mr L—if he should again have occasion to send any thing by Bristol.

After dinner I took a long walk with my Father and heard an application of a word which I think will amuse you – you must know there was a great storm some nights since in this neighbourhood, My Father stop'd to speak to a turnpike Man about it but observ'd he could not be much allarm'd as it was at some distance. 'I beg your pardon Sir,' said the Man, 'we had it pretty *handy* here' – how do you like handy thunder and lightening? This day I walk'd a little in the morning – saw Miss Lidia White – or as She is call'd 'the witty Miss White', but positively the dose of affectation is too strong there to suit my taste. The whole Evening has been sacrificed to quadrille[1] and I am sleepy and weary.

Monday – Yesterday we lost our tall Clergyman so the Dr is now our whole stock. Walk'd with my Father who chose to stroll into Spring Gardens, very little company and not of the best sort, the Evening not pleasant; on my return call'd at

[1]The card-game, not the dance.

Handcocks and walk'd with Miss H: in the Crecent Fields where every one was assembled. Saw young Lister who married Miss Bourroughs – I hear the marriage is dissolv'd. At nine return'd, drudged at picquet till ten, retired at eleven.

This morng. Miss H. call'd and we walk'd for two hours before breakfast. At dinner The Fletchers had a guest, a gentleman who formerly boarded here but who would be no addition to our party – a Mr Marant who last year married one of the Duke of Athol's Sisters – he is very plain in his person, dissagreable in his manners and has apparently very little understanding; and to compleat his wants very little fortune so that one cannot guess the Lady's inducement to the match.

I left the table early and my Father again chose to go to Spring Gardens. Under the trees there was a party seated among whom was Lord Nugent. Upon seeing my Father 'pray,' says he, 'have you seen Lord Buckingam?' – 'Yes my Lord' – 'Well, he stutters as much as ever, doesn't he?' I felt extremely provoked at the impertinence of the Old Vagabond and took no pains to conceal what I thought at least by my looks. My Father I thought much too condescendingly enter'd into conversation, and as I was unemploy'd I felt rather awkward standing by a set of People who honor'd me with no other notice than an impertinent Stare, in particular Miss or Mrs McCartney who was sitting with her poor palsied head dress'd with flowers and painted up to the eyes, so I walk'd off to a sufficient distance to escape from their nonsense yet still in sight that my Father might join me when he quitted them: when he came up he said he beleived Lord N: was doating. I said I should hope so as the only appollogy for his total want of good manners. I was glad he should see I felt that We were not properly treated as I think he is too apt to pay a hommage to fortune and titles when he meets them, tho' to say the truth he does not seek them – this I attribute in some measure to his mixing so little with the world of late and admitting only such as yeild to him in every point, so that when he is with those from whom he can not expect that manner, he has nothing for it but recollecting the usual forms of good breeding he formerly practised with the persons of real fashion he once knew, but which are no match for the self-sufficiency and unfeeling impertinence of many of our present titled people. We then continued our walk for some time and as usual concluded the day with picquet.

Friday Morng. – This is a most Stupid journal and I have delay'd sending it only in hopes of a letter from you that I might have something to answer – My head is still in pain so I can neither think or write so I will close this.

27: BATH, 10TH JULY 1786

Monday July 10th – Saterday Evening I received yours of the 3d. I thank you my dear Woman for the share of good sense you allow me but I am afraid you give me more credit for wise and good qualities than I deserve. Our situations have been materially different – tho' you have had more than your share of vexation in this world, still from your infancy you have had some one being whose chief object you were and in whose tenderness you naturally sought comfort. I believe you loved me better than any other person did but for years the difference in our age (tho' trifling) made it impossible for me to treat you as my equal and so to expose my various little grievances to a person I look'd up to. As to religion I hope I am not defficient but there are occasions on which one is almost ashamed to fly to it for relief. Under severe afflictions one has that comfort, but under the daily vexations there may not be one circumstance of sufficient consequence to trouble heaven with our complaints. All this is idle talk but your opinion of me led me into it. At present I will endeavour to banish these ideas as much as possible and to think only of our meeting. My Father has not waver'd as yet so I allow myself to look forward to that event with some degree of certainty.

In speaking of Dick now he is the first to say what you or I or any of his friends last year would have wish'd to insinuate

[92]

but in vain. He acknowledges his neglect of him, and that even
in the Theatrical business which so severely hurt him he did not
wonder at his Conduct when he reflected that tho' it was done
with a view to serve him and the other Patentees, yet still he
so thwarted Dick's schemes and wishes that he was not surprised he opposed him. When I compare this with the last year's
violence and execrations on the same Son, who has since done
nothing to make him alter his opinion, I can only wonder at the
effects of Passion, which could so far blind a Man of my father's
understanding and morality to the destruction of his own peace
and that of his friends.

Yesterday Evening I had promised Mrs Fletcher and the Dr
to walk with them – accordingly we set out to a House call'd
St James's Palace beyond where the Bagatelle was formerly;
that House is now quite forsaken and the garden overrun with
weeds. When we arrived a little Girl inform'd us thro' the gate
that we could not be admitted as it was Witcombe *revel* – on
those occasions they shut up all public places here so fearful are
they of anything that might promote mirth. She would let us in
but no tea was to be had. Mrs F. is neither young nor very light
so even a seat was acceptable and we stroll'd round the gardens
which are really pretty. I then proposed our returning quietly
home to tea as I am not fond of those public places. I call'd for
an hour on the Handcocks – he press'd me much to visit them
at Bristol. It was kindly meant but I can be dull enough at Bath
without trouble. Tomorrow morning they go so I lose my only
walking companion. This day it has rain'd incessantly and I am
going to cards, so God bless you my dear Woman.

28: BATH, 13TH TO 16TH AUGUST 1786

Sunday – Our weather my dear Love still stormy and dissagreeable – of course no Vauxhall last night. My Father went to
Lord Cunningham's where there is a constant rout on Sater-
days. As I thought all the Gentlemen out I stroll'd into the
Garden for a little air and there was pursued by Bogle who

swore I must and should play quadrille with him so I was forced to go in and play till ten. I thought it best to comply as I shall probably want his assistance at the card table much oftener than he can want mine. This day has been unpleasant, we drank tea with the Patersons and return'd early as there was no walking and my Father I beleive wish'd for a little picquet. Good night my dear.

Teusday – Still wind and weather against us. Last Night the Prince's birth day was celebrated at Spring Gardens and above fifteen hundred people ventured their health at least in his Service – much as I regard him I durst not venture tho' well inclined and strongly press'd by our poor Doctor who leaves us tomorrow. Last night as I gave up the gardens I engaged the company to tea and work'd while they play'd cards. This day I have not been able to get out but my Father brought me from the Coffee House some Copies of letters written by Mrs Jefferies to a Priest in her neighbourhood – they do her credit and plainly prove that whatever active part She took in the disturbances at Blarney was from the best and most humane motives. A few more of her disposition might be of real service to the unfortunate poor of Ireland. We have lost our pretty Neighbours, but Mr Cobbe is here figuring with the *Bird of Paradise*, as if no such being as his Wife existed. Mrs Fitzherbert is also here with her Father who has been dangerously ill. She received the news at Brighthelmstone[1] while sitting at Breakfast with the Prince; She instantly set off and made what haste she could to Bath where her reception was very different from that given to her – (I dont know what to call him) – who when he flew with the utmost expedition to Windsor to rejoice at his Father's safety, was not permitted to see him, so after eating his dinner at the White Harte Inn he return'd from whence he came. Can you bear such sulky people?

Wednesday – We are going to dine at Patersons, so I must dress as I find they have a party to meet us. Last night we were at home, the weather shocking, and quadrille the word. After

[1]Brighton.

[94]

supper my Father again confirm'd what he has told me of leaving this the first week in September and our stay in London is to be short as possible. If he can possibly settle his business in a week he will not exceed that. He had talk'd of the expence of taking over his Horse and Servant, but I would not on any account have him part with either as he would not easily replace them in Dublin and at his time of life those privations are almost misfortunes. His Horse is the safest Creature I ever saw, and Riding is to him of more service than all the Phisicians can do for him – à propos to Phisicians our Dr went early this morning. My Father told me he took leave of him last night after I went to bed, and express'd sincere regret at the loss he should sustain in his conversation. He had avoided seeing me in the course of the Evening and this morning at breakfast John deliver'd me a parcel enclosing a card from him to thank me for the pleasure he had received from my company, with wishes for my happyness etc – if good wishes could give happyness I ought to possess it, as I have at least through life had the good fortune of making few Enemies and some well wishers. Poor Mrs Fletcher has been with me crying after her departed friend, tho' he gives her hopes of returning in a couple of months. She has much too feeling a heart for her situation which necessarily subjects her to perpetual separations. Her eyes also begin to fill at the mention of our going as she looks upon my Father's journey to Ireland as a more serious separation than any She has yet known. Luckily she likes me or I beleive I should stand in no very pleasing light to her as She considers me very much as the occasion of this move. I own I am too well pleased with it to think much about what any of the People on this side of the water may think of it. Bath August 16th.

29: BATH, 29TH AUGUST TO 3RD SEPTEMBER 1786

Teusday – Yesterday our Sky clear'd a little and, as your orders are de me bien porter, I sallied out in the morning and took a very pleasant walk. In the Interval between coffee and cards I again set out to visit my old walk by the River which after the first little unpleasant sensations excited by the recollection of former times became my favorite solitary walk. I had not proceeded far before I saw Mrs Lynn and a young girl of the age of a Neice She had at Aixe when we knew her, walking just before me. I totaly forgot the impossibility of its being the same girl and began to fancy that Time had really made an extraordinary effort in stepping back some years purposely to oblige me. I immediately accosted my Old Friend (who is exactly what you remember her) but here the illusion vanish'd – She look'd earnestly at me but could not recollect me – Yet said She was certain She knew my voice. When I named my self, without more ceremony She put her arms round my neck saying She was indeed happy to meet me as She had ever loved me dearly. Then a variety of enquiries about you – If you still had those spirits that used to delight her: and she has preserved little scraps that you used to write at that time. In short we talk'd over pass'd scenes and I found the time pass insensibly, so true it is that there is a delight in recalling the days of our Youth even when not mark'd with happy events. We walk'd on together and She then brought me to her Lodgings which are in Beaufort Square. She is only return'd to Bath within this fortnight, but we have promised to meet often while I stay.

Saterday Septr 2d. – A long interruption my dear Love but quite unavoidable. Teusday I left you to go to dinner, in the Evening the Fletchers and Mr Bogle made up the quadrille party while I ran through the Second Volume of Caroline, which (soit dit en passant) I think much inferior to the first. Well, Wednesday I rose in miserable pain, spent the whole morning cooling myself with penny royal water – no releif, Yet I dined below and drank tea and play'd cards with Mr B., still ready to cry with pain and not daring to complain. Thursday worse and yesterday my head in such a condition I could not take it off the pillow. I got up however in the evening and sat by them while they play'd cards. I did this in preference to staying alone as when my head is so attack'd I lose all use of my eyes, so that I can neither read nor write. This morning I got up much better and walk'd out a little after breakfast and call'd on Mrs Lynn who had visited me in the course of the week. I gossip'd some time with her and ask'd her to Tea for this Evening. At my return I wrote to Mrs Cologan – only a few lines to recommend John to her as it was at her recommendation my Father took him originally and as he does not part with him for any fault he wishes to provide for him before we go, so my dear Love I trust you will be able to get some one to replace said gentleman before we arrive, which will be the latter end of *this* month or the first week in Octobre. Our Stay in London is positively not to exceed a week, but my Father seems inclined to take as much of his rides and the good air of the Downs here as he can before he sets out. Je ne m'amuse pas trop en attendant as you may suppose, but the great point once decided I don't let trifles trouble me much. This morning the Post Man brought a letter here directed for Dick. It had already travel'd to Weymouth, Exeter, Plymouth etc – so where they are God knows, but by the letter being forwarded here it looks as if they had some notion of coming. We have seen nor heard nothing of Linley, which I think odd after the reconciliation, particularly as he never stood on ceremony with my Father before. God bless you my love, again summon'd to dinner – I have eat none two days so you will allow me to be hungry.

Sunday – A most dreary wet day – no stirring out, no company at home, my sad story. This morning my Father told me that he has fix'd this day fortnight for our quitting Bath and so I must write to Thompson to know if we can be in his House the few days we stay in London or to bid him take a lodging near him which will be quite as agreable to me as I think I have before mention'd his wife is a meer Savage. I like these preparations for tho' I have for some time had no reason to doubt my Fathers keeping his purpose yet still these little preparatory steps stamp a degree of certainty on our motions. I must write to Charles to bid him prepare for his reception of my Father, as to my share of their intended civilities, I believe I may resign

[97]

them without any violent effort of self denial. God bless you my dear love.

I have nothing to add in the way of news – I have been reading Lavater and intend becoming wise in my judgements on the cut of people's faces – for he does not advance the general idea of particular passions and dispositions impressing certain lines on the countenance, but positively insists, that a nose, or mouth of a certain formation almost invariably belongs to particular characters. I can not say I am a convert to his opinions but his book is pleasingly written, and so I proceed with the same sort of pleasure one has in conversing with a sensible person tho' one may happen to have a different opinion. 'Tis true in this case the conversation is not very equably devided, but we find that so often with our living companions that one would not quarrel with a leathern coated gentleman on that score. My Father's kindest love ever attends you. As to his not having answer'd your last, attribute it to the true cause *Laziness*, for he is come to this pass now that he almost always makes me write for him.

30: BATH, 11TH TO 16TH SEPTEMBER 1786

Monday 11th – Saterday after I had sent my last I was seized by Mr B: to drink tea and play cards with him, as my Father was out and I was not positively to be left alone. Today he left us for some time and we shall be gone before he returns. In our present dearth of company he is a loss as he was good humour'd, sociable and had the manners of a gentleman – he lent me books and sometimes supplied my place at the card table so I regret him, but he threatens a visit to Dublin next Winter and has got my direction, but there I shall not want him. At present we have no one left but old Mr Brooke – a very good sort of Man in the main, but who neither speaks, plays at any games, reads, or writes from morning, 'till night; with that tho' a Man of fortune so good an Oeconomist as to have no drawing room of his own so that he invites no one and if invited by us only occupies a

[98]

chair as he takes neither tea nor coffee. Yesterday I had a good deal of conversation with my Father about Mr Orde's resignation. It does not in the least affect his intentions with respect to Ireland and I am happy to find that he seems to rest a good deal on his own former connexions and interest, and his health is now so perfectly reestablish'd that, from a hint that drop'd from him, should his expectations on the great point not be answer'd, he is both able and willing to get money in another way. The appointing of W: W: Grenville looks very like an introduction to the return of the Marquis of Buckingham to Ireland – I wonder what Charles thinks of this change? – Interrupted.

Thursday – Still a succession of Storms – absolutely no venturing out but with the risk of being blown away or wet to the skin. Yesterday I was busy all the morning packing a trunk to send by the Waggon. 'The labour we delight in, etc:' I may say on this occasion, but truth to say it is labour. If *many hands* make light work certainly the reverse is true and I never 'till this last expedition to England experienced what it was to be entirely depending on *a pair* – tho' pretty well accustom'd to attend myself. Teusday we had an addition to our family – A Mr Corbett from Cheshire – a Man of Fortune – about as young as my Father but well bred and plays quadrille. Mrs Fletcher has been ill for some days so I am forced to be alone with the Gentlemen. Mrs Paterson has been sending me cards and invitations, but when I have dullness without trouble I always give it the preference. No letter from Dublin this Evening so good night my love.

Friday – I concluded with wishing you a good night but a most unpleasant one I have pass'd owing to a small defect in my constitution whenever I either suppose or see danger. I had scarce done writing (it was near Eleven) when I received a message from Mr F: to request I would go down. I apprehended Mrs Fletcher was worse, but the Maid who brought the message said that her Master wanted me to interpret for him to a French Gentleman, who came for lodgings and whom he could not make sensible that he could not be accommodated.

In the Hall sat a Porter loaded with Portmanteaus etc, and when I enter'd the Parlour I found Mr Fletcher with a Swaggering looking Fellow, who told me had been recommended to this house by a Gentleman whose name he did not recollect. I told him at F's desire that the House was full but there would be a vacancy in a few days. 'Et où Diable voullez-vous que j'aille coucher, dans les Rues?' said the polite Frenchman. 'Non Monsieur, il y a des Auberges, des Hotels en abbondance où vous pourrez être logé en attendant qu'on puisse vous recevoir ici,' resumed I very civilly. 'Et Sacre Dieu qui avez-vous dans cette Maison qui est si bien remplie?' 'Plusieurs Messieurs,' said I, beginning to be a little frighten'd as he rivetted two very wicked looking eyes on my face while he put his right hand in his pocket, to search for a Pistol as I thought. After a few more questions in which he added words the most shocking that you can concieve, finding he would take no denial from me I went into a little room on the same floor where Mrs Fletcher was – here he follow'd me in a most violent passion: 'Did we take him for *un Aventurier, un Gueux?*' 'Troth, little better,' thought I. I then told him he could have a bed at the Inne he came from. 'Pray, was he to walk the streets in Search of a bed?' 'By no means,' Fletcher said, 'he was welcome to stay in his Parlour 'till the Porter should go and bespeak one for him.' I ask'd him if he was totally ignorant of English – 'Tenez, je parle huit langues mais pas un mot d'Anglois.' He then ask'd if the Archeduke of Milan had pass'd this way, to which being answer'd in the negative he return'd to his old amusement of cursing, swearing and blackguarding. Upon his quitting the Room I return'd to my Father, fully resolved if they could not make him leave the house in plain English that the Watchman should be the next Interpreter applied. He call'd after me as I was going and Fletcher told me he attempted to follow me up, but that had he insisted he would certainly have call'd the Watch. When the Porter return'd to tell him his Bed was ready, he still refused to go but insisted passing the Night in the Room he was in, and at last partly by force he was got out. What the Fellow's design was I know not but the whole night I never closed my eyes from a violent palpitation at my heart which the fright had brought on. I slept towards morning and am now pretty well but it is a Sad thing to be such an Arrant coward.

I have just received one of the kindest letters you can concieve from Mrs Cologan, in answer to one I had written about John. She is not only an Amiable but a good creature, and at present one of the happiest of human beings. She is at Southampton with her Mother and her little girl so I fear I shall not see her again, and I really shall regret both Mother and daughter more than any of my London acquaintances. But this said John of ours has been very ill for some days and as he is to ride the journey to Town it delays us 'till Monday or Teusday. I mind this the less as while this weather lasts I should only be a Prisoner in London and we could not cross the Sea. And it still allows us to be with you the first week in Octobre.

Saterday – I have kept this open in hopes my dear love of a letter but these villainous winds or something have dissappointed me. We do not leave this 'till the latter end of next week so I wrote to Thompson to forward any letters you send me to London. The French Man sent from the Inn where it seems he has remain'd, to know if there was a lodging ready for him yet. You may suppose he will not easily get admittance again.

[From October 1786 till July 1788 Betsy kept no Journal, as she was in Dublin near her sister.]

CHAPTER 4

London and Margate, July and August 1788:
Thomas Sheridan's last weeks

31: LICHFIELD, 21ST JULY – DAVENTRY, 23RD JULY
1788

Litchfield Monday noon 21st July – I sent you a few hasty lines from Chester just to inform you of our safe arrival, and having a little time at command I will endeavour to get into our Old regular method. I told you we parted from Mrs Crewe at Pargate, not indeed with out every mark of kindness on her part. We walk'd out together a little time and I found She was very curious to find out the terms my Father and my brother Richard were on. As I found She really knew nothing of the matter I kept on the reserve and attributed a coldness of manner She remark'd in my Father on that Subject entirely to his very bad state of health which gave him an appearance of indifference to everything – The ladies both promis'd to visit me at Chester but were I beleive apprehensive of intruding on my Father and so I saw no more of them: but just before I set out I received a kind farewell note from Mrs Crewe.

We then travell'd on with tollerable ease to my Father, as far as Stone where we pass'd the night. I could not help observing an odd circumstance during Supper which was that the whole Family took their turn to wait on us, as they were pretty numerous this bred no small degree of confusion. In the morning we understood the matter – We had got into Staffordshire and the good Gentlewoman of the House having learn'd our

[102]

name from Allick, a general curiosity to look at Mr Sheridan's Father had seized the whole Set.

This day he seems rather fatigued with going Post so we have put up here to rest and tomorrow he means to hire a Chaise to London which will certainly be the best method – upon the whole I think he has kept wonderfully well. He is much pleased with his new Servant who seems perfectly to understand the proper attendance on an Invalid and is besides exceedingly active and careful. Indeed he seem'd so very careful that I could not help remarking it to him – he told me it was very necessary to look sharp in *this* Country for that they were very fond of robbing the Irish. As this opinion can only be of service to us I have left him in quiet possession of it. Since my arrival here I walk'd out and bought my Father some Magazines which he is now reading by a good fire, so good that I dread returning to it but for that I see no remedy.

I feel vex'd to spend a whole day at Litchfield without the smallest chance of seeing or hearing of Miss Seward. Having no assistance from outward objects one unavoidably returns to self – and when I do I cannot but feel how very different this journey is to that we sometimes talk'd of and which even I almost hoped might have been realised, or even under some distressing circumstances how much your society would have relieved all parties. I have no means of reconciling it to myself but considering it as one of those events which reason and duty compels us to submit to however painful the struggle.

Our plans for the future are as unsettled as ever, but my Father has determined to go first to Thompson's, and I have written a line to him to desire him to look out for some lodging that may suit us but not to engage any. I once wish'd we could have been accommodated for a short time at Dick's House, but my Father chose to begin a conversation last night in the stile of that he held at your House once to which I dared not give any answer, so that must not be thought of. But at last however he said he meant to meet on civil terms, even that is something. Charles's Wife is with child again as we guess'd so I suppose She will be very domestic and good. He did not desire me to write 'till I reach'd London and I do not feel tempted to do more on that occasion that what strict propriety requires. God knows I am sufficiently sick of the whole farce they have acted so that nothing can be more irksome than the necessity I am under of assuming an appearance of kindness where I owe so little.

Daventry, Wednesday 6 o clock in the morning – I could not my dear love send off my letter from Litchfield, as I did not leave my Father 'till he went to bed and by that time I was so roasted and so tired I could not hold my head up. We could not accomplish our plan of hiring a chaise but he was so well restored by our day's rest that he bore posting very well and tomorrow we hope to reach London very early. The hurry and fatigue I have suffer'd has brought on one of my old attacks. I was in so much pain yesterday that my Father proposed stopping at Coventry, but I got some brandy burnt and proceeded as well as I could. Last night sleep was quite out of the question so I make no merit of my early rising for I have been up long before I could even procure pen and ink, but I hope the worst is over. I have no patience with the general want of feeling of men when they can not be ignorant of the Sufferings we poor Females must undergo even in the most comfortable situations, when we are to encounter cold and fatigue necessarily every thing is doubled on us, and I have had my share on this occasion for I lay on the floor on shipboard 'till the Captain took compassion on me and dragg'd my bed out of the birth and having made it as well as he could settled me on it. What I suffer'd from at Sea was constant faintness without the smallest releif from my stomach so I have no hopes of future benefit. This is a true sick woman's journal. God bless you my dear love – ever kindest love to Mr Lefanu. It is impossible to feel more gratitude than I do for his constant kindness to me – My Father's best love attends you and yours – remember us kindly to Mr H: Lefanu; to my other friends I shall write when I reach London. I hope poor Fidele is not troublesome to you.

At last my dearest love I can tell you we are safe arrived in London. We slept Wednesday at St Albans and yesterday at about three o clock reach'd Marlbro' St. My Father very little fatigued. Thompson was out looking as I had desired for some lodging for us, But Mrs Thompson received us most graciously and immediately produced a good roast fowl and some mutton broth which they had prepared for us at a venture and to crown all some very fine Madeira which Mr Beaufoy had given to Thompson. My Father had quite drop'd his plan of going to a Hotel, so I dispatch'd a note to Dr Morris and set out in search of a lodging. I recollected Mrs Wilson had an excellent one in Frith St so I proceeded there immediately and was lucky enough to find it dissengaged. I took possession of it and return'd with this good account to My Father. In a few minutes Dr Morris and George came to us and paid my Father a very long visit. He does not at all approve of his going to Lisbon in his present State, but as my Father seems to think the Sea air would agree with him reccommends Margate where he means himself to spend part of the Summer. I had no opportunity of speaking to him in private but I thought all he said was encouraging.

Kitty Angelo as usual was the first to come to me. She seem'd really happy to see us and made many kind enquiries about you and I gave her all manner of pleasing intelligence about her Sister. At about nine oclock we sent for a Coach to remove ourselves to Frith St., but just as we were setting out it occur'd to the Doctor that my Father could be better in his Carriage so he took him and put George in the Coach with me. As I had shewn no sort of recollection of his letters to me I thought he would have follow'd my example, but the moment we were alone he began appologies, explanations. I beg'd he would think no more of the matter and immediately began telling of my Father's situation. They left us at our Lodging and Thompson soon follow'd with new laid Eggs and more of the good Madeira which my Father had praised. He sup'd with us and as my Father retired early he staid with me to indulge in talking of his dear Master Richard. I should tell you that he praised him most warmly to my Father repeatedly saying 'Sir, your Son is the first Man in England – You will find every one of that opinion'. I thought my Father seem'd rather pleased. When we were left alone he began his praise again and got up to give me an idea of his concluding words, and bad as the attempt must have been yet it convey'd some idea of the manner in which he spoke those words 'My Lords I have done' which so haunted you. He regretted very much he could not provide for us, could he have spared one Bed for my Father, Doctor Morris provided one for me at his House if I would have accepted of it – My Father is not yet up and I am distracted with the Mob's huzza's for Hood, whose Standard is under my Window while our opposite neighbour is distributing purple Ribbons to all who ask for them.

I wrote so far before breakfast – I have since seen Dick and his Wife. I went out with Thompson about some business for my Father and going near Bruton Street I took that opportunity of calling. Mrs Sheridan received me very kindly, but my Brother seem'd very much affected. His eyes fill'd with tears and his voice choak'd. After embracing me very affectionately he hurried out of the room. Mrs S. said he was *nervous* but would return to us soon which he did and then enquired for you in the most affectionate manner, he spoke very kindly of my Father, who would not let Thompson go to him yesterday, but I hope they will meet today. Mrs Sheridan was surrounded by Townshend's Ribbons one of which She pin'd to my hankercheif and proposed to me to go out with her on her Canvassing tour, but I had already rather trespass'd on the time I could spend. Mr Crewe and some more Gentlemen came in who seem'd to think Lord John will certainly be ellected. They were very civil to me as my ribbons proclaim'd me as a friend to the cause. Mrs Crewe remains at Crewe Hall.

Doctor Morris was with my Father during my absence and

Dr George M: since my return. I took an opportunity of asking the latter what I might hope with respect to my Father – His answers were friendly but cautious. They do not apprehend immediate danger but seem to think much care and time will be required to restore him to any degree of strength. I have the firmest reliance on their skill and friendship and for the rest I endeavour to hope the best and put my trust in the Almighty. Whatever be the event we have the consolation to think that nothing has been neglected that could be serviceable. We shall leave this in about a week and 'tis more than probable Dr Morris will go with us to Margate.

'Tis time my dear Love to thank you for your very kind letter which I found on my arrival, the more kind as you do not dwell on what I am sure you feel. I did not tell you Mrs Sheridan made a thousand kind enquiries about you and your dear little ones; tell me how they are. My Father's kindest love attends you. He told Thompson last night you had got the finest little Girl in the world – He joins with me in kindest wishes to Mr Lefanu and your Brother.[1] Thompson begs to be remember'd to you in the kindest manner. He is very busy and important just now.

London July 25th

As a friend to the cause I enclose you a cockade.

33: LONDON, 27TH TO 29TH JULY 1788

Sunday Eveng. – I have slip'd away from my Father while Mr Beaufoy and his youngest Brother are with Him, to resume my Journal. But to begin with what I suppose you most wish to know, I must tell you we had a long visit today from Dick and his Wife. All pass'd off very well – My Father a little stately at first but soon thoroughly cordial with his Son who staid 'till near Six but could not dine with us. And now to *recede* – I had just sent off my letter yesterday when Mrs Angelo call'd, as usual all life and spirits and full of news, amongst the rest She

[1] i.e. brother-in-law, Henry LeFanu.

told me Anthony Angelo had last year Married his Maid – that he had taken her Sister, a House-Maid in the neighbourhood, to live with them and to complete the group had envited their Mother a very honest *Washer-woman* to be of the party – he is bless'd with an heir to his Fortune by this illustrious Bride. While She was with me yours of the 22d was brought to me enclosing Harry's note which I shall certainly answer that he may not accuse me of Prudery or unkindness. With regard to what he *feels* for me I can truly say I am wholly at a loss what to think; but as to his intentions being such as your regard for me might lead you to wish I confess I have not the smallest reason to suppose it. He has been so very particular in marking his attentions to me to be chiefly the result of his strong attachment to my Father (an attachment of which he certainly gave proof when I was totally out of the question) that I can not think he means I should place them to my own account.

Mrs Angelo dragg'd me out with her and at my return I found Mrs Sheridan with my Father. As kind and attentive to him as possible, strongly pressing him to spend some time at Dibden, offering to be his Nurse, to play with him – in short everything that could flatter or induce him to comply, but he keeps to his own intentions. Thompson dined with us and has done so at my Father's desire ever since we came. After dinner Dr Morris and George with a fresh cargo of books – Whyte came in bien Poudré and in high Spirits. He perceived my Father seem'd exhausted and so shorten'd his visit.

Well this Morning first Thompson, then Dr Morris, who kindly went to Bruton Street to see Dick and to talk about my Father – then Mr and Mrs Crauford and most of her young ones, all well and full of enquiries. Then Angelo as young and handsome as ever – then Patty Whyte very kind and quite well after her journey. Then a drive to Florida Gardens with my Father – during our absence a visit from Mrs Fitzgerald. At our return Dick – every thing that was kind, and pressing us much to go to Dibden – repeating the offer they had already made of their Carriage while we remain in Town. In short every thing we could wish – very kind in speaking of you and by no means relinquishing his plan of visiting Ireland. Mr and Mrs Linley remained in the Coach during their visit so I went down and spoke civilly to them and they were as kind as possible. My Father eat a little dinner and the Beaufoys came in while we were at our wine which I left them drinking, and having scribbled so far must go down to make tea. I thank you for your care of my poor Fidele.

Teusday Morng. – When I went down Sunday I found Mr Yarker below full of joy to see us and kind inquiries for his old flame. The Morrises spent the remainder of the Evening with us. The Doctor strongly recommended to my Father a visit to Dibden before he went to Margate. He seems I think to give up his plan of going immediately to Lisbon with great reluctance. But Dr Morris entirely dissapproves of it 'till he has gain'd some degree of strength; He seems to devote almost his whole time and thoughts to him, and Studies not only the most efficacious medicine, but is perpetually bringing some little palliative that if it has no violent effect yet affords a temporary releif. He is also of use in directing his diet, Slops, etc, which, as I must act by my Father's orders, is a great comfort to me. You may suppose I should fear the loss of such a friend, to encounter the fatigue and risk of a voyage of at least a fortnight, probably without any medical assistance at hand; yet I can not but apprehend that my Father will make the attempt if he does not find immediate benefit from Margate. Tomorrow we set out – It is 72 miles from London so we shall be two days on the road. Your next direct to the Post Office Margate.

Yesterday I received yours of the 23d.: I hope you received a letter I wrote from Daventry. I am glad your good Brother has recover'd his spirits. I enclose a note for him – Unseal'd as his was, so you may cast your eye over it and if you think either the contents or the act of writing to him at all in itself improper, you will oblige me by burning it and substituting such a message from me as will answer the purpose, As I should wish to avoid if possible equally an appearance of forwardness, or on the other

[109]

hand of distance or unkindness where I feel a very sincere regard.

Yesterday Dick had promised to send the Coach at twelve, accordingly a Coach did come at that hour but he sent me a note to tell me some thing had happen'd to theirs and so he sent Ld. R. Spencer's. I knew my Father would not mind the livery so I said nothing of this change 'till we set out and he was very well satisfied. We drove to Kensington and got out to enjoy the air for some time and with the help of my arm he walk'd about a little. He seem'd the better for his airing, and at his return I procured some Turtle which Dr M: said he might safely eat – and he seem'd to relish it. We could not expect to see Dick as yesterday was a very busy day with them. We shall have the Carriage this morning and might have had it from the first had my Father chosen it. I am sure we shall see them. I rose at seven to finish this I do not expect one minute to myself after breakfast.

London July 29th   Frith St.

34: MARGATE, 1ST AUGUST 1788

Margate Friday – August the 1st – Here we are my Dear Love settled for one month if nothing very particular happens to change my Father's plan. He bore the journey tollerably. We left London Wednesday Morng. and slept one stage short of Canterbury – Yesterday a little after two we arrived here and put up at the Hotel. In the Evening I sallied forth in search of a Lodging. After a tedious walk I at last found what I thought would suit us. It is a very small House in the Highest part of the Town. A fine open ground before us and a full view of the Sea. We have a parlour and Kitchen – two good Bedrooms and two garrets – every thing of china, glass, etc, etc, found us – for this we pay two guineas a week. I had then a Cook to hire and a thousand little domestic matters to mind so no time for writing, but this day I think we are quite settled. My Father seems not dissatisfied with my arrangements which is some comfort, for he has been most dreadfully irritable ever since we left

Dublin. He does not gain strength but he does not lose ground and he complains less of his head than formerly. This morng. we drove by the Sea side. He seems to enjoy the air – nothing can be finer than the face of the Country here and the Sea is a pleasing prospect from the number of Vessels perpetually sailing near us. As to any thing else, I can tell you nothing more of Margate nor shall I probably see much of it while I remain. I can hardly tell you how much I have been hurried and harrass'd since we parted but I sometimes think I have been the better for it, as it has kept me from reflections that would have injured me much more than any bodily fatigue can do. I shall begin to bathe as soon as possible. My Father intends to try the warm Sea Bath tomorrow.

Teusday as I expected Dick and his Wife call'd on us and paid us a very long visit. He declares positively that he will come to us here as soon as the Election is over. They seem'd both tollerably tired of it. He gave us some account of his transaction with Sir Samson Wright – much the same that the Herald gives. He said that he desired Sir Sampson to make the Soldiers draw back on which the Justice sneek'd behind a Grenadier crying drive them off, that being provoked a *little* he did take the Fellow by the Collar and having dragg'd him forward gave him a shaking. I hear they have made a Print of the Scene but did not see it. Mrs Sheridan told me she had just given ten guineas (a collection she made) to the poor Black who at the risk of his life had step'd forward and received a cut on the head that was intended for Charles Fox. They seem'd in good spirits and quite certain of success.

Friday Eveng. – I have again driven out with my Father. But the weather is cool and he has got a fire in our small room enough to kill us. I see no remedy for this as he evidently suffers so much from cold that I am forced to be the first to propose fire, for the Doctor says whatever injury he may have done his constitution by the practice that warmth is absolutely necessary to him. He has got a book that amuses him which has procured me an hour's liberty.

I had desired my letters to be forwarded, and have sent twice to the Post Office in vain – tomorrow I shall hear from you but I will prepare this for the Post least you should be uneasy at not hearing from me. This day two years you wrote to me a chearful letter on the prospect of our meeting – and now at a still greater distance, I can not look back on that period which promised us so much satisfaction with any pleasing reflections – how it was embitter'd by dissappointment, ill treatment and sickness, on my part you know, and on yours by the uncertain state of your health. Let us hope our next meeting will compensate for all. I think it will be on this side of the water where we have not to apprehend the machinations of art or malice – where my Fathers health will I trust be better, and where I am sure you will find many enjoyments which must not be thought of in Dublin and many Friends who will truly rejoice to see you. My airing and roasting have disagreed with me.

I had forgot to mention that I should be glad to have my Trunk sent as soon as you can by Long Sea to London, addressed to Thompson's. I shall write to him to take care of it and supply us with linnen any where and other common necessaries. My Father's Cloaths, books etc. etc. remain as we settled before we left Dublin.

35 : MARGATE, 2ND TO 4TH AUGUST 1788

Last night my dear Love when I had finish'd my letter I return'd to my Father who complain'd greatly of his stomach. In a few minutes he was seized with vomiting which seem'd to releive him and he then went to bed. This happens now frequently, and tho' Dr Morris said it was not an allarming symptom yet I can not help feeling a degree of terror whenever he is attack'd in this way, now that we are so far from any Friend or assistance of any kind. We do not expect the Dr 'till thursday next. This morning he seem'd rather better and we took a long drive. He is now gone to the warm bath from which he expects releif – God grant it. As I never leave him you may

[112]

suppose I see little of this place. Our Lodging is almost out of
the Town which I prefer'd as the amusements of the place were
not our object, And being obliged to keep a chaise it makes no
difference with regard to the convenience of bathing – Monday
I begin.

We took a beautifull drive this morning and pass'd thro'
several little villages all well provided with Lodgings and
accommodations for bathing. The Country as I before told you
is uncommonly fine – but conveys only the idea of wealth, not
pleasure. Every foot of ground is cultivated to the utmost – they
seem even to grudge what is necessary for roads, for tho'
remarkably good they are so narrow that two Carriages can
never pass each other but at particular spaces left for the purpose. As to Hedges they too I suppose are consider'd as en-
croachers, so scarcely an inclosure of any kind is to be seen.
Corn, beans and Clover join each other, and the eye wanders
over this rich carpet with out the smallest interruption – And at
first (perhaps from accessory ideas) with pleasure; but I begin
now to feel a little like the Coquette in the fairy Tale who was
condemned to wander over a most beautifull Lawn and under
a perfectly serene sky, as the greatest punishment that could be
inflicted on her. Some times the scene is enliven'd by the reapers
who are in some places very busy – In some others the Harvest
is quite finish'd. Before I quit fields I must mention one that we
never saw together, which is a large field of Canary seed. It is
the prettiest thing that can be, and gives me the idea of Lilli-
putian Wheat. Part of our tour is allways by the Sea side. At
no great distance there is a very good banqueting Room where
the company go to breakfast and dine and breathe the Sea Air.
Near it is a House built by Lord Holland, a heavy mass of
building of a most gloomy aspect. Il y a vraiment semée des
Tombeau as everything is built of black and white Stone in the
true funereal stile. The house is at present uninhabited, but as
we pass'd we had a view of the pleasure grounds behind it,
which were so crouded with black and white buildings that one
might very easily mistake it for a Church Yard. Near it are some

Mock Ruins very *neatly* finish'd, intended I suppose to be fine Objects to be view'd from the Sea. If they do not inspire one with the feelings of reverence that are excited by the sight of those reliques of former times which have withstood the injuries of time, at least they give the idea of future duration, a more comfortable one if not quite as well adapted to the subject.

At our return sent to the Post Office and no letters – Some blunder of my friend Thompson's I am sure. I am not so unreasonable as to fret, yet I do feel in this little Island most terribly cut off from every friendly tie. If my Father finds benefit all will be right. He is just return'd and has lain down for a little time. He complains very much of his stomach, yet it is impossible to take less or lighter food than he does. Good night and God bless you my dear love.

Sunday Noon – We are just return'd from our drive and I think my Father rather better than yesterday. While we were out Mr Sharp call'd, he is no great favorite of mine but he is sensible and conversable and may so far be a releif to our Tête à tête.

Monday Morng. – Mr Sharp is now sitting with my Father so I have slip'd away to finish this Cargo. Yesterday pass'd heavily – My Father seems doubtful of receiving benefit from our excursion, he retired early to bed and I was not in a frame of mind to take up my pen. This morning we have taken our drive and he seems better both in health and spirits. At seven I went down to the bathing House where I found a great Number of Ladies and Gentlemen waiting to take their turn in the Machines which are comparatively few in number. They are much better contrived than those we had at Scarboro' – I enclose you a card which gives an idea of their form. The Canvass which is behind when you are at a proper depth is let down into the water and forms a compleat bath where the Guide stands to receive you. It is quite light as the Canvass is very thin. I never bathed so comfortably in my life and find myself much revived by my dip. I have settled to go before Seven every morning which is the time I can best be spared. I saw no one I knew there but Mr

Sharpe. No letter still from Ireland. How sincerely did I wish I had you by my side this morning. God bless you my dear Love – You and yours. My Father ever desires his love. Remember us kindly to your Brother and to all Friends – adieu for the present I shall probably begin to scribble again this Evening.

[On 14th August Thomas Sheridan died at Margate, and Betsy went at once to her sister-in-law Elizabeth at Deepdene, the house near Dorking which R. B. Sheridan had been lent by the Duke of Norfolk.]

CHAPTER 5

Deepdene, Dorking, August to October 1788:
In the country with Mrs Sheridan

36: DEEPDENE, 18TH AUGUST 1788

Dibden, August 18 – Though you have ever been uppermost in
my thoughts, yet it has not been in my power to write since the
few lines I sent from Margate. I hope this will find you, in some
degree, recovered from the shock you must have experienced
from the late melancholy event. I trust to your own piety and
the tenderness of your worthy husband, for procuring you such
a degree of calmness of mind as may secure your health from
injury. In the midst of what I have suffered I have been
thankful that you did not share a scene of distress which you
could not have relieved. I have supported myself, but I am
sure, had we been together, we should have suffered more.

With regard to my brother's kindness, I can scarcely express
to you how great it has been. He saw my Father while he was
still sensible, and never quitted him till the awful moment was
past – I will not dwell on particulars. My mind is not sufficiently recovered to enter on the subject, and you could only be
distressed by it. He returns soon to Margate to pay the last
duties in the manner desired by my Father. His feelings have
been severely tried, and earnestly I pray he may not suffer from
that cause, or from the fatigue he has endured. His tenderness
to me I can never forget. I had so little claim on him, that I still
feel a degree of surprise mixed with my gratitude. Mrs Sheridan's reception of me was truly affectionate. They leave me to
myself now as much as I please, as I had gone through so much

1. *The Linley Sisters*, by Thomas Gainsborough

2. 'Sheridan threatening Sir Sampson Wright', by Gillray

4. Alicia Sheridan

3. Henry LeFanu

5. 'The Prince's Secret Wedding', by Gillray

fatigue of body and mind that I require some rest. I have not, as you may suppose, looked much beyond the present hour, but I begin to be more composed. I could now enjoy your society, and I wish for it hourly. I should think I may hope to see you sooner in England than you had intended; but you will write to me very soon and let me know every thing that concerns you. I know not whether you will feel like me a melancholy pleasure in the reflection that my Father received the last kind offices from my brother Richard, whose conduct on this occasion must convince every one of the goodness of his heart and the truth of his filial affection. One more reflection of consolation is that nothing was omitted that could have prolonged his life or eased his latter hours. God bless and preserve you, my dear love. I shall soon write more to you, but shall for a short time suspend my journal, as still too many painful thoughts will croud upon me to suffer me to regain such a frame of mind as I should wish when I write to you.

37: DEEPDENE, 22ND TO 24TH AUGUST 1788

Dibden, Friday, 22 – I shall endeavour to resume my journal, though my anxiety to hear from you occupies my mind in a way that unfits me for writing. I have been here almost a week in perfect quiet. While there was company in the house, I stayed in my room, and since my brother's leaving us to go to Margate, I have sat at times with Mrs Sheridan, who is kind and considerate; so that I have entire liberty. Her poor sister's children are all with her. The girl gives her constant employment, and seems to profit by being under so good an instructor. Their father was here for some days, but I did not see him. Last night Mrs S. showed me a picture of Mrs Tickell that she wears round her neck. The thing was misrepresented to you: – it was not done after her death, but a short time before it. The sketch was taken while she slept, by a painter at Bristol. This Mrs Sheridan got copied by Cosway, who has softened down the traces of her illness in such a way that the picture conveys no gloomy idea.

It represents her in a sweet sleep, which must have been sooth-
ing to her friend, after seeing her for a length of time in a state
of constant suffering.

My brother left us Wednesday morning, and we do not
expect him to return for some days. He meant only to stay at
Margate long enough to attend the last melancholy office,
which it was my poor Father's express desire should be performed in whatever parish he died.

Sunday – Dick is still in town, and we do not expect him for
some time. Mrs Sheridan seems now quite reconciled to these
little absences, which she knows are unavoidable. I never saw
anyone so constant in employing every moment of her time,
and to that I attribute in a great measure the recovery of her
health and spirits. The education of her niece, her music, books,
and work, occupy every minute of the day. After dinner the
children, who call her 'Mamma-aunt', spend some time with
us, and her manner to them is truly delightful. The girl you
know is the eldest. The eldest boy is about five years old, very
like his father, but extremely gentle in his manners. The
youngest is past three. The whole set then retire to the music
room. As yet I cannot enjoy their parties; – a song from Mrs
Sheridan affected me last night in a most painful manner. I
shall not try the experiment soon again. Mrs S blamed herself
for putting me to the trial, and after tea got a book, which she
read to us till supper. This I find is the general way of passing
the evening.

They are now at their music, and I have retired to add a few
lines. This day has been more gloomy than we have been for
some days past; – it is the first day of our getting into mourning.
All the servants in deep mourning made a melancholy appearance, and I found it very difficult to sit out the dinner. But, as
I have dined below since there has been only Mrs Sheridan
and Miss Linley here, I would not suffer such a circumstance,
to which I must accustom myself, to break in on their comfort.

Wednesday – Yesterday our little quiet circle was broke up – Mrs S: and I had walk'd and had just agreed that we would save ourselves the trouble of a second toilette when a note from Dick changed our whole plan. He announced his return to dinner and also a visit from the Duke of Norfolk who has been expected here for some days past. I was obliged to change my quarters immediately as it seems a very pretty Room in which I have been establish'd ever since my first arrival is the one he always sleeps in. At about six he made his appearance – Dick not yet arrived and what was worse some fish and game he had promised to bring was expected for dinner. Mrs S: put the best face on the matter and order'd up dinner such as it was. Some time after the cloth was removed arrived our Brother who had been detain'd by a variety of cross accidents. This was a great releif to Mrs S: who began to fear a total dissappointment. In the Evening we had music – Miss Linley's voice goes charmingly with her Sister's in Duets. Mrs Sheridan's voice I think as perfect as ever I remember it – That same peculiar tone that I beleive is hardly to be equall'd in the world as every one is struck with it in the same way. We had no cards.

The Duke in appearance gives one the idea of a good honest Gentleman Farmer, dress'd in a plain Grey frock, and brown curly head, his face is hansome but his Person very large and unweildy. He is very civil, very good humour'd seemingly, and perfectly unaffected – tomorrow he leaves us but will probably pay another visit before we leave this part of the World. I ask'd Mrs Sheridan about the Microcosm – Young Canning was one of the writers. She has not got it but I will get it for you from Town the first opportunity.

Excuse my again recurring to the Subject of your Brother[1] – After what I have said I wish to know from you whether I ought to continue a correspondence for which I see no very good pretext. He certainly can know from you what ever he wishes

[1] i.e. brother-in-law, Henry LeFanu.

concerning me, and as the motive for his first letters no longer subsists I own I am rather doubtful whether he would himself expect me to continue to write to him – he says nothing on the subject. And his not letting the correspondence drop on his side was a thing of course – a meer matter of common civility. I should be very glad if by means of Mr L— you could find out his real sentiments on that Subject. At all events I shall not write 'till I hear from you, as the length of time he has suffer'd to pass since I last wrote does not entitle him to expect an immediate answer. Enough and too much of this.

We have nothing but wind and rain – no stirring out – This does not agree with me. Your interviews with Charles always distress you – do not my dear Love encrease them on my account. I fear he is callous to every right feeling, Yet I have brought myself to write to him in a stile I think he cannot object to. I accept the addition to my allowance and have drawn accordingly. He does not mention his Wife's name in his letter to me. My way of life furnishes me with few materials for entertainment and always self is a tiresome Subject.

I heard the other day an account of Miss Burney[1] which makes her rather an object of compassion than envy for having attracted Royal notice. It seems the employment She has about the Queen is litterally of that kind that requires absolute servile attendance. At Eight oclock every morning She must be drest for the day in great form and always be within call, and so far from deriving any advantages from her litterary talents The Queen has made it a point that She shall write no more Novels. It reminds one of poor Madam de Staal's promotion to the Duchess de Maine's favor. Dick's best love and Mrs Sheridan's ever attend you. Dreadful accounts of Suicide in Dublin – Swan's seems very extraordinary.

39: DEEPDENE, 2ND TO 5TH OCTOBER 1788

Thursday – This morng. my dear Love our Visitor left us.

[1]See Fanny Burney's Diary.

Yesterday the dinner made up for the plain fare of the day before – Turtle Venison etc – and he did such honor to it as shew'd he must have been punish'd the first day. To see him eat his bulk is at once accounted for, as any four reasonable men might be satisfied with what he takes in a day. In the Evening Cribbage was proposed which I play ill but as there was one absolutely wanted and the Duke was my partner I ran no risk in playing as Dick and I were to settle together so I lost without being the poorer. Today we shall return to our regular hours which I am glad of for late ones do not do with me nor with Mrs Sheridan who has not been well these few days past. She is very uneasy about her Father and I am afraid with too much reason. He had it seems some time ago a kind of paralitic attack in his head – so violent that his life was in the greatest danger. Ever since he has suffer'd constant violent pain in his head. It is really distressing to see him, and she says She can not divest herself of the horrid dread of seeing him fall dead before her – loving him as she does you must suppose what she suffers. Her attentions to him are unremitting. She is now working hard at some music they are preparing for Drury Lane to save him the labor as much as possible. Indeed I think she exerts herself rather too much for upon the idea of keeping herself constantly employ'd I think she exhausts her spirits.

Friday – Today my Brother went to Town. The weather is bad but Mrs S: order'd the carriage for her Father to take the air and ask'd me to accompany him as She is so busy. Miss Linley and the Children were with us. I rather liked the drive as the Country about here is very beautiful. Mr Linley as usual very low. I can not but think that his disorder is very much on his spirits. His daughter has prevail'd on him at last to follow his Physicians direction, which is to have his hair cut off and try a blister. She has the greatest hopes from it. As I have nothing but unpleasant ideas to day I will write no more.

Sunday Morng. – Yesterday I was not well in the morning and could not accompany them in their airing. Mr Linley seem'd much better. His daughter tells him the sight of a blister and wig She had got from Town was the cause of this amendment. In the Evening Mrs Linley arrived in a great fright about her Husband. She brought with her a Mr Pratton an Apothecary – The same my Brother made me see in London and a person it seems they have all a great opinion of. A fresh attempt was now made to prevail on Mr Linley to part with his hair but in vain – And they proceeded to play whist. Mrs S— still busy with her music so I sat down to the first rubber but was so worried with Mrs Linley's incessant prate at the end of it I deputed Tom to play for me. If the poor Man had no other cause of illness such constant teasing would be sufficient to account for his headakes. The incurable vulgarity of that good Lady is something astonishing, and in another disposition of mind I should find entertainment in her. Yet She is not without some good qualities that secure her the regard of her friends – really affectionate and fond of her family, where their health or comfort is concern'd She never spares her own, and tho' her avarice often leads her to the meanest actions to save a trifle, Yet her purse is freely open'd to those She loves should any extraordinary occasion require her assistance. My Brother gave me an instance of this which I think does her real credit. It seems she has some little profits arising from her Theatrical interference, which She reserves wholly for her own use, by constant saving and putting the money out as She received it it accumulated to a tollerably large Sum – last Year when poor Mrs Tickell's illness began first to allarm them, She went with her whole stock to Tickell and with tears in her eyes beg'd he would accept it for the use of her poor daughter, that She might not want any assistance or alleviation that money could procure. This is no Woman of sentiment.

Pratton has been blistering and bleeding poor Linley from which they hope to give him temporary releif. But certainly it is very cruel in him to deny his Friends the satisfaction of trying at least the only remedy which his Physicians think would be effectual. It distresses Mrs S: very much and I do not wonder at it. She is however well again since we have return'd to our

regular hours. I am better I think for Dr Morris's last pre-
scriptions. I walk out when I can as our weather is now tollerable and even when Stormy the woods afford us delightful
shelter. Yours of the 30th is just brought me – I would desire
you not to think of using your Pen on my account 'till your
finger is quite well but that I hope it will be cured long before
this reaches you. Mr Lefanu's very kind letter I deffer answering 'till I hear from Ireland again, as I wrote to him last
Monday a long letter that relates to the business he now
mentions. To you my dear Love I write as I talk in all modes
and tempers – Also as to the only person who truly knows my
real sentiments on all subjects. Mrs Sheridan's kindest love,
She will write soon. At present her Father and the music leave
her scarce a minute to herself. Mrs Linley enquired very
kindly for you and your family.

40: DEEPDENE, 10TH TO 13TH OCTOBER 1788

Last night after supper We got upon the topic of Animal
Magnetism with Tessier who professes to understand the whole
business and told us many wonderful stories. I ask'd Mrs
Sheridan whether there was any truth in what We had heard
concerning her having experienced the effects of it. She confess'd that she had and entirely confirm'd the account I had
heard from Col: Faucette. The first time She went to Dr
Maneduke,[1] She staid only a short time and found no effect
from his experiments. She promised to return to him again and
to allow him what time he thought necessary. This she did in
the course of a few days in company with Mrs Crewe. She was
that time thrown into a state which She describes as very distressing. It was a kind of fainting without absolute insensibility.
She could hear and feel but had no power to speak or move.
The fit gradually went off and she told Maneduke She was not
even then convinced as She thought such effects might be
produced on a nervous person by the effects of imagination.

[1]Mainauduc.

[123]

She continued ill all day and when She went home told my Brother what she had been doing who blamed her very much and made her give him a solemn promise never to try the experiment again.

She had engaged herself to go with the Duchess of Devonshire which she did but with the intention of being only a Spectator. She sat down at the end of the room and engaged in conversation with some of her acquaintances without the smallest expectation of being affected, when in a few minutes She found herself attack'd as before but in a more violent degree her limbs being now convuls'd. She made a violent effort to express what She suffer'd and to insist on immediate releif. She could hear Maneduke say that the crisis was near and that it would be better to let the fit go off of it self, but on her continuing to make violent signs of impatience he did something which brought her almost instantly to herself but She continued ill and exhausted the whole day. In excuse for trying the experiment without consulting her the Doctor alledged the wish She had express'd to be convinced of the reallity of such a power – The Duchess of Devonshire was thrown into Hysterics, Lady Salisbury put to sleep the same morning – And the Prince of Wales so near fainting that he turned quite pale and was forced to be supported. To what good purpose this amazing power can be turn'd I can not at present conceive.

Tessier told us no bad anecdote of himself if it be true – When they were getting up the Farce of 'Animal Magnetism' at Covent Garden Mr Harris ask'd him to shew the performer who was to magnetize the proper motions to use. That accordingly he put himself in his place opposite to Mrs Mattocks and *really* magnetized her, in such a way as to throw her into convulsive fits of laughing – that on her recovering herself she made him many apollogies and attempted to go through the scene. But he continuing his experiments She was again affected and it was not 'till he had tormented her some time he confess'd the truth. He told me that he knew the extant of this strange power to be so great that he could strike me dead with it. You may suppose I have no intention to try any experiments as even allowing greatly for exageration still mischeif enough may be done to make one pay too dear for a gratification of curiosity.

Our weather is very fine today and I have been taking advantage of it the woods affording us very pleasant shelter against the northern blasts that begin to visit us. I made an attempt to shoot, but a very bad one. I had a letter this morning from G— Morris that affected me. It is written in such a strain of real affection, at the same time of acquiescence to my wishes that I sometimes think I have put away a real blessing, for the indulgence of hopes that may never be realized.

Mr Linley continues to mend. Tessier I find remains here some days – this Evening he is to read to us and Mrs S— has been telling her Mother the story of the peice that she may make out some amusement for herself out of it to console her for the loss of cards. God bless you my love. I have scribbled this much out of my own stock. Tomorrow I hope a letter from you will give me fresh materials.

Saterday – As I expected this day I received two packets from Ireland – Yours of the 6th and Mr Lefanu's enclosing some papers. I must see Dick which I expect will be today before I can answer him fully. I sincerely wish you were with us to hear Tessier for I know you would be amused – He gave us 'L'Avocat Pattelin' last night but did not I think read with as much spirit as the former time. As a companion he sometimes entertains us more than he intends as his marvellous stories make us a little enclined to laugh at him as well as with him, but he is quite unconscious of this so all is very well.

In answer to what you ask about my Brother, it is true that he is the purchaser of Dr Ford's share but he does not chuze to have it generally known. The Duke of Norfolk did not lend him the money, but who did is I beleive equally a secret to Mrs S. and myself. She declares She is often astonish'd at the points apparently almost impossible which he accomplishes. He now says his great object is to make as much money as he can and she is certain he will succeed. His time has latterly been entirely engross'd by the Theatre which he has been putting in the best train he could, Mr King having (luckily I think) deserted them at the Eve of opening the House.

Sunday – I was call'd away yesterday to take an airing, we drove to the House of a Mr Lock remarkable for commanding a very fine prospect, but it is of that kind I can not admire from there being a total want of water. Linley mends daily and would I think be soon well if his good wife would leave him. One is obliged perpetually to call to mind that She possesses some virtues to support one's spirits under her excessive vulgarity to which is also adjoin'd a most ungovernable temper. Mrs S: is as you may suppose heartily weary of the visit, but she conceals her vexation as well as She can. Not to feel both vex'd and mortified under such circumstances is I think impossible. Dick did not come last night and Tessier who had taken up his abode at Dibden in the full persuasion of his coming down immediately look'd very blank on the occasion. This morng. he left us as he had staid to the last minute he could command. The fact is I beleive that notre cher Frère sent him to us to get rid of him for a few days as he plagued him in Town. He says positively he will be here at dinner today.

Monday – Last night my dear love Dick came to us. I had a long conversation with him this morng on the contents of Mr Lefanu's last letter. He means to write to him himself and wishes me to send the letter on which account I still defer my answer. He left us this morng and Mr and Mrs Linley also went to Town.

Tomorrow Mrs S— and I go for a few days when I shall make it my business to go to the Bankers to settle the matter as Mr Lefanu proposes as soon as possible. The portion of the *Dictionary* I have recieved I sent to Dilly immediately – I mean to see him Wednesday morng.

Mr Tickell came last night and goes to Town with us tomorrow. We are to dine with him at the Stamp Office. You know how I love him and I beleive Mrs S— not much more partial – but these things cannot be help'd.

This day my dearest love I received yours of the 15th. As to your thoughts about the Duke of Norfolk I certainly should have made the attack had he been as you suppose a *Maiden* Duke, but alas He is a Husband for the second time. His first Lady lived but a short time – and his present Dutchess is out of her senses; so that she is not known in the World but She is at times well enough to dine at table with him, with a very private circle.

Mrs S— had an answer this morng from Mrs Canning. She has taken a lodging for me on very reasonable terms and writes in the kindest way possible. She insists on my being set down at her House and that I should give them as much of my company as my health or spirits will allow. Thursday I have fix'd to go.

Mr Tickell left us today. I have been walking with Miss Linley in a Park that joins our grounds that I had never yet visited – nothing can be more beautiful than it is. Our weather is charming but Mrs S— durst not venture with us as her cold is still very severe.

22nd – No Dick last night but a note from him to mention that he was under promise to go to Brighton with the Prince today and that they should probably call at Deepden on their way so we were all prepared for the visit betimes but they did not come and I am glad of it as Mrs S— has been really ill all day – She is rather better this evening. There is a kind of influenza in the House almost all the Servants are laid up and poor Tom as bad as any one. He is at my elbow playing with a Dormouse he made me a present of some time ago. Tho' not desirous of keeping any more Pets I could not refuse him as he seem'd quite pleased with having procured it for me and had at his own expence got me a proper cage for him at Dorking. He leaves us in a day or two, and I shall really regret him as it is impossible to conceive a more amiable disposition than his united to spirits that make it impossible to be entirely sad in his company – I have defer'd my journey 'till friday as I hope by then the family will be in a better state than now.

By the papers you have no doubt seen that the King has been ill. It is perfectly true and he still continues very ill. We have heard nothing from London yet but it is not unlikely that the King's indisposition may have been the cause of putting off the Brighton party. When we hear I shall add something to this. Good night my dear Love.

23d – This morng. your most welcome pacquet of the Seventeenth was deliver'd to me. To say it did not give me the highest satisfaction would be gross hypocrisy, my anxiety to know the truth must have convinced you how material it was to my happyness. I might have spared some of my last journal but, as our Friend Mad: de Sevigné says, that is one of the plagues of absence that we are often concern'd at greifs that no longer exist. Your kindness and Mr Lefanu's adds greatly to my joy at the pleasing prospects before me. Yes I will now admit of hope which has been so long a stranger to my heart. I will write to your Brother and as you desire avoid a prudery foreign to my character and feelings. Yet I feel awkward – to say *no* to a person who is indifferent to us is much easier than to say yes with a tollerable grace where we are conscious the explanation has been long desired on our part. I entirely agree with you as to the propriety of defering any farther engagement 'till circumstances shall put it in our power to do it with comfort and credit. From my Brother Richard's latter conduct to me I have the strongest reason to rely on every act of real friendship in his power. And Mrs Sheridan assures me that nothing would give him more pleasure than to see me so happily and ellegibly connected. As to my return to Ireland tho' as I have before told you my heart is with you I believe the *wise Head* you allude to is perfectly right. Dick now considers me as under his immediate care and protection and will I am certain act in the best manner. To leave them now that I have a prospect of seeing you so soon in England might bear the appearance of unkindness which in me would be wholly unjustifiable. He gave us a

[128]

flying call today on his way to Brighton where he was engaged to dine with the Prince. He regretted much he had not been able to give us notice of his motions or he would have taken me with him – but I am better pleased as it is, as Mrs S: is by no means well today and I hope to leave her better tomorrow. She sends her coach with me the first Stage and I then shall proceed in a Chaise. Saterday they set out for Stafford. God bless you my dear Woman I must write a few lines to my Gentleman.

I enclose my answer to Harry unseal'd – If it requires any comment I beg you to make it as you know my meaning tho' it is very possible I may not have express'd myself clearly. You will seal it or not as you think best.

Mrs Sheridan desires her love and bids me tell you she will write as soon as she gets to Mrs Bouverie's. She will talk to her good Gentleman on the subject of your letter when She gets him to herself in the Chaise.

CHAPTER 6

The Regency Crisis:
London and Deepdene, November 1788 to April 1789

42: LONDON, 16TH AND 21ST NOVEMBER 1788

I am here in the midst of news and politics. Ever since Breakfast
Mrs S— has had a constant Levee and the present situation of
the king of course the only topic of conversation. I have been as
you may suppose chiefly a listener. I have been a good deal
amused by their various conjectures which were all suited to
their different interests. Among the last group came Mr
Erskine, to me the most pleasing man of any I had seen. There
is so much fire and sense in his manner that it is impossible for
the moment not to be entirely of his opinion. What might perhaps influence me in his favour is the knowledge of his being a
respectable and amiable private character. The fact is that the
reports of the king's amendment relate only to his health. His
mind continues in the same state it has been for some time past.
If any alteration happens tomorrow I shall add a line to inform
you, but from the kind of life I must lead here I think it best to
snatch any moment I can to write, as I might otherwise be
entirely prevented.

Novr. 21st – We are as unsettled and uncomfortable as you
can conceive. Ever talking of going to the country and the
house all confusion so that I litterally can sometimes hardly find
a place to sit down and write a line to tell you of this to account
for the brevity and confusion of my latter journals. Tuesday, we
dined at home and alone. In the evening Tickell and Richardson as usual. Dick with us but so engaged in thought he hardly

seemed to hear or see us, and so went to the play, Confederacy and Sultan, Mrs Jordan delightful in both. The usual intimates came home to eat oysters. I now have got the method of going to bed as I could not hold out a month of Mrs Sheridan's town life.

This morng I was just reading yours of the 17th when Sir Watkin and T. Grenville were announced. He recollected me almost immediately and I think I should have known him anywhere, just the same pleasing ingenuous countenance you remember.

The news just the same. But certainly something will soon be settled and according to our wishes. I scribbled a few lines to you on the subject which you in your wisdom will reflect on. I also wrote to Harry some of my ideas which he will communicate to you. I wish to God you were on the spot. As I am certain that once he has the power there is nothing he wishes more than to serve you by employing his interest for Mr Lefanu.

Cher Frere has been gone since four o clock this morning to a private conference. He is the head they all apply to now, and he will be if things turn out as we have reason to expect just what he chuzes.

Among the numbers that drop in we hear a variety of anecdotes relative to the K—'s situation. One I heard yesterday shocked me very much. It seems he had been anxious to go to the Queen but they were obliged to prevent him. This he complained of bitterly, repeating frequently 'I am eight and twenty years married and now have no wife at all, is not that very hard?' And then said, looking at the Duke of York 'I love you Frederick, but I love the Queen better, she is my best friend.' These sort of ideas have however seldom troubled him. He is generally very busy about some particular object. Latterly he has been making commentaries on the Bible and Cervantes which he dictates to the pages in waiting. They have not been able to prevail on him to get up or to be shaved. Nor has he lately liked to see the Frince, who however is constant in his attendance at Windsor. Some nights ago he went softly into the room and put his eye to a hole there was in a large screen that stood between the bed and the door. While he looked at the bed the K— happened to look up and immediately perceived the eye. The Prince withdrew at the instant, but the K— called to one of the pages and said 'I have seen my son.' They assured him he had not, however he persisted and when he found they still denied it he gave no other answer but a most significant glance at the screen.

43: DEEPDENE, 27TH AND 28TH NOVEMBER 1788

I did not write yesterday as our life here now affords no materials for correspondence and I have of late you know been pretty communicative of my own sentiments and opinions – This Morng my hopes of enjoyment here were damp'd on my first rising by finding the ground entirely cover'd with Snow: I had scarce time to grumble at my bad fortune when the Post came in with three letters from Dublin – 20th – 21st – 22d – enclosing two from Harry – and at the same time a few lines from Mrs S— She had scarcely set eyes on her good Gentleman who was taken up entirely with Charles Fox and the P. of W—. I should tell you the latter Gentleman has more esteem and friendship for him than for any Man in England. Matters at Windsor *exactly* in the same State, and You may depend on My *Bulletins* (as Dick calls it) before any accounts you hear or read. I have already written fully to you on the ideas the present situation of affairs suggested and shall wait impatiently to hear your opinion on the matter. I begin to doubt of their returning to Deepden now that winter has fairly made its appearance, and as my cheif motive both for coming and remaining here was to have some chance of talking with our Brother which I knew to be impossible in Town I shall only stay here 'till I find what is their determination.

As to your questions concerning Mrs Crewe and Mrs Bouverie I can not entirely satisfy you as I do not know the cause of their difference. That Mrs Crewe hates Mrs B— is certain – And to such a degree as to be distress'd if they accidentally meet. Mrs B— neither seeks nor avoids her and by what has drop'd from Mrs Sheridan I fancy She is the injured person of the two. Some love affair I beleive to be the origin of the quarrel. As to Mrs Crewe's coldness with regard to Mrs S— it is partly jealousy of Mrs B— to whom Mrs S— certainly gives the preference. You know also that Mrs Crewe among other Lovers (favor'd ones I mean) Has had our Brother in her train. As his fame and consequence in Life have encreased, her charms have diminished, and passion no longer the tie between them, his affection, esteem and attentions return'd to their proper channel. And he never has seem'd or I believe never was in truth so much attach'd to his wife as of late, and this her *dear friend* can not bear. And Mrs S— tells me that while they were at Crewe Hall, she took little pains to conceal her jealousy. A strange system you will say altogether and for such people to associate and disgrace the name of friendship is truly disgusting. Yet such I am told is the universal practice of the great world, Or as poor Jenny Linley calls them 'the *fine* people' of whom She seems to have a comfortable dislike. There is something good and quiet about her that makes her improve much on acquaintance. She feels that she is not form'd to figure in the sphere chance has placed her and yet She has no retreat – for her Father and Mother seem glad to get her off their hands at any rate and give her grudgingly the small allowance that is necessary to cloath her. The Old Gentlewoman has been even so ungenerous as to reproach her with not having contributed to her own support, tho' they are really in affluent circumstances; and what is more her Father never gave her any instructions. She has however pick'd up a good deal of musick, and has the Linley toned voice, tho not a powerfull one. She accompanies herself with a Luth which I think a very sweet instrument. Her Sister is fond of her and my Brother is very kind to her, but her mind is depress'd and tho' pretty and accomplish'd She will never feel at her ease in the circle in which She is placed. In Mrs Sheridan's absence She takes charge of her little Niece and continues to give her the same lessons as when She is here. The Boys as yet learn nothing, but they are fine children – And Tickell seems to idolize them.

Friday is come and as I expected an excuse from Mrs Sheridan on account of the badness of the weather. She still says Dick means to spend some days here before the meeting of Parliament – but if he does not come I shall certainly go to Town whether the rest of the family move or not, for I know it is very necessary to look after one's own interest in this World and my being absent might hurt me. We are block'd up by snow and I feel vex'd to be so caught by my fear of fatigue which I need not have incurr'd as I could have remained in Town when I was there but they all seem'd so determined to stay only a few days that I did not like to go against the general opinion which seem'd to be that I had best keep quiet.

Mrs S. tells me She has written to you so you have now the best intelligence relative to important matters. All the House here have caught colds by this violent change of weather. I have as yet escaped very well by keeping very quietly by the fireside. God bless you my love I must leave you to talk to the Gentlemen. I have two long letters from Harry as kind as possible. I can't write a separate letter to Mr L— as the fact is I have not another sheet of paper in the House. Give my Love to him and tell him the quarter of the pension is not £50. but 47., owing to deductions that of late years have been made at the Exchequer. The £30. I received from Mr Powel has already repaid me the twenty I sent, together with the expence of proving the Will which I enclosed to Mr L—. I am rejoiced to hear from Harry so good an account of your dear little ones, a kiss apeice to them, and my love to William.

44: LONDON, 3RD DECEMBER 1788

Pitt has sent impertinent restrictions to the Prince and in an impertinent manner by a common Livery Servant, but the Prince, in compassion to the unsettled state of the nation, does

accept the Regency even on these terms and has informed the
Cabinet of his intentions in a letter sent last night to them. For
he did not chuze to address his answer to Mr Pitt in particular.
Nothing can be better than what he says on this occasion. The
most perfect moderation blended with a strong sense of the
unworthy manner in which he is treated by the Minister.[1] The
answer will soon be made public and I shall send it by the first
opportunity. The K— continues the same – Their new word
'Comfortable' meaning nothing more than his not being out-
rageous.

Mr Grenville is talked of very positively as Speaker. He is
just nine and twenty. No doubt of the Prince's constancy to my
Brother. I have already told you that I saw Mr Fox. His
manners are certainly plain and unaffected in the greatest
degree. If one did not know he was a great man, the idea one
would take up would be merely that he was goodnatured and
goodhumoured to the greatest degree.

45: LONDON, 12TH DECEMBER 1788

Still you see nothing is determin'd. Pitt is determin'd to fight
every inch of ground and gains time and gives trouble to others
tho' there is not the smallest probability of his holding out long.
Dick came home to dinner yesterday at seven. He seem'd much
harrass'd for added to the trouble that naturally falls to him,
every difficult negotiation, every mistake to be rectified is put
upon him. Teusday will be a day of great consequence to them –
And will we hope decide every thing favorably.

They went in the Eveng to Mrs Bouverie. Mrs S— ask'd me to
go with her but I can't yet reconcile myself to the idea of going
among Strangers. I almost regret I was not tempted to go as
She told me this morng Mr Fox was there, but the fact is I have
not been well these two days – My head torments me and
exhausts my spirits. Tickell dined with us but went away in the
Eveng. Our Brother was with the Prince 'till 4 this morning and

[1]Sheridan drafted the letter, and Mrs Sheridan made the fair copy.

as usual I have not seem him today for he never leaves his dressing Room but to go out. I shall take an opportunity of speaking to Mrs S— about what you say of Swan's place and She may tell Dick, for in the present situation of things I can not get his ear for a moment and the sooner he knows it the better.

You are very kind my dear Love in what you say of my future prospects with Harry. You know how long I have esteem'd and loved him. I have every reason to be satisfied now of his attachment and I should be compleatly happy If my very uncertain health did not throw a damp over my satisfaction. Yet I make it my study to regain a better state, as I find the Spirits will sink with the body. I am sure he is perfectly amiable and had we met sooner I think I should have been more worthy of his affection, however as it is I certainly would not resign my place in his heart for any good this world could give me. No Post goes out tomorrow or I should not have written today for my head akes very much, but I could not bear to leave you in suspense about the grand business. God bless you my dear Love. Kind love to Mr L and *votre cher Frere* –

46: LONDON, 20TH DECEMBER 1788

Yesterday my dear Love you see nothing material was done. Tickell and Richardson were here all day, part of the time preparing an address to come from different parts of the country to counteract Mr Pitt. Mrs S— continued really ill all day. In the evening Dick sent Dr Turton to her and he seems to consider her complaint a violent nervous attack. She certainly goes beyond her strength at times. Last Teusday She sat up at Mrs Bouverie's till six in the morng to hear the event of that day's debate – part of the time without fire – so that fatigue, cold and anxiety united may well account for her present indisposition. To day She is better and I hope a little quiet and care will set her up in a day or two. Miss L— has got down as far as my Room, and I go all over the House – this is the present state of the family. Mrs S— was in her drawing room and Tickell fidgetting and sentimentalizing all day. Mr L and the good Lady dined with us but went away early. George Canning drop'd in at night and they all supt here but I made my escape to bed at the time Mrs S— retired. This morng Mrs Bouverie came to see her. She certainly is a woman of most engaging manners. I saw le cher Frère for a minute but that was all. He was uneasy about Mrs S— but otherwise in good spirits, as far as Politics are concern'd we are so secure that matters are only delay'd. Bishop Dixon left his Card here Thursday, I beleive they are all here upon the look out. No Post tomorrow so I send these few lines –

47: LONDON, 22ND AND 23RD DECEMBER 1788

Monday 22nd Evng – I sent you my dear Love a few lines while dinner was waiting that you might not be uneasy about us. The Debate of this day is of consequence. We have had one note from le Cher Frère but as yet no particular intelligence. He has not yet spoken.

I have not been out of the House these eight days 'till this morng that I got the Coach for an hour and went to the Yarkers who were truly glad to see me and I have promised to dine with them on Friday. I will make it a point to see Miss Hamilton but indeed my dear love I can not follow my own inclinations in my present situation. I never can get out but when the Carriage can be spared and tho' they are very willing to oblige me with it yet it is so much used by my Brother as well as Mrs S— that it is seldom I can get it for my own use without inconvenience to one or other. My taking a Hack would obviate this inconvenience but that would not please them I know and I am obliged for the present to sacrifice to the opinions of others. Yesterday we were all at home – Mrs S— really very much indisposed. Dick meant to have the day to himself to read over Precedents and prepare for this day's business. Before he was up comes a message from the Prince to beg to see him immediately – he sent word he was not very well and had taken a medicine that made it necessary for him to keep house. In less than half an hour the Duke of York was in Bruton St. and shortly after him the Prince himself, both boring him and preventing him reading said papers, And to compleat all, they beg'd him to see another person who idled him two hours more. In the Eveng Tickell and Richardson call'd as usual. Miss L and I dined tete a tete.

Today Mrs S— is considerably better, Tho not yet able to venture down. This morng I saw Miss Townshend who call'd on Miss L, and was sorry to hear from her that Mrs Greville is ill – much in the same way She was in Dublin. Mrs Crewe is here this Eveng so as I don't leave Mrs S— alone I got away to write this.

As to Fashions I have not yet had an opportunity of seeing much. Mrs S—[1] has not much taste I think and what She has she leaves under the direction of Charles who has none. Bonnets I see most generally worn and some with very deep Curtains, The Bonnet itself is small. Hats are also worn, like riding hats. The Hair universally dress'd very loose in small curls – as many in curls down behind as otherwise. What caps I have seen just of the same kind we had last year all made on very deep round headpeice. As to gowns all kinds – Chemises – Round gowns with flounce or not. Great coats made very open before to shew the peticoat – in Undress – half dress, Night gown and peticoat with fine muslin Aprons – full dress I have not seen, but from what I can gather the same as we had last year in Dublin. I give but a flemish account but you must consider I have not been once in company since I came over. A few chance Men, and women quite in undress are all I have seen here, so what little I have seen was at the play House.

The accounts from Kew are worse and worse. For several days past he has had the Strait waistcoat and has been obliged to be lash'd down in bed beside. Great Wars and Rumours of Wars among the medical Tribe – Willis abuses the regular

[1]Presumably Mrs Charles Sheridan.

Physicians and they Scout him. He certainly acted a Strange part on *Teusday* last – In the course of the debate a Note from him was deliver'd to Mr Pitt informing him that within a few hours the K— had had a very great and sudden change for the better and that he had continued some hours in that State of amendment and that he (Doctor Willis) had now the strongest hopes of a perfect recovery in a very short time. The note was circulated thro' the House and 'tis not a very unreasonable supposition that many might be influenced in their vote by such a prospect being held out to them. Dr Warren who had been at Kew in the morng and had not perceived these violent symptoms of approaching amendment set off immediately to enquire into the matter and found the K— in the State I have already described, and on questioning all the Attendants was inform'd by them that he never had been worse than during the precise point of time that Dr Willis had mark'd as the period of amendment. Dr Warren was in a great passion almost call'd the other a Villain and other names of the same import.

All the regular Physicians are in a kind of disgrace at Court since the Examination at the House of Lords. The Princess Royal has been ill of a fever and soar throat, But the Queen would not allow Sir G. Baker to attend her, Assigning for reason that he never could expect favor from her after having answer'd in the manner he did when examin'd before the House of Lords. The others will probably be all dismiss'd in their turn, as being question'd on Oath they could only answer according to their consciences.

I am perfectly of your mind about *reccomendations* and told Dick so the first opportunity I have had of speaking to him and he seem'd to mind me, but your letters will best enforce the argument. At present they talk of the Duke of Northumberland for Ireland, I don't like him as well as any of the others. The D: of Devonshire will not go positively. The D: of Norfolk is afraid of drinking himself out of the world, and Ld: D—[1] I suppose won't leave Miss Farren. I have now written all my

[1] Lord Derby.

budget of news, tomorrow I shall add the event of this day and hope it will be pleasing.

Harry talks with some certainty of coming over as soon as the Regency is settled, this hope has raised my Spirits very much tho' beleive me I would not purchase the pleasure of seeing him by any risk. Yet it certainly would be a great comfort to me in the interval that must still ellapse before we are all united. I have here people who wish me well and treat me kindly but no friend to whom I can fairly unfold my thoughts. Mrs S— always amiable and obliging has adopted ideas on many subjects so very different from what mine must be that we can never converse with that freedom that minds in some sort of the same kind indulge in. She told me last night She had converted Mrs Canning who was *uncommonly rigid* in her notions, and therefore was not without hopes of bringing me over to her way of thinking. I assured her, her chance was much worse with me than with Mrs C – for that so far from being *rigid* I was convinced I was *indulgent* to the utmost verge of propriety, and that therefore I must *err* to extend my latitude in the smallest degree – That my opinions on some points were as fix'd as my principles and that I was now too old to change either – That I allow'd others to indulge their own way of thinking and should no more quarrel with a woman for thinking differently in point of morals that I should on religious matters if She had happen'd to be brought up a Mahometan. In this manner I always treat the subject and we end in good humour.

I must add to my chapter of Fashions that furr Muffs (very large) and Tippets are universal. The tippet tied round the throat makes a very good imitation of a brown beard. Your chapter on fine people puts me in conceit with myself. Certainly Ease and assurance are more the striking distinction of a Woman of Fashion than polish'd manners or ellegance of deportment.

Teusday – The event of yesterday has not proved what they wish'd – Pitt's majority I see is encreased tho' we had every reason to expect otherwise.

London Dec 29th – Saterday my Dear love I dined with Dr
Morris and stop'd in Pall Mall to buy your gloves. I have fitted
you as well as I could by analogy, if they don't answer send me
a glove and I will endeavour to do better for you another time.
Our day pass'd off very well – no awkwardness or unpleasantness of any kind. Charles was to set out for France the next
morng and gave me at parting one of the prettiest french boxes
I ever saw. The Dr sent his carriage home with me and well he
did for ours was not forth coming and the night was so severe
there was hardly a coach to be had. I had been invited to go to
Mrs Bouverie's where Mrs S— went after dining with a Mr
Crawford who gave a dinner to Mrs Fitzherbert, Dutchess of
Devonshire, Prince, etc., but I was tired and cold and prefer'd
staying at home – the more so as I knew my hopeless passion
was out of Town.

Yesterday the report was that the K— was much better –
mais n'en croyez rien. Those accounts are always sent at the
Eve of the meeting of Parliament. We dined at home, Mrs
Linley came to spend the day, not much to the joy of Mrs S—
who expected her Eveng party of fine People, but the evil could
not be avoided, Mr L— and William came also and I play'd
whist with them to oblige Mrs S—. The same Women as before
but more Men, among the rest Mr Grenville – but somehow we
are not acquainted now. The same set will probably be here
tonight and this is the life always when Mrs S— don't go out.
Dick dined with us by chance, The Prince waiting to see him
all the time. I never can get out of a morng as the Carriage
being kept out almost all night is never order'd till four and my
walking dependence Miss Linley is still in a very weak state – I
think her really ill, ever since her last attack She has continued
low and weak and entirely lost her spirits and good looks tho'
she has both care and advice.

I do not expect any news to send tomorrow so shall not
write again till Wednesday, but now I think of it I will trouble

you with a little commission which is to buy for me at Reilly's two poplin gowns and petticoats – 22 yards I think for each gown. The best half tabinet.[1] The coulour I wish is a kind of silver grey which may be worn in slight mourning, but is also to be worn out of mourning. I suppose you need not pay Reilly directly and I shall send you the money at the time I remit Mr Powell's ballance. I mean one for a present to Mrs S— and one for myself. If your good Brother will take charge of them when he comes I shall be very much obliged to him. Kind love to both your Gentlemen.

49: LONDON, 3RD TO 6TH JANUARY 1789

I have sent a long Letter, my dear Love, to Harry and now return to my journal for You. Yesterday we were at home but Mrs S— did not admit many Visitors as She was busy writing out a fair Copy of the Prince's answer to the Restrictions which was to go to the Council that very night. Nothing could be better than it was; for we made her read it to us. Dick (Wrapp'd up in a fine Pellisse the Prince has given him) then set off with it to Carlton House. Mrs Crewe came and was admitted, And Tickell who supp'd with us. I have received Harry's letter today which has been a great comfort to me tho' I did not allow myself to be very uneasy.

Monday, 5th – Saterday Eveng the usual set – In addition Bishop Dixon, who looks I think very old. Dick was at home most part of the Eveng and supp'd with us – Mrs Crewe as usual in the little room *listening* to what pass'd in the next.

Yesterday J. Linley and I dined with the Angelos, Osias Linley just come from Oxford was of the party. He is rather a handsome young Man and has a sensible countenance; but has such invincible gravity of manner that it is difficult to avoid laughing at him. Part of his gravity may be owing to timidity of which he seems to have a great share. The Church is the profession He has chosen and Mrs S— has got the promise of a

[1]A watered poplin, half-silk half-wool, chiefly made in Ireland.

living for him. William Linley was there and he and his Sister sung very pleasantly after Supper. We had also Mr Vernon that you may remember to have seen there – exactly the same only a little fatter with his Second Wife a very pretty Lancashire Girl who fell in love with him within this last year. He determin'd to make us admire her musical talents which among the Linleys did not appear to advantage. Osias who plays charmingly on the Piano Forte gave us a short lesson which was really delightful – and She immediately took possession of the instrument evidently to the edification of no one but herself or her Husband, and almost every song from Miss L's really sweet voice was purchased at the expence of one very ill sung by the same Lady. Upon the whole however the day pass'd off very well. Kitty's intended was there – a good humor'd rather *chubby* well looking Young Man.

This day the House meets to chuze a Speaker. 'Tis universally thought that W: Grenville will be the Man. Dick Sheridan[1] has just left me and has promised to call on me tomorrow to take me *abroad* which is a thing I find impracticable of a morng now, As I can get neither Carriage nor Servant, Notre Frère employs them so constantly and I *must* not go out alone. Tomorrow – Twelfth night, I am ask'd to Mrs Craufurd's and mean to go as 'tis within a Chair distance. This moment yours of the 31st is brought me and a little note from Harry. He complains still but is in good hands and soon I trust all will be well –

I thought I had told you all about the Dutchess of Devonshire. She cannot I think be call'd fat but upon the whole I think there is too much of her. She gives me the idea of being *larger* than life. I do not think her Ellegant – She was here last night and with her Lady Elizabeth Forster who lives with her and is her bosom friend, but is supposed to be more particularly the friend of the Duke – such is the system of the fine World. As to the Dutchess, tho' we Who stand at awfull distance consider her character in a respectable light I find among her *friends* She is by no means supposed to be sparing of her *smiles* at least – Voilà le monde, as you used to say.

Teusday Morng – Yesterday the Event was what We expected – W: Grenville chosen by a great majority. Dick return'd to us to dinner with the news. He had not voted as he went too late and was shut out with a number of others of both parties. They don't consider this as a matter of any moment. This day the Limitations come before the House and they expect great things. Dick stay'd at home all yesterday Eveng preparing for this day as I beleive he will speak. You shall know the result tomorrow. We all drank your health yesterday being the 5th of January – May you see many happy returns of it. We had the usual party and in addition Lady Williams – W: Grenville's Sister.

I am now waiting for Dick Sheridan to go make purchases for his Lady. 'Tis a bitter day and I expect to be frozen. Nothing can equal the severity of the weather. They say it is beyond the year 40 – And to comfort us there is a dismal prophecy handed about of: Fourteen weeks' frost, a Bloody riot, and a dead King. I go tonight to Mrs Crewe's. The little Tickells are going to Devonshire House, the Dutchess has a party for all the children. They meet at five and are to break up at eight, a very rational plan I think. I have already sent you all I could observe of fashions, when I see more I will communicate. As yet nothing has come up. All the Women I have seen have been dress'd in muslins or white gowns of some sort.

50: LONDON, 20TH TO 22ND JANUARY 1789

Teusday 20th – Yesterday my dear love when I had sent off my letters I went to dine at Mrs Wilson's, I had been ask'd to Mrs Craufurd's in the Eveng But J. Boileau lent me his Carriage to take me there so I brought my own excuse and return'd. I think it must have been rather dull – Et pour cause. I have written to Harry this morng. No news but things are going on quickly and well.

Just now a visit from Lady J. Townshend – She has lost her

beauty in a great degree but is still a pleasing looking Woman very like Miss Townsend. She had a fine Baby with her of which She seems very fond – She never had any child by Mr Faulkner. Last night the usual party at home, but a kind of farewell to Cribbage as Lady Julia[1] goes to the Country to day, so tonight we go to the Opera.

Thursday – Our Opera Teusday was detestable in all its branches and we closed the adventuring by waiting a full hour in the Coffee room which from not being properly air'd smell'd so offensively I could hardly bear it. Mrs S— I fear got cold there as she has not been well since. Turton who is just gone says She must absolutely be kept as quiet as possible for some days or that he will not answer for the consequence tho' he does not apprehend her present situation to be dangerous, but She has an ugly cough and spitting of blood in a slight degree these two days. Yesterday She had her party as usual but today he insists on her not going down stairs. I dined with Mrs Craufurd yesterday and took her to the play in the Eveng, where I got a complete headake which still remains today, but the weather is absolutely stifling, I was forced to sit with my window open half the morng to keep off the most oppressive faintness. Of course it is bad for our Invalide. I shall certainly tell Dick the moment I see him what Turton said about Mrs S— in general keeping too late hours, as he perhaps may have influence to make her give them up. I have answer'd Harry very fully. My head will not let me or I should answer more fully yours of the 16th and 17th received yesterday. I saw Tickell for a minute this morng who tells me all goes on well and will be finally settled in ten days. The K— still *worse*.

51 : LONDON, 9TH AND 10TH FEBRUARY 1789

Monday 9th – The Deepden party still hangs over us my dear Love, and the fact is none of us wish to go but *le cher Frère* and I beleive it will end in my staying in Town as travelling would

[1]Howard.

[145]

be particularly unpleasant to me just now and I know Harry had rather not go. Yesterday he dined with us – Dick out but Tickell and Richardson with us. In the Eveng Mrs S— had her party the same as before her illness; in addition Mrs Marant, a Handsome Woman above forty, the bonne Amie of the Duke of Gloucester these many years. Harry left us early and I went to bed being tired with two nights' Raking, for Saterday Night Mrs S— was anxious about the debate and we were not in bed 'till near three. Tickell came to us after it was over and gave a pleasant and satisfactory account of it; the attack on Mrs Fitzherbert had been scouted by all parties.

Mrs Bouverie who had been at the Opera brought us an account of the Riot going on there, and certainly they did not complain without reason as there never was any thing more infamous than the entertainment Gallini chose to provide for the Nobility of this good Town – Tho' call'd for very loudly he did not chuze to make his appearance. I told you I had got Mrs Craufurd, Mrs Sheridan's Box for that night, and She sent to thank me not only for the pleasure of the Opera, but that the riot afforded her.

This day I have promised Harry to go with him to dine at Wilson's. I have been driving out with Mrs S— who is very uneasy about her friend Mrs Canning – She writes her word that She is now absolutely ruin'd, all hopes of the reestablishment of the House being at an end. We drove to Devonshire House as Mrs S— wishes to get the Dutchess to exert her interest for Mrs C—, as She thinks She might essentially serve her in that way without clogging Dick with any further demands. The Dutchess was not at home so she was obliged to defer her application. She wishes in the first instance to get one of the Boys appointed Page to the Prince, for the report of such a thing being already done was groundless. Mrs C comes to Town immediately. She has ask'd a bed in Bruton St and Mrs S— gives her half Miss Linley's the only spare corner in the House, for mine I beleive I already told you is Tom's Room and bed. We then call'd on Mrs Crewe – very civil, has given me an invitation to dine there every day while our family is out of Town, but that is not my plan. She told us anecdotes of the K—. He has been quiet now for some time but not one bit more rational. His present fancy is to think himself a Quaker and he is dress'd like one from head to foot. He carries the Queen of hearts in his pocket, and calls it Lady Pembroke's picture, for She is the object of his affections ever since his mind has been disorder'd. So much for his amendment. The clauses are not yet gone thro' but they expect the business will be over today or tomorrow and the Prince appointed by Monday next. God bless you my dear Woman I am summon'd.

Teusday 10th – Still all in Town. The clauses are not yet gone thro'. Dick can't stir and Mrs S— will not go without him, nor when there stay without him, so if they go at all it will end in a two days' expedition, so Harry and I have determin'd not to go. It would be both expensive and troublesome to him as he must hire a chaise for him and me, The Coach being fill'd with Children, Maids, etc., and answer no purpose.

We spent our day very pleasantly yesterday at Wilson's where were all the Boileaus assembled. I do not think the Girls that are going abroad either handsome or elegant but quite well enough for their intended expedition. They were in all the bustle of preparation. Harry brought me home at night but the House was not yet up. This morng he was here and saw Mrs S— but Dick was hardly out of his first Sleep for he was not in bed 'till nearly five. Harry dines here and we go to see Coriolanus, which I am told is very finely got up indeed. We shall certainly see nothing of Dick today, all this is tantalising but unavoidable. Harry behaves as well as possible, never by a look betraying the least impatience or vexation when things have not turn'd out exactly as we could wish, but all will end well I trust and as you say should our political hopes fail in any degree, how great a portion of happyness shall we still possess, for the more I see of a certain Gentleman the more convinced I am that If I have any chance for happyness it is in a connection with one who unites real gentleness with great frankness of

[147]

character and of whose attachment I have every reason to be convinced. I fear I shall lose him soon as he tells me his stay must not exceed the going over of a new Ld Lieutenant. Whenever that does happen his return will I hope be for the advantage of all as even if the meeting between him and Mr Pelham should not take place in London, he will go over provided with such a letter to him as must secure us success in that quarter. In the mean time I am determined on patience and on no account to be induced to think of a union 'till it may be done to the perfect satisfaction of his family. His spirits are much better than at first and these ten days of conversation have brought us to a better understanding than could have been accomplish'd in as many months' correspondence. I have not yet sent the gloves – I got some but they were so inferior to those I sent before that I kept them for myself and determined to wait 'till I could go out to chuze them myself. You shall have them in a day or two.

52: LONDON, 12TH FEBRUARY 1789

Thursday 12th – Yesterday my dear Love I rec:d yours of the 5th and 6th. Harry had before brought me his letters from Dublin with an account of the Majority in our favor. I told the news to Dick who was much pleased but surprised at Charles's absence from the House. While we were talking of it there came a letter from him to Dick in which he gave a particular account of that day's business, making use through the whole letter of the words *we* and *us* – at the end he says he did not sit in his *usual seat* in the House – was he in it in any part? That he had sent notice to the Ld Lieutenant that he no longer consider'd himself as in employment, and had not been at his Office for some days. If this is true all this unlucky, for the K— for these last three days has been *certainly* mending – So much as to damp the hopes of the most sanguin people of the party. The Regency bill must go on and the Prince will be in power for a time, but they all now think the Period will be so short that nothing of consequence can be done. Charles will certainly be restored to his employment, if as report says, it is true he has resign'd, but if the Regency proves a short one I fear he must lose it without a prospect of any compensation. With regard to us our hopes stand much where they did as it will be in the Prince's power to dispose of moderate things and there is little probability of persons being changed who were obnoxious to neither party. What I sincerely wish is that Dick would endeavour to secure for himself any *Patent place* the Regent may have to dispose of in Ireland as the Restrictions on that subject only relate to this Country. Mrs S— and I have been talking over this matter, but She says that such is our Brother's shyness of applying for any personal favor that tho' She knows the Regent would rejoice in the opportunity of providing for him, She has no hopes of his taking one Step in the business. So you see at present there is a heavy Cloud over us but we will keep up our spirits at all events.

Yesterday Harry gave me a letter he had recd from Peter,[1] In which with very little ceremony he desires that he and I will desire application to be made in his favor to Bp Dixon – loaded as Dick is with applications and precarious as his own situation now is nothing could be worse judged than the introduction of any new solicitation. I told Harry so very frankly, who seem'd vex'd and express'd himself apprehensive of this circumstance producing a coolness between him and Peter; but I shew'd him so evidently the total selfishness and indelicacy of the good Gentleman's troubling him at this time, that I satisfied his mind entirely on the subject and he writes to him by this day's post to inform him that the K— 's amendment and the total uncertainty of what the Event will be with regard to the Regency, makes any application *impossible* at present. I mention the purport of his letter (as Peter will probably communicate it to you) to account for Harry's giving the least favorable representation of matters. But to say the truth we have had a tedious time of anxiety and suspense. I have one

[1]His younger brother, see the list of characters at page ix.

[149]

great comfort that Harry seems perfectly reasonable on the occasion and turns his thoughts with real cheerfulness to the prospect of our union unaided by any favors on this side. Could the allowance I recd from Charles be made even to appear to the Old Gentleman a permanent thing, he seem'd to have little doubt of obtaining his consent. At present my hopes in that quarter have little to rest on, as his losing his employment necessarily leaves me without a guinea for at least some time to come, and I fear he has now gone too far to recede. I have seen Harry this morng but avoided touching that string as he pleased himself with the idea of a possibility of our being sooner united from my dependence there. The facts will appear soon enough, en attendant I do not wish to embitter one minute that we can snatch in these troublesome times. He dines here and we mean to go to the Play for an hour litterally to be private, for in this House we find it difficult to get half an hour's conversation uninterrupted. He did not dine here yesterday but came in the Eveng, we had beside Mrs Bouverie, Mrs Dixon, and Tickell as dismal as a prospect of dissappointment could make a Man possess'd of a good share of both vanity and ambition. Dick came to us between twelve and one and we did not break up 'till past two. He confirm'd the news we had heard, but he has a spirit unacquainted with despondence, and tho' fatigue was added to the anxiety he must feel, yet there was something cheering in his manner that in a great measure conquer'd the glooms that hung over us before his return.

Mrs Crewe dined with us and She has a little the art of communicating her own dismal feelings, but She certainly has good qualities that attone for some failings – last night She gave an instance both of feeling and generosity. Mrs S— was talking to her of Mrs Canning's distress to induce her to exert her interest with the Duke of Portland, as I before told you She wishes to avoid drawing on Dick's interest on this occasion, And in the course of her narration mention'd that Mrs Canning was almost litterally reduced to her last guinea. Mrs Crewe seem'd interested yet made little display of fine feelings, but when going away took Mrs S— aside to beg She would convey a note of 50£ to Mrs Canning as a loan from herself, as She did not think her acquaintance with Mrs C— would authorize her offering any pecuniary assistance. There was I think real goodness and delicacy in this. You will be glad I am sure to hear that your favorite Mrs Greville[1] is recovering very fast. I desired Mrs Crewe last night to mention you to her as a person sincerely interested in every good that happens to her.

The morng was rather fine and I walk'd out with Harry which help'd me to banish blue devils, and I had the comfort to see his spirits quite good before we parted. A few days perhaps will clear all matters. The Deepden party is for the present at an end. The Cook who had been sent down last week came yesterday to know what was become of us and brought with her all the Pies and Stewes She had been preparing since Friday last. She says the House is both cold and damp so that our going would be a very bad plan. Tho' I am a little vex'd I will not *fret*.

53: LONDON, 28TH FEBRUARY 1789

I yesterday received yours of the 23d with the enclosures which to use your own phrase I *backward* to you. They will probably arrive about the same time as their lawful owner does. You may judge how much I miss him and how anxiously I shall wait for an account of his reception in Ireland. I hope the best and the cheerfulness which Dick's conduct to him inspired has greatly strenthen'd those hopes. On Thursday for the first time we sat down to a quiet family party to dinner – all kind as possible to me. In the Eveng there was a croud of fine people, but I sat in my little Room and saw none but Miss Bouverie. Yesterday again alone. I spent the Eveng with Mrs Canning whose little Boy is still confined. The Eveng party was small and we supt a female party quarré. The cloth was just removed when Mrs Crewe came in tired and harrass'd from a large assembly, Very

[1]Mrs Crewe's mother.

[151]

much of a fine Lady. Dick had dined at the Duke of Portland's with the Delegates[1] – People attempt to be witty on their expedition but I hope it will not be so idle a visit as many suppose.

The K— they say is quite well[2] – But to a certainty he is incapable of talking on any matters of importance. Willis leaves him but he has instructed the Queen how to control him, which it seems She does very compleatly – His own Pages are removed and four of Willis's Men appointed his constant attendants – Yet so circumstanced they talk of bringing him forward very soon – Suspence being over for the present we go on much better than we did. Le Cher Frère is quite himself and Mrs Sheridan infinitely more cheerful than for many weeks past. The most dissappointed faces are those who had least right to be sanguin.

Will you my dear love take charge of my letter to Harry and deliver it to him yourself as Mr L. you know sometimes forgets a letter for a few hours and I wish him to get this one soon.

54: LONDON, 2ND AND 3RD MARCH 1789

I was sorry my dear Love to find you so much indisposed as your last of 23d which I recd this day represents you. But as to your Rheumatic complaint – bad as it is we must not add to its imperfections by supposing it intends takings its residence with you on any ground of right. The fact is it is a universal complaint this year. At the time I got your letter Mrs Sheridan was groaning with it beside me. The pain in one of her thighs is so bad today that it is with the greatest difficulty She limps about. I read her your account of yourself and She says like Mrs Forseight, "Oh! Sister, Sister, Sister, every way." Miss Linley was in the same way for above a month this winter. And I hardly know a person who has not suffer'd more or less from it so we must hope the fine weather will remove these ugly pains.

---

[1] The delegates from the Irish Parliament.
[2] The King's recovery was officially announced on 10th March.

I rejoice that our dear Bess is well. Harry says She is a darling Girl. I had a letter today from Shrewsbury so that if the wind was fair this day he may be now in Cuffe St. He writes cheerfully and it was a load off my spirits to know him so far safe. I shall anxiously expect the account of his having reach'd your fire side, where next to my own I certainly wish him to be. Please God all will go well.

Today the K— parted with his own four Pages and as a farewell gift gave each a pair of Razors. Willis's Men have taken their places. The Windsor Apothecary who attended him got a fall lately which confines him, so his Majesty walk'd to Richmond,[1] where he is, yesterday and sat two hours with him, saying often 'You took care of my illness, its my turn to nurse you now.' He has a plan in his head of going publicly to St Paul's Church to return thanks for his recovery. All these are facts.

Saterday Eveng the Party was larger than usual. Mr Fox was here in perfect health and spirits – I supt with them but slipt away early. Yesterday the Linleys at dinner and a croud in the Eveng – Mr Fox both morng and Eveng. I got to my room before one and that by not going into the Supper Room. I can not stand their hours. Today we Ladies dined alone and I have stole away to write this. Dick dined at the Prince's with the Delegates of whom they Speak here as of so many Indian cheifs. Dick has been of all their dinners: Duke of Portland, Lord Spencer, etc. At an Assembly of Lady Buck'amshire's some of the Ladies on the Opposite side groan'd and hooted them as they came into the room, what say you to Female delicacy? – Wednesday They all sup here and there is to be quite a croud which I can not escape, so I make up a *new dyed* sattin Gown on the occasion. We are to have the Prince, Duke of York, Mrs Fitzherbert, all the fine people and I should be very glad to give them the slip if I had any decent pretext. Thursday The Dutchess gives them a Ball at Devonshire House, where Mrs S— very good-naturedly got me invited but I have

[1]From Kew.

[153]

no thoughts of going for various reasons. J: Linley goes and Mrs S— if She is able, as She has a reason for appearing in Public of a curious nature. Among other infamous falsehoods propagated against our Brother it is now said that he locks her up and uses her in every respect ill – Even to beating and starving her; how such ridiculous falsehoods can ever gain credit! And yet the eagerness for scandal makes them wellcome.

Teusday – I was interrupted by Miss Bouverie coming up to shew me her Ball dress. I then went down and found no one but Mr Fox, Lord John[1] and Lady Julia Howard. Dick came home and the supper party was to me more pleasant than usual as I had an opportunity of seeing and hearing Mr Fox more at my ease than hitherto. The good humour and simplicity of his manners is truly delightful. Today I have walk'd out and call'd on Mrs Fitzgerald to get Jenny Linley ask'd to Mrs Cologan's Ball, which I found would please Mrs Sheridan, and on that account I go, tho' otherwise sore against the grain as I am no dancer and do not much delight in crouds and noise, but at least I shall be able to make my escape from thence with more ease than from Devonshire House. We are all busy making our gowns and aprons for tomorrow Eveng, So I must leave off – God bless you. The K— was bled yesterday, another fact. I have always the love of the good people here – Dick quite well in health and in good spirits and good humour.

55: LONDON, IST APRIL 1789

My dear Love by some accident or other yours of the 21st and twenty fourth came together Monday [30th March] and the letters of the 23d came Saterday [28th March]. With regard to my own affairs I will say as little as possible, all seems to be suspense and uncertainty, of course I can not write cheerfully on the Subject. The life of uniform vexation and dissappointment I have led for years has indeed been hitherto a painful one perpetually kept between dependence and unkindness.

[1]Townshend.

I am very thankful to you for your kind offer as to my drawing on Mr L—, but that is what circumstanced as you are I could not think of doing. My Dissappointment with regard to Charles tho' unpleasant was not wholly unexpected, as I was convinced whenever a retrenchment was deem'd necessary by him his first views of oeconomy would be directed towards me. Therefore I kept cautiously within bounds and tho' forced to spend more than in reason I ought at least I avoided all unnecessary expence and have kept clear of debt or difficulty. I have at length received the remainder of the Ballance in Powell's hands which, for what reason I could not well make out, amounted only to 16£, which with the 30£ he before paid makes forty-six; twenty I sent to Ireland; the remainder I will give an account of and our ballance remains still less than we thought.

			£		
The expences of proving the will –			7	3	10
	Godfrey's bill			10	0
Bills brought by	Oliphant's for Hats		2	1	0
Thompson	Holyland's for wine		1	2	3
	Allick for wages		2	2	0
			12	19	1
laid out in lace	2 13 6	Sent to Dublin	20		
Gloves	0 9 0	Total spent	32	19	1
	£3 2 6	Received	46	0	0
			32	19	1
		remains	13	0	11
		half	6	10	5½

I have stated our little account as it stands with regard to what has gone thro' my hands, in your answer let me know what I am in debt to you for Tabinet and whether any other bill has been sent in on my account.

And now we are on the subject of money I wish you could inform me what Quilca is really likely to produce, that I may judge in what time Smith will be pay'd off. I confess I should be glad now to dispose of my share in it for a sum of money in present. I have never mention'd this matter to Harry but I think he would not dissapprove of the idea, as a little money would be of more use to us now than a small addition of income hereafter. If it was fairly valued (and I should think Smith could do it) and that it appear'd an advantageous business, perhaps your Old Gentleman might be induced to advance what might make you sole possessor. So small a property is nothing devided, but altogether might be worth something and settled on your Son or Daughter as you thought proper. This is not a sudden start but from the first was my own and Dick's idea, as the very little I was entitled to by inheritance could never have supported me but by being sunk to produce an income, and even before that could be done I must *contrive* to live for a couple of years –

I am glad Charles is avowedly safe: that he was so in his own mind I beleive firmly from the first, for he would have taken due time to reflect before he resign'd. He has never written one satisfactory line to me, I mean relative to Harry etc. nor do I expect he will, but if I do not hear from him when things are got into the old track I intend to draw on him as usual.

Mrs Sheridan is going to the country next week. Her Sister has gone to Norwiche and I could not decently leave her to go alone, for alone She would be, as Dick never stays two days at a time with her.

Last night was the Grand Ball at the Pantheon for the King's recovery. Our Butler Mr Edwards went there as a waiter and we were laughing at the idea of his being perhaps forced to attend Mr Pitt in the course of the Eveng, But the Servants I assure you consider him as a kind of *Rat* for voluntarily engaging in the Service of the Enemy, so do Politics descend. The Duke of York also gave a Ball to his most intimate friends and twenty of the most beautiful Women in London of *no Character* – Our Brother was ask'd but very properly did not go. Their Club at Brooks's is to give a grand Gala the 23d – And all for what? for truth to say I do not think the recovery exists.

My kindest love to Harry, I shall write to him tomorrow. I have recd all his letters safe but I have nothing pleasant to say to him and I am already fatigued with what I have written – for these easterly winds as usual disturb my head. Pray answer me particularly as to Quilca.

CHAPTER 7

London, May to June 1789: The Great World

56: LONDON, 16TH TO 19TH MAY 1789

Saterday 16th – This day my dear Love I received from Harry the account of Mrs Lefanu's release[1] for in that light we must view her death when we consider what her sufferings must have been for some time past. Yet I am sure at the painful moment of separation her Sons must have felt sincere sorrow and I fear your spirits are unequal to the melancholy scene you have been engaged in. Harry seems truly affected tho' prepared for this event and I am certain Mr L— who valued his Mother sincerely has felt his share of distress. Is the Old Gentleman much affected?

Since Wednesday my Journal is soon told: I spent the Eveng at home alone – Mrs S— went to Mrs Bouverie. Thursday She went to the Opera, and Tom and I went to see part of a play. Friday I had promised to accompany Miss Patrick, who is in Town for a short time to Drury Lane to see the *Heiress* and *Critic*. Mrs Canning dined with us and is quite pleased with her new Habitation which is about seven miles from Town. This day we dined at Mrs Crewe's and as usual dispersed after dinner – Mrs S— gone to Mrs B—,[2] Tom and his Father to the Opera, and I prefer'd coming quietly home. This last week a vile North East wind has prevented my walking, but I accompany Mrs S— in her daily visit to Norfolk St for the sake of the old people. Sometimes Mr L—[3] goes out with us but I think his health seems in a very precarious state.

[1] She had died on 9 May, aged 80.
[2] Bouverie.
[3] Linley.

Sunday – This day uncommonly bad, I went only to Norfolk St, dined at home – a quiet family party. Mrs S— is now gone to a Concert at the Dutchess of Bolton's, and I prefer'd staying at home to going to Mrs Crewe's Sunday party. Tom has spent the Eveng with me and 'tis now bed time, so good night and God bless you.

Teusday 19th – I waited for my letters yesterday before I sent off my packet and had scarce recd your journal from the 7th to the 14th before the Coach came to the door for our Morng airing. I had promised the day to the Yarkers and determined to be set down there early and finish my letter, but I had hardly got there before dinner was on table, so different are the hours kept by regular people. As I knew the Box was disengaged we went to the Play in the Eveng and found my Old Flame the Bishop of Down establish'd in the Box. I can not help wondering at his Wife preferring a round of cards and dissipation to the society of such a Man, but he doats on her and thinks She must always be right. Mrs Yarker was quite taken with him and squeezed herself into the smallest compass imaginable that he might have a front seat.

At my return I found Mrs S— at home. I thought her gone to a great assembly, but her raking at Bolton House which was 'till near 4 o'clock had quite knocked her up. She seem'd quite faint and had been so ever since her return from airing. She was better this morng and goes tonight to a grand fête at Cumberland House. A momentary return of health always tempts her out and I can not help fearing She will at last exceed her strength. Before the family was stirring this morng the Yarkers and Mrs Hargrave call'd on me to go to Shakespear's Gallery.[1] I liked some of the pictures very well, in particular two from the *Winter's Tale* – One by Opie representing the moment the King is ordering the Infant to be exposed, the Other by Wheatly when Polixenus and Camillo are in the shepherd's hut.

---

[1] At the end of 1786 Alderman John Boydell commissioned paintings of scenes from Shakespeare, to be engraved for his sumptuous edition, from the leading artists beginning with Sir Joshua Reynolds.

Thursday 21st – Teusday My dear Woman I sent my last – spent the Eveng. at home. Yesterday walk'd out with Tom to Dr Morris's. None but the little Lady at home who half kill'd me with kindness and various attempts to make me eat, which I with great difficulty escaped. In the Eveng there was a party at home, Mrs S— did not go to Ranelagh to my great joy –

This morng I went with Mrs Crewe and Mrs Dixon to the Trial. We sat in the King's Box, which directly fronts the Managers and the place where Mr Hastings stands. With the help of my glass I could see him very well and could perceive him a good deal agitated at times. Mr Burke spoke first. His manner is so much against him that it must require time to grow in any degree reconciled to it, But that once done it is impossible not to admire his flow of language and force of imagination. Next Mr Fox – his voice I don't like, but his manner is so clear that a child must at once comprehend his meaning, and at the same time so earnest as to force conviction. Last Our Brother – I felt a thousand pulses beat as he rose, and gulp'd down the tears that were almost choaking that I might not appear too nervous (the fashionable expression for feeling of any kind). It recall'd too the remembrance of my Poor Father who had ever so blindly driven from him the pleasure he might have derived from that quarter. I was also reminded of him by his manner, which is certainly very like my Father's tho' not an imitation. There is a calm dignity in it, yet animated to the greatest degree where the subject admits of it. His voice is uncommonly fine, and his utterance so distinct that I did not lose a syllable, which is surprising as you know his general way of speaking is rather slovenly.

The sight in itself is certainly fine and from accessory ideas must strike the imagination of any Person. I thought of You and wish'd my poor Neighbour Mrs Dixon quietly at home and you in her place. When they adjourn'd we stroll'd about in some of the Outward courts and met several of the Managers.

Mr Burke came up to take care of Mrs Dixon, and Irishman-like insisted on the *Young Lady* as he stiled me taking his other arm, so under the care of this Friend of the Begums I got thro' the croud –

At Dinner we had Dr Parr, who desired his respects to you; you have no great recollection of him I suppose? He is a good Scholar and has many good qualities but so foolishly vain as to make him more often laugh'd at than admired. In speaking of one of his own compositions he said that after reading it over, he took down a volume of *Junius,* and was astonish'd at the flatness of the stile. I went in the evening to Mrs Bouverie with Mrs S., at Eleven I came home and have written so far while the rest of the ladies went to Cumberland House and from thence to the 'Je ne sçais quoi' Ball. Good night my dear Love.

Sunday 24th – Friday was bad and we staid at home all the Morng. Mrs S— had a small party in the Eveng and they all went together to a late Assembly. Yesterday we went to the Shakespear Gallery again.[1] There was less company and I saw the pictures better. 'The death of Cardinal Beaufort' by Sir Joshua, and 'Hamlet and the Ghost' by Fuseli are uncommonly fine. This kind of Painting has long been wanted to show the real genius of Painters. We then drove to Hyde park and walk'd for some time and were join'd there by Dick. Dined at Home. Poor Mr Linley who had been taking the Air was set down in Bruton St and dined with us, His first wish being always to be near Mrs S—. I think he seems much better. In the Eveng we went to the Opera. Mrs Bouverie brought me home and Mrs S— went to an assembly.

Today we drove to Kensington gardens and walk'd there some time. I saw the Princes, some on foot, some on Horseback. The Gardens very full of all ranks. Dined at home – Mr and Mrs Linley and Miss Lee. Our Brother dined out having forgot he had ask'd Kemble who dined with us yesterday also. We made out the day very tollerably. Mrs S— went late to a

[1]See letter 56 and footnote there.

Concert and I took care of her Guests for the remainder of the
Eveng. Yesterday I recd your little journal from the 15th to the
18th and was glad your cold is better – good night my dear
Woman.

58: LONDON, 2ND JUNE 1789

Tonight they are all going to a ball given by the Duke of
Clarence. I will tell you a *fact* that sets our amiable Queen's
character in a true light. Friday last [29th May] the Duke of
York went to Kew for the first time since his duel.[1] He found
the King sitting in an outward room with a door of com-
munication open to that where the Queen was. The minute he
saw the Duke he went softly to shut the door, then running to
him embraced him most affectionately and with tears con-
gratulated him on his safety – in short in his whole manner
was quite the father. On the Queen's entering, he drew back
and fell into the reserved manner he has assumed lately. She
took no other notice of her son than with a cold and distant air
asking whether he had been amused at Bootle's Ball, which was
the evening of the day he fought [26th May]. It is no wonder
that all her sons are disgusted with a conduct so unfeminine.
They showed their displeasure by leaving the Ambassador's
grand entertainment before supper, and this step of course has
given great offence.

Our brother is much with them all, and when a head is
wanted they have recourse *to his*. He has great influence and
will no doubt rise one day as high as his utmost ambition could
wish. Mrs Sheridan told me a little circumstance that happened
at Bootle's that shews the footing he is on. The Prince in the
fullness of his joy for his brother's safety had taken rather too
many bumpers to his health. Some one told our brother that
they feared he was setting in for drinking and desired he would
try to get him away. He accordingly went up to him but finding
that he did not readily yield to persuasion, he pushed the bottle

[1]With Colonel Lenox at Wimbledon.

away from him saying '*You shall not* drink any more.' The
Prince fired at the idea of control and said, 'Sheridan I love
you better than any one, but *shall not* is what I can't put up
with.' However with the help of one of the Conways, they got
him away, and no doubt his Royal Highness was thankful next
morning for having been prevented from giving a handle to his
enemies for increasing their abuse.

Just as I received your letter yesterday, I was setting out for
the trial with Mrs Crewe and Mrs Dixon. I was fortunate in my
day, as I heard all the principal speakers – Mr Burke I admired
the least – Mr Fox very much indeed. The subject, in itself, was
not particularly interesting, as the debate turned merely on a
point of law, but the earnestness of his manner and the amazing
precision with which he conveys his ideas is truly delightful.
And last, not least, I heard my brother! I cannot express to you
the sensation of pleasure and pride that filled my heart at the
moment he rose. Had I never seen him or heard his name
before, I should have conceived him the first man among them
at once. There is a dignity and grace in his countenance and
deportment, very striking – at the same time that one cannot
trace the smallest degree of conscious superiority in his manner.
His voice, too, appeared to me extremely fine. The speech itself
was not much calculated to display the talents of an orator, as
of course, it related only to dry matter. You may suppose I am
not so lavish of praises before indifferent persons, but I am sure
you will acquit me of partiality in what I have said. When they
left the Hall we walked about some time, and were joined by
several of the managers – among the rest by Mr Burke, whom
we set down at his own house. They seem now to have better
hopes of the business than they have had for some time; as the
point urged with so much force and apparent success relates to
very material evidence which the Lords have refused to hear,
but which, once produced, must prove strongly against Mr
Hastings; and from what passed yesterday they think Their
Lordships must yield. We sat in the King's box by which means
we had a full view of these noble personages as they went out,

and I do think them as ugly a collection as ever I beheld.

59: LONDON, 8TH AND 9TH JUNE 1789

Monday June 8th – Saterday my dearest Woman – I staid at home and alone, Endeavour'd to continue *Zeluco*,[1] but when the Spirits are oppress'd reading is not always the best resource. Yesterday the family were engaged out and I determined not to stay at home, meerly that I might avoid my own reflections. I call'd on Mrs Craufurd intending to stay there if they were at home, but She was out. That I have been little with them has not been my fault. The fact is I have never once been ask'd to dine with them, even the days I took her to the Play, when it would have been a real convenience to me, but I beleive She had some foolish notion that I might introduce her to the family I live with (which I could not), as you know of old how ambitious She is of getting among what She considers as fine People. Every other civility in my power I have shewn but I could not attempt to introduce one acquaintance unless I introduced all.

Well, dissapointed in that Plan I went to Angelo's, found them at home and spent the day there – Rather pleasantly as no Horne Tooke's or Men of that kind came in.

This day they are all engaged to a Ball so I dine with the Yarkers and go to the Play in the Eveng. I have been often with them so they seem perfectly to understand my situation and are uniformly kind and attentive. I gave them two Prints of my Father, one was for Luke, and they were very thankful for them. I also gave one to Angelo, and one to Kitty who beg'd one for herself. I have got Harry's Picture and am quite pleas'd with it, Every one is struck with the likeness.

Teusday Eveng – This Morng I recd your journal which affected me most painfully. I could not think it possible you could be affected in the way you describe by Charles's conduct.

[1] A novel by John Moore published in 1786 and very popular in the following years.

You have long known he was worthless and should therefore have expected that the moment he *dared* he would act ill by me. However distress'd by what has happen'd, Surprise or Sorrow have had little share in my feelings – Indignation is uppermost and he shall yet experience the effects of it. I told you my dear love your letter distress'd me, and that I was so was evident when I met Mrs S— at breakfast, But not perceiving it at first She began talking to me about a masquerade I had promised to accompany her to on Thursday next. I said something that shew'd I wish'd to decline the party, and She then hoped there was no bad news from Ireland. I could not say there was, but still the unpleasantness of my present situation, which what I had been reading had more forcibly impress'd on my mind, brought a thousand sad thoughts and I only said in general I was not now in Spirits to enjoy such a party. This She could not understand: Amusement was the way to banish dissagreeable reflections. As to Charles, I ought to think no more about him, that I never had more than his word to trust to, and She had no doubt that Mr L— would have equal reliance on Dick's. To all this I could answer very little, for there are circumstances of immediate inconvenience that I must feel from what has happen'd that I never could bring myself to mention to her. And as to my Brother Richard's promises, I have so many daily instances of his engaging for what he is wholly unable to perform that where one's support is at stake it cannot be look'd on as a bright prospect; And no one more conscious than She is of the difficulties he involves himself in from that very custom! I enter'd into no further explanation for to People who only hear of difficulties at large, but never feel the want of the comforts or even Elegancies of life it never occurs, that others can be without them.

While we were talking the Stuffs for our dress were brought in. Mrs Bouverie had undertaken to provide them for all the Party that go with us. We are to be a group of Gypsies. The dress very ugly I think – brown stuff jackets and blue stuff peticoats, straw hats tied under the Chin, and scarlet silk cloak

[165]

hanging behind in imitation of the red cloak worn by those Ladies. Our Maids were set to work and I have consented to go with as little prospect of pleasure as ever I did anything in my life, but as my feelings are not even understood I think it my best method to endeavour to conceal them and to conform to the opinions of others where I can. Our party are Mrs and Miss Bouverie, Lady Julia Howard, Lady Betty D'Elmé, a Mrs Stanhope a very Beautiful Woman, Mrs S— and I. The Masquerade is given by Mrs Sturt (a very fine Lady) at Hamersmith, where it seems She has a very beautiful House and gardens. The scheme has been long talk'd of, but I thought to have got off with more ease.

This whole day I have been pretty dismal. We drove out for a little time with the Children, little Dick getting well again, dined at home. Mrs S— gone to the Opera, from thence goes to a late Assembly. I quietly at home and alone, part of the time I have been reading Zeluco, the rest Scribbling this.

I am happy to hear of the happy conclusion of Mrs Cotingham's[1] History. She should be ever grateful to you for the part you have taken. I thank you my dearest love for the influence you exert with your Old Gentleman, But unless we have something secured to us it would be impossible we could live *near* him on Harry's allowance. Here at least we shall have House rent free and a better chance for assistance from the only quarter I can now expect it, by being at hand. So the Old Gentleman must consider this, if he should wish for his Son's return. Till he comes I cannot tell what arrangements will be made and of course can form no plan, But I trust he will not hasten his departure at the expence of his health and I have written to caution him on that head.

As in my present situation I can not go on without money and am determin'd not to mention my distress at home, as I know they are at this time under particular embarrassment, I have thought of a method to extricate myself. When Thompson brought back the *protested* draft, with some hesitation and con-

---

[1]Mentioned in earlier letters as Miss Woolery.

fusion, he beg'd I would not want for any money he could supply me with, which offer however I positively declined. But I have since seen Dilly who spoke so favorably of the sale of the *Dictionary* that being able to give him that security I mean to apply to him for what is indispensably necessary, that I may at least be entirely clear with the world – I suppose there can be no impropriety with regard to Harry in my doing this? When Mr L— writes to Dilly he will inform him more accurately what profit we are likely to have, So you see I am endeavouring to counteract Charles's kind wish to cross my future plans. Tomorrow we go to Mrs Canning as the badness of the weather prevented our keeping our appointment with her last Friday. As we go early and for the day I will have this ready for the Post.

60: LONDON, 14TH AND 15TH JUNE 1789

Sunday 14th June – I must now my dear love fulfill my promise of an account of our Masquerade –

We went to Hammersmith about ten o'clock – Mrs and Miss Bouverie, a Mrs Stanhope (a very beautiful Woman), Mrs S: and I all as Gypsies and our dress, which I thought ugly enough, was however very much admired. Mrs Sturt's House formerly belong'd to the famous Lord Melcombe. The Hall and Stair case very lofty and ornamented with coulour'd Lamps. The Duke of York's Band playing. We enter'd first a very fine Gallery paved with different sorts of Marble and ornamented with some uncommonly fine pillars, lighted with coulour'd Lamps and ornamented with a transparency representing the Prince's Crest and devices of the professions of the Two Brothers, Natural flowers in abundance – from thence we went through two or three pretty Rooms to a very Spacious Ball Room and then through small rooms again Round to the Gallery, so that tho' there was a great deal of company there was no unpleasant croud. I stuck close to Mrs S— and we unmask'd very soon. She was of course accosted by a great many with abundance of fine things and I came in for a share of civility.

About One the Princes arrived all dressed alike as Highland Cheifs; nothing could be more Ellegant or becoming than their dress. The Prince came up to Mrs S: to enquire for Dick and gave such an enquiring Stare at me that She thought it best to introduce me, for he has his Father's Passion for knowing who and what every one is.

At two the Supper Rooms were open'd. The Etiquette is always to have a Room for the Prince who chuzes his company, So that neither Rank nor the Lady of the House decides that point. He as usual ask'd Mrs S— and She kept fast hold' of me 'till we got in to the Room. The Duke of Clarence took the head of the Table and the Prince placed himself on one side, Mrs S— at his right hand, The Dutchess of Ancaster (as *Hecate*) on his left. I sat next and le Cher Frère next to me (who by the bye is always particularly civil to me in Public, unlike a certain sneaking Puppy of our acquaintance). Opposite to us Lady Duncannon as a *Soeur Grise*, casting many tender looks across the table which to my great joy did not seem much attended to, A Young lady with her in the same dress; Lady Jersey and her Daughter (very pretty Women) as black veil'd Nuns; Dutchess of Rutland in a Fancy sort of Dress without powder and not looking Handsome; then Duke of Clarence, and then Mrs Fitzherbert in a White dress and black Veil but unlike a Nun's dress. These were all the Women. There were a good many Gentleman at table and several standing behind.

When Supper was near over Some excellent Catch Singers belonging to the *Je ne sçais quoi* Club sang some very good catches. After a little time the Prince call'd them round and proposed to Mrs S— to join him in a Trio, which She did at once tho' She has not practised any thing of the kind for many months and was taken quite by Surprise. The Company as you may suppose were all delighted with this unexpected pleasure. The Prince proposed a couple more and then gave over for fear of tiring Mrs S—. He has a good voice and being so well supported seem'd to me to sing very well.

We sat about an hour at table and then return'd to the Gallery. We intended going home at first, but Dick who came in a black domino put on a disguise after supper and made a great deal of diversion, as he was unknown to every one but us; having plagued several people sufficiently he resumed his Domino and return'd to the company, pretending he had just left a party at supper, and at length at a shamefully late or rather early hour we return'd to Town. I saw Miss Cholmondeley there in very bad preservation. Time has used her but scurvily and She has unluckily retain'd all her little affectations.

I could not help thinking while I was Supping with Princes and great people that my situation was a little like poor Gil Blas at the Court of Madrid, but mine is only temporary and I look beyond it to real comfort and happyness. I have had a peep at the Raree Show of the great world without trouble or risk, and not being young enough to have my brain turn'd shall enjoy my broil'd bone in Cuffe St with as much pleasure as ever, and shall have the advantage of having a great deal of talk to myself as I expect to be as much question'd as dined when I get among you.

There was also a Room for the Duke and Dutchess of Cumberland and a third for the company at large. After we all unmask'd Dick walk'd about a good deal with us and several of the masks remark'd that having such a Partner it was no wonder he kept by her: I think I never saw Mrs S— look handsomer. As Mrs Sturt had given out Dominos were not to be admitted, it enliven'd the scene very much, for those who did not venture to assume a character at least wore handsome dresses; she admitted Friends however in Domino's.

You see that I could not have been sufficiently awake to write you all this yesterday and perhaps you don't thank me for such a long account – the intention however is good so at least I shall be forgiven.

[169]

I went as I promised, Yesterday, to Craufurd's and dined there with a Dutch Man and his Sister. In the Eveng there came in one or two Gentlemen and I got off pretty early to make up my arrears of sleep. At my return I found a note from Mrs Oddie to ask me to dine there today and a Card from Lady Palmerston to Ask me with Dick and his Wife to dine there on Teusday. I never saw her but the night I supp'd last at Mrs Crewe's when I sat next her at Supper, so her inviting me is civil. Tomorrow we are all ask'd to dine at Mrs Crewe's.

Monday – I was call'd away suddenly yesterday to be set down at Mrs Oddie's where I met the usual party. All very civil to me, and Mrs Yarker brought me home. I have been watching for the Post all this morng but have got no letters. Harry's last announced his intention of setting out the 13th and from your account of him I scarce know whether to hope or fear his keeping to that intention. I unluckily call'd on the Angelo's in my way yesterday and by her indiscretion have had my mind a good deal disturb'd – She read me a Paragraph in a letter of Mrs St Leger's[1] relative to Harry's illness that distress'd me very much. Her doing so was the more inexcusable as Mrs St Leger expressly says She supposes me ignorant of the circumstance. I did not from your account think he had been so very ill and I can not suppress a thousand allarming ideas that this sort of attack naturally gives rise to. My anxieties I must keep to myself for I see now less of the family than ever except I join in the croud, which I sometimes do to avoid my own thoughts, as I am necessarily quite alone when I decline accompanying them, no Friend visiting me here. I feel now unable to fill up my own time: in the midst of all quiet occupations the most painful ideas occur, and I have nothing for it but letting myself be led 'till this state of painful suspence is ended.

I think I must have a letter tomorrow and shall then be able to determine what to do. At present Dick talks of our sleeping at Richmond tomorrow night after leaving Lord Palmerston's

[1]Mrs Angelo's daughter Ann.

[170]

which is in that neighbourhood. But if Harry is really set out I shall not leave Town 'till I see him. Today we dine at Mrs Crewe's, a sort of farewell family dinner. I had hoped no melancholy thoughts would occur in the course of this letter – The next will I trust be free from them, but indeed that little foolish Woman has made me very uneasy. Mrs Sheridan always desires best love and Dick's too.

61: LONDON, 17TH TO 22ND JUNE 1789

At length my Dear Love Charles and I have come to a perfect understanding. I mean that he has fairly thrown off the Mask. I received two packets from him yesterday, the one of 5, the other of 6 Sheets of Paper – litterally Pamphlets, paged and tack'd together. I had no curiosity to read them but perceiving a line that inform'd me he had sent a duplicate to my Brother, I thought it necessary to see the nature of the lies he had most probably invented. I waded accordingly through this maze of gross abuse, falsehood and the basest ingratitude to my Father, as he recur'd to all the misrepresentations he on a former occasion sent him in a letter equally voluminous. He affects to tax me with abusing him to my connexions here, to whom I never mention'd his name, my own family excepted who had little to learn on the subject of his conduct and character. He speaks of a Lady intimate in the family having written in this stile to Ireland; Mrs S— suspects Mrs Crewe, as she confesses that to her she has spoken her sentiments very freely. Miss Handcock he also names as having said things that she had from me, he calls her my particular Friend; You know how little we were together and in my life I never had any conversation of the kind with her, tho' Mrs H— who saw many things she dissapproved of often endeavour'd to draw me out on the Subject.

With regard to Mr Lefanu his behaviour is if possible more base and cruel: I had told him in my latter letters that as I had promised Mr L— to marry him whenever his Father's consent was obtain'd, I had therefore no alternative now, as to recede at this time might expose us to the risk of the Old Gentleman's withdrawing a consent not easily obtain'd and obtain'd on the idea of his continuing to enable me to live. In answer to this he says: 'You are not candid, *I know as much of the matter as you do.* Mr Lefanu's consent is of such a nature as to bring you into the family under the circumstances of total dissapprobation, and such as you will hereafter feel the effects of. *You set every engine to work. You almost brought your Sister into a quarrel with her Husband's Father* and your intended Father-in-Law. There is no personal objection to be made to Mr L—, but where people chuze to act for themselves without consulting their nearest Friends they must take the consequence. All I have to add is that you have not *a Friend or acquaintance who does not think as I do on the Subject.*' Now as this paragraph directly points at you and Mr L—, the only friends whose opinion I think of any consequence, I mention it to shew you the degree of falsehood he is capable of. That I approved of Harry's speaking to his Father is certain – But in every letter decidedly declared I would not proceed one step without his approbation, and so far from setting every engine to work, both Harry and I endeavour'd to keep you clear of the business. That you did take an active and a successful part we are very conscious, and must ever feel sincerely grateful for it; but it would have added greatly to my unhappyness had your interference been attended with the consequences my kind Brother supposes. I have written only an extract from that part of his letter, but if you wish to shame him for the mean attempt to hurt me where he thought me most vulnerable, I will enclose you the whole Sheet. I wrote him a few lines simply contradicting the most palpable falsehoods, at the same time bidding him an everlasting farewell, as it is my sincere wish we may never meet in this World.

He has sent me no money, and as near two quarters were due I am endeavouring to borrow some to extricate myself, as I know Dick is particularly distress'd at this time. His sending a duplicate of his string of falsehoods to my Brother was an action worthy of Blifil[1] and could have been done only with a view to injure me with the only Person who could serve me, and in that light I was vex'd and distress'd beyond what I thought it in his power to make me suffer. Indeed the reading of this strange work affected me in such a way I was unable to accompany Mrs S— to Sheen (Lord Palmerstone's) for my stomach and head were most violently attack'd.

Dick did not go 'till Eveng, and as I still felt too low to wish to speak on the subject I wrote him a few lines to beg he would give me an opportunity of talking to him when he had read Charles's letter, as from the misrepresentations contain'd in it I fear'd I might appear in an unfair light to him. He came to me immediately, kiss'd me very affectionately, and assured me nothing from that quarter could ever hurt me in his opinion; at the same time he said he had hardly leisure to peruse such a parcel. He then set off to meet Mrs S— and as they were to sleep at Richmond I have seen nothing of them since, tho' we expected them in Town early.

I pass'd but an indifferent night but am better today, and a letter recd from Harry has proved a real cordial to my poor broken spirits. He gives a good account of his own health and still talks warmly of your kind attention to him. His Father he says speaks kindly of me and is affectionate to him. In short his letter has in a great degree dispell'd the gloom my *Evil Genius* had endeavour'd to spread over my prospects.

Eleven at Night – Dick return'd alone today, as Mrs S— had been prevail'd on to give the day to Mrs Greville who has a House in that Neighbourhood. I dined alone and took a walk in the Eveng and have seen no one but Tickell who call'd for a minute.

I was roused from my book just now by an allarm among the servants and going out to enquire what was the matter I met the little Boy's Maid frighten'd out of her wits, crying 'my Sammy' and 'fire' alternately. On looking up I saw the sky in a blaze but soon perceived the fire was not near us, so prevented

[1] The villain in Fielding's *Tom Jones*.

[173]

her taking up the Children which in her fright was her first thought. The allarm they had at the beginning of the winter accounts for the poor Girl's terror. Miss Tickell's french Woman was echoing her and all the Maids in confusion. The Men went out to enquire where the fire was and have just brought me word the Opera House is burnt to the Ground – luckily this was not Opera Night, and it is also fortunate that it began so early there is no chance of any lives being lost, tho' they say many Houses are burning so that many poor People may be ruin'd by this Calamity. You may judge with what fury it blazed when the allarm in our family arose from the appearance of the sky thro' the skylight, which was so very red it was impossible to think the fire at any distance, and when I look'd out of the Window I saw the flames so distinctly I thought it could not be farther than Bond St, and you know what a distance we are from the Haymarket. It seems now going down so I hope the mischeif will go no farther – Good night my dear Woman.

Thursday – This Morng another *last letter* from Harry in which he bids me expect him this Eveng or tomorrow morng. He writes in unusual spirits so I trust he is well. He gives a good account of you too, which has taken off a great deal of the load that was on my spirits.

Monday, June 22nd – I am quite proud of Tom – indeed Harry gives a delightful account of both your little ones. He tells me your Old Gentleman speaks kindly of me. If you think it right present my respects to him and tell him I should be happy to have the confirmation of his approbation before we are united, but in that my dear Love act as you think best – Suppress the message if you think it improper, or say in my name what ought to be said and I will agree to it. I have had a joint letter of congratulation, kindness, etc. from Peter and Fanny[1] which I shall answer tomorrow –

[1]Peter LeFanu, the youngest brother of Joseph and Henry, had married Alicia's and Betsy's first cousin Fanny Knowles, daughter of John Knowles and Hester Sheridan.

Wednesday 24th – Nothing new my dear Love since Monday that I sent my last – Harry dined and spent the Eveng here. Yesterday the same story. His spirits are good and his health seems to mend daily. Mrs S— has been out in the Evengs cheifly with Lady Williams. Poor Sir Watkin quite unconscious of his situation is delighted with her company and talks of going to Italy as soon as Lady Williams is up. Her reckoning is out, and she has now the dread of confinement and the particular fear of being deceived about her husband when she can no longer attend him, for hitherto she has never slept out of his Room, nor has suffer'd any one about him but herself. Tom Grenville never quits the House but to sleep, and she made him promise last night that he would religiously tell her the truth during her confinement if Sir Watkin should not be able to be with her – In short it is impossible to conceive a Scene of greater distress. Mrs S— says T: Grenville is an Angel upon Earth, his behaviour on this occasion is indeed very unlike most Young Men of fashion.

This day we heard great matters were expected at the Trial, and I gave Harry a ticket for the King's Box and went to meet him there, but it turn'd out a day of dissappointment. Nothing was done, and in the confusion coming away we miss'd Mrs S— and with some difficulty got a Hack to convey us home as it rain'd most powerfully. He dines with Mr Gilbert, but I expect him in the Eveng.

Thursday – Last night quiet at home with le cher Harry. He came this morng with a Licence, and the Ring you know is already provided, so he fancies himself half married already, but he must wait a few days for some necessary arrangements. As Mrs S— could not accompany me to the Country she sugested the idea of asking my Friend Mrs Wilson to be with me for a few days, and I have written to propose it to her. Sunday we go to Richmond. Monday Harry and I go to look at our future habitation to see if anything is wanting. Teusday we return to

Town, and then I beleive I remain a very little time my own Mistress. The particular day must depend on le Cher Frère as he gives me away.

We heard a most shocking Story today which is however too true. I beleive in the course of the Winter I mention'd seeing Miss Beauclerc here with Mrs Bouverie. She is daughter to Lady Di: B:, the same that occasion'd the Divorce from Lord Bolingbroke. The present Lord Bolingbroke, his Son (of course her Brother[1]), has been married about six years to a very charming Woman. Miss B— was invited to spend some time with her Brother and the consequence was a most infamous connection between them: So compleatly criminal that the Young Lady was with Child. Lady Bolingbroke to prevent if possible the horrid story getting wind, went abroad with her and nursed her in her lying in. Yet so harden'd were they in vice, that she was soon after with child again. Lady B— again acted the same part, and then the family return'd to England. You may judge what the poor Woman must have suffer'd who doats on her husband, tho' cruelly treated by him, and three Children she has by him entirely neglected. Yet the hope of saving from disgrace the family she was connected with made her submit to her unfortunate Lot. However Miss Beauclerc has put an end to the business at once by going off with her Brother Lord Bolingbroke. She left a letter to her unfortunate Mother informing her of her connection, of the birth of the Children, which she had taken with her, and ended with advising them not to pursue them as they had changed their name and had determin'd to spend the remainder of their life abroad. An Express however was sent after them with an offer of free pardon from every branch of the family, if they would return, to save them from the horrid disgrace their crime entails on them, but the Messenger return'd with a positive refusal. Poor Lady Di: was near dying and is now very ill. You know Lord Rt. Spenser is her Brother, and these facts Mrs S— had today from Mrs Bouverie. She heard from other reports but

[1]Half-brother.

[176]

had hoped they were groundless. Miss B— is about one and twenty but does not appear more than eighteen and I thought had a look of innocence and simplicity – I saw her frequently this winter under the protection of Mrs B—, as her Mother has never gone into Public since her divorce. She was with us most part of the Eveng the night of Brooks's Ball. I think a more shocking circumstance altogether cannot be conceived.

Harry has been here all day and is now gone home. Mrs S— not yet return'd from Mrs Bouverie's where I was ask'd. It is late, so good night. I hope for a letter tomorrow.

[Betsy and Harry were married on Saturday 4th July 1789.]

CHAPTER 8

Hampton Court and Bath, July 1789 to March 1790

63: HAMPTON COURT, 7TH TO 9TH JULY 1789

Hampton Court July 7th 1789 – My dearest love, My hasty letter of Saterday[1] will naturally have prepared you for a little interruption of the journal. As the change of scene and bustle of moving could not allow me much freedom of thought or time for writing. We are now settled as comfortably as the hurry we left London in would admit of and soon I hope we shall feel quite at home.

Saterday we went according to our settled plan to Richmond with Mrs Sheridan and Richardson, Dick having been taken from us by very particular business, but before we parted he took me apart to inform me that he should remit to me in a very few days a deed legally drawn up to entitle Harry to receive the income he had proposed giving me – Cocker who transacts all Law business for him had promis'd to have the thing done by Saterday but unluckily was press'd too much by a hurry of business. We had no wish for any such security but his doing it is certainly truly generous and like himself – He took the most affectionate leave of me at the same time assuring me that he thought from the choice I had made he was certain I should be very happy. You will readily suppose this scene affected me a good deal but I struggled and did not suffer my agitation to appear.

At Richmond we found Mrs Wilson who dined with us, and in the Eveng Mrs Sheridan sung to us at my request as the best

[1] 4th July, her wedding day.

[178]

celebration of a day I consider'd as happy. The moment of parting with her was another trial and my shedding tears in abundance could hardly be consider'd as any way derogatory to my affection to Harry. She had received me with the affection of a Sister at the most melancholy period of my Life, and during the Eleven months I had been with her I could only look back to constant kind and friendly treatment – And that when my situation was most dependent. She was affected too, tho' She reiterated her request that we would consider her House as our home when ever we chose to be from Hampton. I dried up my tears as soon as I could and the rest of the Eveng was chearful. You know Mrs Wilson is an Old friend and favorite of Harry, so he was quite happy to have her with us.

Sunday we walk'd a little in the Gardens, which are flat and in the dutch taste but spacious and kept in very tollerable order. We did not walk at the Hour of company but I am told during the Summer that one walk is every Eveng quite crouded with company. There are no less than 47 families that inhabit the Pallace. The remainder of the day we pass'd very well as besides the Library I mention'd there is a Book Case in the Drawing Room that contains all the best books of entertainment both french and English. Yesterday the Morng was warm so we let Harry walk out alone and we took to our work and our Books. Mr Nallegan a friend of the Craufurds has a House very near us and the whole family came to visit me but of course were not admitted. However Harry met Mr Nallegan riding home and in spite of an Asthma that almost Stifles the poor Man had the conscience to bring him up our 80 stairs to pay his devoirs to me. He was civil and friendly in offers of good Neighbourhood in his own and Mrs Nallegan's name and press'd one offer which I think of accepting, which is to send regularly to his Garden for vegetables of all kinds of which he has very great abundance, and you know in these sort of places one is not easily supplied and he tells us we shall find it worse when all the familys are settled here for the Summer.

In the Eveng we again walk'd a little in the public Garden,

but soon left to follow the Gardener who shew'd us the private Gardens in which in future we may walk when we please. They have little beauty but one is at least safe there from the Sunday Visitors that croud here during the fine weather. The Hot Houses and Green Houses are very Noble and supply the King with a great deal of his fruit. One vine he shew'd us that extends over a Hot House near a Hundred feet long, it is always loaded with fruit and the whole proceeds from one Stem. There is a dark walk of Lime Trees that must be delightful during the sunny part of the day, which he told us was planted by the Hands of William and Mary – several very fine Orange trees brought over by them and now very flourishing and a number of other memorials of those times. We shall visit the appartments at our Leisure.

Today Harry is gone to Kingston, which is quite near us and where I am told we may be supplied with every thing almost as well as from London. Our friend is deeply engaged reading 'The Recess' and I have scribbled thus far in the midst of the noise of Bell-hangers who are rectifying all negligence of our predecessors. We find our appartment quite comfortable but not as Roomy as we had supposed with regard to bedrooms, as in our former visit we had reckon'd the same Rooms twice over. Our numerous Stairs I don't mind as they are not steep and I have placed a chair half way for the benefit of any visitor. To save the servants we use a contrivance of poor Mrs Tickell's – It is a well stair case and there is a Basket tyed to a long Rope at the Top, which they let down when the Tradesmen (according to the English fashion) bring home the provisions. They ring the Bell at the bottom of the Stairs, call out their business, the Basket is let down, and the bread or meat rides up in perfect safety. So you see we have obviated the cheif inconvenience of our Habitation.

Harry seems quite happy and satisfied and I do not doubt that when we have time to look into our little domestick arrangements we shall be able to do very well even with our small income. We can live here as we please and if we should hereafter associate with the Inhabitants of the Palace, society can be kept up on easy terms as I am told they meet cheifly in the Evengs. Tho' the Nallegans are not very bright they are good people and as the Craufurds will be with them part of the Summer that will also be a very pleasant circumstance to me on Harry's account as well as my own. I ought to call myself the happiest of Women and run out in Raptures on having got the best of Men, according to all rules of bridal Epistles, but you know the worth of your Brother and I need not enlarge on the Subject.

Having now *the care of a family* upon me I shall in future only send one packet a week but to that I will be punctual. I am hardly accustomed to my new name yet, and felt some doubts about opening a letter directed to *Mrs Lefanu* which I received this Morng from Charles Morris. It contain'd the most friendly congratulations of the whole family and many polite expressions respecting le Cher Henry with whom he dined one day in Bruton St. This letter was pleasing to me as I have every reason to esteem and value that family. As yet I have received no letter from you here, as they must go first to Bruton St and I must depend on the vigilance of Edwards,[1] who is not uncommonly bright tho' very civil. My Brother's family are now all settled at Richmond and I shall probably see them on Sunday, and I mean to dine with them the first day I am at liberty.

July 8th – If Charles does send the money I shall be glad of it, as we have of course many little purchases to make, and whatever my Brother R— had intended doing in the way of a little present towards Housekeeping was I know out of his power at the time. And notwithstanding Charles's assertions to the contrary, to delay was not in my power, unless I had been content to appear *indifferent* not only to Harry but to have been supposed so by the friends I was with, who wish'd to promote my happyness by hastening the Match.

I have only lately look'd over the trunk you sent me, and am sorry you did not send me over the little square Box I

[1]Mrs Sheridan's butler.

mention'd – the spoons I should also be glad of. I found several pr of Harry's Sheets so coarse we can only use them as Servants' Sheets. I left 4 pr of tollerable finer ones behind and should be glad of those that remain and any thing that you think would be useful as we must buy else and have not as you know much money. My *Dictionary* too I wish'd particularly as it was a gift from my Father to me and I value it as the only token of remembrance I possess from him.

China, delph and glass I never expected for they are troublesome to move and may be of use to you, so never consider them as mine nor the tea Urn which you will also want. Of my own private property I shall thank you to enquire about a little inkstand of Ebony with glass bottles and plated tops which I kept for my own use, as I have nothing of the kind and for reasons aforsaid want to buy as little as possible. I had no intention of mentioning this little business when I began, but when I speak of Charles I think the idea becomes connected with tiresome details.

So my dear love to plague you no more with these sort of things, if you will order these things to be put up in either of the trunks I left behind and sent as I before mention'd by long Sea, we may have them in a fortnight at this Season of the Year. The plated candlesticks will also be very useful to us, pack'd up with Hay they will come very safe I am sure.

Thursday – I gave Dilly my note for the Twenty pounds he advanced me which serv'd to clear me. I am glad to tell you that he gives a favorable account of the Sale and will shortly be prepared to make the first Settlement from which we can not expect much; but the profits afterwards will he thinks answer very well.

Yesterday Mrs S— sent over Jenny Linley to see me who return'd only on Teusday from her Norwich Expedition. She is a good humour'd Creature but not troubled with those feelings that keep her Sister from me, as I could not perceive the smallest emotion on her entering these Appartments which She had not seen since her poor Sister's death. She brought the Children also to see me, and we have fix'd to dine at Richmond on Saterday.

August 20th – I was at Richmond yesterday and at my return found yours of the 4th and 11th, And am glad for your sake you go on with the Plays. Mrs S: has commission'd me to answer that part of your letter that relates to Mrs Crouch and Kelly. She says She did speak to Dick about it, but that he told her he was sorry it was not his power to do the thing, as Kemble undertook the management on the express terms of his not interfering; that in this Instance there might arise a real inconvenience to the Theatre as all the Performers are for ever applying for a few days' grace which if granted to one could not be refused to others, which might oblige them to postpone opening Drury Lane, or lay them under the necessity of doing so with only the Riff-Raff of the Company, a circumstance that would certainly be injurious to profits of the Season. She would have written to you herself to explain this matter but that for this last fortnight She has been so ill as to be hardly off the Bed. I spent the day with her yesterday, Harry went to Town about business and She sent the Coach for me and sent me home at Night. I found her ill when I first went but She grew rather better towards night. Dick was at Brighton to celebrate the Duke of York's birthday[1] and we spent the day in her bedroom. I got home time enough to sup with le cher Henri who had no hopes of seeing me so soon.

This morng I had a visit from my sentimental Cousin William Chamberlain. Harry contrived not to appear, so I supposed an engagement to dinner and escaped his fixing himself with us for the day and most probably the night. He was full of sentiment and fine speeches and brought me a present of a pr of silver clasps for the Shoes of my unborn Infants. In short he bored me so much on the Subject of marriage and Children, that recollecting that he acts as Surgeon and Accoucheur I was sure his visit was intended in the fair way of trade and was heartily glad when he took his leave. Tho' his extreme regard had brought

[1] He was 26.

him 13 miles to visit Eliza Lefanu, who ranks with his Wife in his esteem. You know how I hate Sentiment so can conceive my comfort at his quiting the Room, Which did not end his ceremonies, as a sentimental note was brought me from the Inn previous to his return to Town.

Tickell marries Miss Lee next week and so ends his sentimentalising. She is very pretty, just Eighteen and daughter of an East India Captain, who before he sail'd last forbad her to think of Tickell. What he will say at his return is more than we can guess; but he is a Young Man and has another daughter so T. will probably not get much fortune. His whole conduct in this business has been shuffling and paltry to the greatest degree and has of course disgusted those whose good opinion he ought to have endeavour'd to preserve. But I beleive he thinks the game up as to any immediate advantage by the connection and is content to appear in his own coulours which are not the brightest hue. The Children are all with Mrs S— and the Boys to remain with her 'till they are of an age for School. It is well these poor little fellows have endear'd themselves so much to her and Dick who truly loves them, while their Father seems quite indifferent, which is the more extraordinary as they are very engaging children.

I always read with real delight the good accounts you give of Bess and Tom. Kind love to Mr L—, I gave his letter to Harry who will write I suppose when the Demon of Idleness will let him. I scold and growl in vain, but still I hope he will mend in time. That his heart is ever truly and affectionately with you I can safely affirm.

65: LONDON, 2ND AND 3RD OCTOBER 1789

Bruton St, Octobre 2d, 89 – Once more my dear Love return'd to my Old Habitation, but with very different feelings from those I experienced on my first entering it. Mrs S— sent us over[1] the Coach this morng to convey us to Town which was both

[1] i.e. from Richmond to Hampton Court.

pleasant and convenient as it saved us some money. We should have dined with them on our way to Town but that they were all gone to Lord John Townshend's to a Cricket Match. So we came quietly on and dined most comfortably in the little Room on a Country Fowl we brought with us. The servants of the House had prepared the House for us so while we stay in Town we are as well and as reasonably settled as can be; and I think it also looks well to the world that this should be our home. Mrs S— in the note she sent me says the Box *of course* is mine while we stay, so this little business has been settled with real kindness and cordiality. We have promised them one day at Richmond before we go to Bath.

My Journal of Hampton is soon told – Sunday I sent my last. Monday, Hillman made us dine with him at a fisherman's across the River, famous for good fish dinners, where we were treated with Water Souchet[1] in perfection. Hillman was our best Neighbour, a good humour'd chearful Creature and of a liberal turn. The rest of the week I kept quiet not being quite Stout. Yesterday Hillman eat a farewell dinner with us, and today I left my card to take leave with the only one of the Dowagers who had visited me or invited me to Cards, paid my farewell visit at Neligans as we past by the door, and left poor Miss Nowlan looking most wistwilly after me. I really think the poor Girl's case a hard one – to be shut up with a very dull Old Mother and still duller Father in Law who adds ill temper to his perfections and keeps those Women without a Carriage and consequently without Society in the Country, tho' he got a large fortune with the Mother, and the Daughter when of age must have twenty thousand pounds.

Teusday I received yours which Harry answer'd in part. I am truly happy your ideas agree with ours as to our destination. It is the only comfortable one within the compass of our finances. Both Fletcher and his Wife have written to me in the most satisfactory and indeed friendly manner and proposed such terms as I take to be reasonable. I have also the comfort

[1] *Water souchet* – a parsley sauce made with water and sugar.

[185]

to find Dick approves of the situation, which I doubted a little as you know he is a little *grand*, but he told me he thought our plan perfectly Eligible. At all Events we know our expences, which is not an easy matter when one keeps House.

Saterday, Octobre 3d – I hope Charles will now think of paying me. I have not recd: a guinea since January last and must of course have been pretty well pinch'd whether married or Single. I trust more to his fear of appearing dishonest in your eyes than any spirit of justice to me, and am truly obliged by the part you have taken in this business.

66: BATH, 2ND NOVEMBER 1789

I have just recd your packet of the 27th Of which to say the truth the contents have vex'd us a good deal. Charles's statement is like himself – if true, it proves a strange degree of extravagance to have incurr'd such debts while in receipt of so large an income as his was. If false, how truly contemptible is his conduct. He does not mention me among his Creditors but he shall find I consider myself as One. Mr L—'s letter relatif to the Quilca business is equally unsatisfactory. We did not conceive ourselves obliged to consult the Old Gentleman about the disposal of any small property belonging to me as he has not in the slightest degree done any thing in consequence of our marriage. Harry's allowance continues the same as when a Batchelor. But since he must be inform'd, what we would wish is that he might be told that we have an opportunity of laying out the money here to much greater advantage than it can ever produce us in Ireland. To you we will candidly own that the money is *absolutely* necessary to us and that if Mr L— does not become the purchaser we must dispose of it at all events, tho' rather on hard terms since so far from benefiting by this business I only get back my own money with difficulty and lose the interest. You know I proposed disposing of it before my marriage.

We have been here now a fortnight and I have gone no where

and that really from oeconomy as the amusements of this place were no part of our inducement to come here, but that simply after much enquiry we could not find any other where we could be provided with necessaries of life on such reasonable terms, so that my dear Woman I am not now in circumstances to furnish a journal of much entertainment.

Since my last I have met Forbes here who visited us yesterday and J. White looking very sulky and very ugly. All Hallows Eve we spent with Mrs Leigh who had a parcel of young People to burn nuts and we play'd cards at a comfortable low rate. I had a very kind letter from Mrs S— who tells me Dick is return'd from Stafford and that he is quite *safe* there. Linley is here and I call'd on him, but he will not leave the Chimney corner, tho' I don't think he seems so ill as he was in London.

67: BATH, 1ST AND 2ND DECEMBER 1789

Yesterday I received yours of the 24th and communicated to Harry your Dublin scheme. Tho' equally sensible with myself of the kindness of your wishes on that subject, Yet he says and with great truth that such a plan is wholly impracticable. Limited as our income must be for a time we can live here because we can live to ourselves. We are neither obliged to receive nor go into company. They may accuse us of liking retirement but the Sin of poverty will not be imputed to us, as it certainly would be in Dublin were we to appear there on a less respectable footing than the rest of the family. Even the Old Gentleman would feel his pride hurt at seeing that his Son had form'd a connection so *evidently* dissadvantageous, tho he would not have generosity to remedy the inconvenience. I know enough of his disposition to be certain that money alone could ensure me such treatment as I should have a right to expect from him, and I know enough of my own not to expose myself to what would make me very unhappy.

Our Weather is damp and dirty but does not confine us as you know we Ladies here trot about in Pattens, a privilege granted no where else to genteel Women. The waters continue to do wonders for Harry so that I hope this winter will quite set him up. I have taken two places in the Green Boxes for tonight to see Miss Wallace – The same little girl you may remember at School in York St. I hear her performance well spoken of. I prefer this mode of going as by avoiding the expence of dress and chair Hire it makes our freedom of the Theatre a real convenience. Bath Decre 1st – Your verses to Patty Whyte are very pretty –

Wednesday Morng – I was too late for the post yesterday, so can tell you about Miss Wallace. Upon the whole we liked her very well. Her face does not appear handsome on the Stage, but her figure is very good and her deportment really Ellegant. She has feeling evidently and seems to have sense and don't doubt will in time be a very good Actrice. The Play was the *Conscious Lovers* which you know is dull enough but the Performers appear'd to me as good as we see any where. The Theatre is very pretty and the green Boxes particularly convenient, as there are backs to the Seats which rise almost as high as your head so that the people behind are not leaning on your Shoulders, and the seats are sufficiently raised to allow every one to see. Lord John and his Lady were opposite to us in one of the upper Boxes. I meet them every day arm in arm when Harry and I take our Walk, So you see what different causes produce the same effect as we certainly appear equally domestic couples. Lord J: is always very gracious, but as I never happen'd to meet his Lady while I lived at Dick's we are not acquainted, which as matters stand is so much the better.

68: BATH, 9TH TO 17TH DECEMBER 1789

Wednesday 9th – Last night my Dear Woman I received your journal from the 28th to 4th Decre. That I write less frequently of late has been owing to a total want of matter from the very retired life we necessarily lead and from want of Spirits to chat pleasantly on indifferent matters, owing to an uninterrupted series of dissappointments of material consequence to us ever since our marriage took place. Tho' often depress'd by present inconveniences yet still I am internally convinced that Dick will keep his promise to me, tho' the hurry he lives in makes him often unconscious of the length of time that passes between his promise and performance. As to Charles he has now pledged himself in such strong terms to Harry, that if he has the means I think he cannot long withhold what he expressly acknowledged as a debt.

The Craufurds are still here but She has been so constantly in Public that of course we have not been much together. Last night I made a little party for Mr Craufurd who had a great wish to spend an Eveng in company with Miss Lee, whom he liked very much. I had beside her Sister Harriet, Mr Linley and an Irish Doctor who boards in the House. Mrs Craufurd and Mr G: Craufurd came to us from the Concert so you see my assemblies are not very numerous, but however the Eveng pass'd off very well. Since my last, General Burgoyne has paid us a visit and that is the only new circumstance in our situation I can remember. Yes I have again got out of J: Whytes good graces, how I know not, except having declined two invitations to Cards from his Mama who took it into her head to visit me. I should have liked the acquaintance of Miss Whyte very well, but as it could only be had at the expence of playing cards with the Mother and being acquainted with the Brother, whom neither of us liked, I found it necessary to keep back a little.

Mrs Forster is also lost to us of late. You know She is a very odd Woman and one of her passions is having vulgar people with her. Her present intimates and companions are her own Maid Charlotte under the name of *Miss Carey* and a Mrs Pritchard who formerly kept one of the Taverns in this Town but who fail'd. Now tho' these may be very good sort of People, they are certainly not company one would wish to appear with in such a Town as this, where every person and every thing is known, so tho' I was always personally as civil as possible to Mrs F: I did not include her suite either in an invitation I

[189]

gave her or in my visits, and for this last month She has drop'd me, which I very naturally attribute to that cause.

Sunday 13th – That Idle fellow Harry has kept me from sending this by saying he would write to you himself today and now it is too late for the Post. I have just read yours down to the 7th and am not a little disgusted with additional dose of selfishness of your old Gentleman. He just stands in the light of the avaricious *Old Man* as described by Bacon – Who he says may be compared to a Person stealing when on his way to the Gallows, but there certainly is this comfort to be derived from that sort of conduct that it consoles one for an event which being inevitable we are glad to consider in the best light. Last night we were again at the Play and were both much pleased with Miss Wallace.

69: BATH, 29TH DECEMBER 1789

My Dear Love I am deeply in your debt – Two long letters of the 14th and 21st, but I have had nothing to say so could keep no journal. Till last night I had not Stir'd out since my last. The rain kept me at home in the mornings and I was not tempted to go out in the Eveng.

Last night I went to the Ball because we have a number of grand Foreigners here and I wish'd to take a peep at their faces. I went with Mrs Ferguson, a Lady Mr L. may remember at Mrs Petrie's. She was a Miss Mitchell. She went to the East Indies where She married a rich Old Gentleman, but the Climate not agreeing with her He allow'd her to come home without him and gives her twelve hundred a year to Spend. She seems however a most unenviable object as dejection and ill-health are pictured in her countenance, but her manners are gentle and I like her the best of my chance acquaintances here. Her Uncle Mr Petrie was of her party: they are a family I like very much.

There was quite a croud on the same account that took me to the Rooms – The Duke and Dutchess of Luxembourg, their

Son, daughter, and nine or ten french persons of fashion of their party. In short the sound of french prevail'd over the Irish accent which reigns pretty generally at Bath and was very distressing to Mrs Craufurd's ears as She told me – Don't you admire the delicacy of such organs? I was myself rather unlucky in that respect last night as I can truly say I met a great deal of bad language. My first Beau was German, of Harry's acquaintance, who splutters french as a Welsh man does English and who chose to give me a great deal of his conversation, and he was succeeded by Our little Italian Marquis whom I before mention'd to you, who is working hard to make a proficiency in our Language in which he has certainly made some progress, but his present method of conversing is not unlike the Pupils of Mr Bradwaite, which tho' of use to him is by no means edifying to his hearers. I was the more provoked with his persevering in speaking English as his conversation in french (which he speaks well) must have been entertaining: for he is a man of Sense and some litterary reputation – His Name Pindemonte. Upon the whole however we pass'd our Eveng very tollerably.

Harry's Friend Mr Baker is here and the Latouches. I think him a very pleasing Young Man and the Boys the very reverse of their Cousins – C'est tout dire. My Good Gentleman has met beside many of his Old acquaintance but I have stumbled on no female friend, which in some measure keeps me from the Rooms as one can't well go without one. Mrs Leigh whom Mrs S— introduced me to has been quite lost to me from a most melancholy cause, which is constant sickness in her family ever since the Eveng I spent with her. I say with you about Mrs Cuthbert's marriage 'the Lord preserve our senses'. You were certainly right to caution Tom, as it is not impossible that twenty years hence Emily might think of making an attack upon his heart.

I heard from Mrs S— about ten days ago. She told me they were to set out for Crewe Hall the next day, where I suppose they arrived by this time. They were all well. Linley has taken himself to London which is a load off me, for I felt that I ought to be kind to him on his daughter's account and yet there was no knowing what to do with him as he seems to be in a deep melancholy.

I have got between the festivals so you must take this for merry Xmas and happy new Year in one. Pray dont forget to make the compliments of the Season for us to our dear *Papa*. As he has been so generous to you I suppose he will send me some capital new year's gift.

70: BATH, 5TH TO 10TH JANUARY 1790

Teusday Jany 5th – Many happy returns to you of *this* day,[1] my dear Love. Last night I was again at the Ball, quite dissipated you see, but the truth is it was Tyson's Benefit, and as he is my acquaintance, independant of being M:C:, it was but decent that at least one of us should appear there. There were near twelve Hundred people there all as fine as Sattins and feathers could make them. I find my millenery and Hair dressing Talents of great use on these occasions, as litteraly since I came here I have not spent a shilling on either article, as some remains of last Winter's finery varied by my own hand have supplied me with caps and tuckers, and as to la frizure I was provident enough never to suffer the Maid I kept to dress me so constantly as to lose the power of arranging my own locks, which by the bye I have so far recover'd that I have compleatly thrown off my Wig. As I have some men acquaintance here I never want one to procure me a tea or put me into a chair, which is all I want with them, my dancing days being long over.

Our Irish Doctor is very civil and talks french in Public, as he says 'to *hide* his Brogue'. I talk'd little but French the Whole Eveng and among the croud met Mr Le Texier just arrived to give us a few Readings. He was delighted to see me, but at first did not recollect me so much am I alter'd since the melancholy

[1] Alicia's 37th birthday.

[192]

time at Deepden. Indeed to confess a truth I can no longer conceal from myself I am grown so fat since I came here that I have no small difficulty in getting into my gowns, but as Harry has the Lefanu taste for embonpoint, without which no Woman can be tollerable in his opinion, I console myself as well as I can.

Mr Le Texier has just left his name at my Door. Harry has never heard him and will not treat himself to the Readings, tho' he wishes of all things to go. The price is a Guinea for 4 persons or 4 readings for one Person, but nothing under the guinea will be taken. I rather hope T: will send me tickets. Tonight we have got places for the *Dramatist*.

Wednesday Eveng – I am just return'd from a dinner at George Craufurd's who now keeps house with his Sister. There were no Women but us but several Gentlemen, among the rest Forbes, very civil etc. I like Miss C— very well but we parted early, as you know an invitation to dinner in England does not engage you a moment after the Coffee is served. She went to the Concert, and I came home to my fireside and the last Volume of Rousseau's *Confessions*, which Harry is delighted with and has now made over to me: but to shew how good I can be I let it lie quietly beside me while I scribble to you. We were not much delighted with *The Dramatist*, but it is the fashion to like it and I suppose you will have it in Dublin. I saw Miss Lee there looking very weary. I have not been in company with her since I recd your letter, but we sup with her next Saterday and I shall tell her what you think of her.

Well, this morng at Breakfast I had a most civil note from Mr Le Texier enclosing a Card of admission for myself and Friends to all his Readings, So I gave the Ticket with great joy to our dear Harry who set off to the Rooms and return'd quite delighted with the performance which he said far exceeded his expectations. It was not in my power to go this Morng, but I do not mean to miss again since fortune has thrown this amusement in our way. Most sincerely do I wish you could share it with us; but these are the Rubs of fortune. Where I feel it most

[193]

is the necessity of separation the want of it produces. Your Old Gentleman is indeed a queer Old Man, but it is a great comfort to me we have not hitherto, nor shall we I trust ever appear to want his assistance.

Sunday – Thursday we both went to hear Texier read *Le Gentilhomme Bourgeois* and were delighted. Indeed the hearty laugh Harry had those two morngs will do him more good than all the water he has drank; most sincerely did we wish we could waft you and your good Gentleman over to share our pleasure. My engagement to Miss Lee made me miss a Reading which unluckily happen'd to be in the Eveng Yesterday, but I do not intend to lose any more for any party. I told Miss Lee what you said of her and She was much flatter'd. As yet I can not tell you more of her as our meetings have been hitherto a little in the formal stile, always cards and a party tho' rather a pleasant one. I like the manners of the Eldest by much the best.

71: BATH, 28TH MARCH 1790

It is a long time my dear Love since I have written and long since I have heard from you. This last week I have been kept idle by one of those feverish colds that you know I am subject to. I have no faith in Apothecaries and no money for Physicians so I undertake my own cure, and with the help of James's powders and dear Harry's care I conquer'd the Enemy but continued weak for some days. While I was ill I got a letter from our poor little Friend Mrs Wilson to tell me that She had that day had a letter from her Husband and that he was in perfect health and wrote in good Spirits. As you must before this have known of the loss of his Ship, this news will I am sure be a comfort to You. We had also a letter from Mr Smith to whom we had written to enquire into the circumstances of the melancholy event, who says that Wilson was fully insured and as the misfortune happen'd in consequence of the Company's orders to try a new passage to China no blame can possibly rest on him. He is expected home in the course of the next month.

Since my last my journal is soon told. I dined out one day with a Mr and Mrs De La Fontaine old acquaintances of Harry's who live here, and the rest of the time at home. We saw in the *Dublin Eveng Post* a most wonderful account of the performance of *Jane Shore*. Tho' I knew Patty had talents I had no idea of her doing so very well, for by the account she must have been really fine. Mr L— I see got his usual share of praise. If you were able to venture to the representation you must have been proud of your Pupil, for I think you told me you gave Patty instructions, which was a double kindness as it assisted her and saved her from being *learn'd* by her Papa.

I have had no letters from London lately so can tell you no news from that quarter. I see by the *Herald* Mrs S— is giving great parties and making up for last year's moderation. I am sorry to see the Pharaoh table always makes a part of the entertainment, as I know her passion for it and the result of a run of ill luck must be dreadful. Lady Duncannon is, thank God, gone to Bruxelles. I should not be sorry to hear she was drown'd on her way thither. Give my kindest Love to Mr L. and your dear little ones. Harry's best wishes and kindest love ever attends you and yours. God bless you my dear love.

Ever yours affectionately

E. LEFANU

Bath March 28th.

Notes

For the quarrel between Thomas and Dick Sheridan see the Introduction.

MRS ANGELO: Elizabeth Johnson, Irish wife of Domenico Angelo, the eminent fencing master.

BALLOONS: the topical excitement. See the note below on Lunardi, and letter 2.

YARKER: Mr and Mrs John Yarker of Leybourn Hall, Yorkshire, and their daughter Ann. 'Your old flirt': their son Luke (see letter 9). 'The old lady': perhaps Mrs Yarker's mother, Mrs Forster.

EMILY: a cousin living with Alicia, aged about twenty.

MRS WILSON: an Irish friend; her husband seems to have been a sailor.

'My father prepared for me': he lodged with his former manservant William Thompson in Marlborough Street.

PANTHEON: in Oxford Street, built as a kind of indoor 'Vauxhall' and later used for operas. Angelo was concerned in its management.

LUNARDI: Vincenzo Lunardi, secretary of the Neapolitan Embassy, made the first balloon ascent in England from the Artillery Company's grounds in Moorfields on 15 September this year 1784, less than a year after the first ascents in France.

NORFOLK STREET: the Linleys' house.

'Angry with the old man': that is, with Mr Linley for taking her father's place in the management of Drury Lane.

For the members of the Linley family see the list of characters at page x.

MRS TICKELL: Mary Linley, Betsy's contemporary.

HAMPTON COURT: the Tickells had rooms in the Gold Staff Gallery, which Betsy borrowed in 1789.

Clandestine Marriage: by Colman and Garrick (1766); *Lord Ogleby* was the principal part.

KING: Thomas King, acting manager of Drury Lane.

O'REILLY: probably Charles O'Reilly.

PARSONS: William Parsons 'the comic Roscius', acted at Drury Lane 1762–95.

MISS POPE: Jane Pope, acted at Drury Lane 1756–1808.

MRS DALY: formerly Mrs Lister, actress wife of Richard Daly the Dublin actor-manager.

DR MORRIS: Michael Morris, M.D., F.R.S., physician to Westminster Hospital.

'My picture': The portrait reproduced in this book.

MRS CRAUFURD: wife of Patrick Craufurd F.R.S., Accountant-General of the Army Pay Office.

MR SIDDONS: William Siddons had married Sarah Kemble in 1773.

'My father's plan': he published *A Plan of Education for the young Nobility and Gentry of Great Britain* in 1769. He was now hoping for help from the Irish Government to put it into effect.

HENDERSON: John Henderson 'the Bath Roscius', acted at Drury Lane and Covent Garden, and joined Thomas Sheridan in his recitals at Freemasons Hall. He died in 1785, aged 38.

'My aunt's death': Miss Elizabeth Sheridan.

BEE: Rebecca Sheen, daughter of Thomas Sheridan's sister Anne.

D'IVERNOIS: Sir Francis D'Ivernois, a Genevese, who promoted the establishment of an industrial settlement at Passage, Co. Waterford, to be called New Geneva. The Irish Government voted £50,000 in 1783, but the Genevese emigrants did not settle.

DU ROVERAY: one of the Commissioners for the New Geneva settlement.

HARRY ANGELO: son of Domenico, born 1756, he married Mary Bowman Swindon in 1778; their children were: George Frederick (b. 1779), Henry (b. 1780), Edward (b. 1787), and William (b. 1789).

MRS WYNDHAM: Frances Mary Harford (1763–1828) married in 1784 William Frederick Wyndham, youngest brother of the third Lord Egremont.

KITTY ANGELO: Catherine (1766–1859) afterwards Mrs Mark Drury. 'The other girls' were her sisters Sophy (1759–1847), a Dame at Eton, and Ann (1763–1833), Mrs William StLeger.

Life of Swift: published in 1784, as the first volume of his edition of Swift's works. Thomas Sheridan was Swift's godson.

MRS HAMILTON: probably Rachel Daniel, Mrs Frederic Hamilton, wife of the Dean of Raphoe. Her husband was a grandson of the 3rd Duke of Hamilton, and brother of Sir William Hamilton the ambassador. Her daughter Jane married the actor J. G. Holman in 1798.

GEORGE and EDWARD MORRIS: Dr Michael Morris's sons: George (1759–1837) qualified as a doctor in 1787 and became F.R.C.P. in 1795; Edward (1769–1815) became a Master in Chancery, M.P., and F.R.S.

NANCY SHERIDAN: Betsy's first cousin, Anne, daughter of her father's brother Richard.

MISS WOOLERY: she acted at the Haymarket in the autumn of 1785 and in Dublin in the following winter season. In 1787 she married a Mr. Cottingham.

COLEMAN: George Colman the elder, the distinguished manager of the Haymarket Theatre. He had a stroke at Margate in 1785, but lived till 1794.

MRS GUINNESS: wife of a Dublin friend of Thomas Sheridan, she appears to have looked after his literary business there.

MRS WARREN: probably Elizabeth Shaw, wife of the fashionable Dr Richard Warren, the Whig physician.

THOMPSON: William Thompson, their landlord, formerly Thomas Sheridan's personal servant.

TISDALE: some member of a distinguished Irish family, one of whom had been a friend of Swift and Thomas Sheridan's father; perhaps Michael, a barrister in London.

BOLTON: probably a relative of Charles Sheridan's wife, Letitia Bolton.

'Your Picture': a miniature, one of several which are still extant.

SCOTCH OFFICERS: on account of Mr Craufurd's connexion with the Army Pay Office.

MRS SIDDONS: for her 'discovery' by Thomas Sheridan, see the Introduction. The riot arose because she was, wrongfully, accused of pocketing the proceeds of the benefit nights of West Digges and Brereton.

HUNT: a bookseller in Frith Street.

Paisan perverti: Restif de la Bretonne's novel was published in 1776.

MR ERKE: Jean Caillaud Erck, a Huguenot and official in Dublin.

MRS HARVEY: perhaps really Mrs Hervey of Aiton (*née* Hamilton).

MISS KEMBLE: probably the elder Fanny (Mrs Twiss) but possibly Elizabeth (Mrs Whitelock).

LETTER 2

SMITH: perhaps William Smith (1728–93), American loyalist, Chief Justice of New York 1779, who was in England 1783–86 and afterwards Chief Justice of Canada.

HAYLEY'S PLAYS: William Hayley's *Plays of three acts for a private theatre* published 1784 include 'Lord Russell'.

BLANCHARD: Jean Pierre Blanchard, who had made three balloon ascents in France, made his fourth with John Sheldon, an English surgeon, from Chelsea on 16 October 1784, his fifth with Dr John Jeffries of Boston from Grosvenor Square on 3 November 1784. Jeffries and Blanchard made the first cross-channel flight on 7 January 1785.

LETTER 3

CARNABY MARKET: Carnaby Street runs north and south in Soho, to the west of Frith Street.

LETTER 4

HARGRAVES: Francis Hargrave (1741–1821), lawyer and legal antiquary. He made the famous argument which Lord Mansfield upheld, that 'Britain is a soil whose air is deemed too pure for slaves to breathe in'.

JODDERELL: Richard Paul Jodrell (1745–1831), F.R.S., F.S.A., an original member of Johnson's Essex Head Club, wrote several plays, two of which were produced at the Haymarket.

LETTER 5

BRAITHWAITE: Daniel Braithwaite (1741–1817), an official of the Post Office, a friend of Thomas Sheridan's publisher Charles Dilly, known as 'Honest Braithwaite' and called by Boswell 'that amiable and friendly man'.

LADY SAVILE: Mary, daughter of John Pratt, deputy vice-treasurer of Ireland and mother of Sir George Savile, 8th Baronet of Rufford 1726–84, to whom Thomas Sheridan dedicated his *Life of Swift*. She married, as his second wife, Charles Moreton (1716–99), principal librarian of the British Museum.

MR VESEY: Agmondesham Vesey, an Irish M.P., and son of the literary hostess, who held the original 'blue-stocking' salons in Bolton Row and later in Clarges Street.

MRS HANDCOCK: wife of Richard, Dean of Achonry, and mother of the first Lord Castlemaine.

LADY DARTREE: Philadelphia Freame, granddaughter of William Penn. She married Thomas Dawson who was created Lord Dartrey in 1770 and Viscount Cremorne in 1785.

MR BINGHAM: Richard, afterwards 2nd Lord Lucan.

MRS CARTER: Elizabeth Carter (1717–1806), the Greek scholar.

MRS MONTAGU: Elizabeth Montagu (1720–1800), the 'Queen of the Blue Stockings'.

MRS AIKENHEAD: wife of a West Indian proprietor at whose villa at Richmond Dick Sheridan spent his school holidays. Mr Aikenhead was an amateur of the theatre and an old friend of Thomas Sheridan.

LORD DEERHURST: afterwards 7th Earl of Coventry.

John Gilpin: Cowper's ballad was first published in November 1782 and made popular by Henderson's recital.

MRS GILBERT: possibly related to Thomas Sheridan's Dublin publisher and to Harry LeFanu's friend mentioned in letter 62.

LETTER 6

CUMBERLAND: Richard Cumberland 1732–1811. His tragedy *The Carmelite* was produced at Covent Garden in December 1784 and his tragedy *The Arab* at Covent Garden in March 1785.

HANNAH MORE: the authoress (1745–1833), as a girl she had written verses in honour of Thomas Sheridan.

SOAME JENYNS: politician, satirist, and philosophical writer (1704–87).

LADY SPENCER: Georgiana Poyntz, wife of the 1st Earl Spencer, and mother of the Duchess of Devonshire and Lady Duncannon.

MISS PULTENEY: Henrietta Laura, heiress of William Pulteney, Lord Bath. Her mother was a daughter of his first cousin Daniel Pulteney and her father William Johnstone assumed the name of Pulteney. She married Sir James Murray in 1794.

LETTER 7

LADY LANDAFF: Lady Catherine Skeffington, daughter of the 1st

Earl of Massereene, married in 1784 Francis Mathew, Lord Landaff, as his second wife.

THOMPSON'S EMPLOYMENT: William Thompson was employed in the Stamp Office.

MR BEAUFOY: Henry Beaufoy M.P., commissioner of the Stamp Office, had been a pupil of Thomas Sheridan.

MISS BROOK: Charlotte Brooke, poetess and Irish scholar.

MLLE D'EON: a notorious case of real or assumed change of sex. After serving as a soldier and diplomat, d'Eon was compelled to adopt woman's dress in the later part of her life.

DE GUERCHY: French ambassador in London, accused of persecuting d'Eon.

MARIA: apparently the same as Mary Walker, mentioned earlier.

LETTER 8

MISS BROOKE'S FATHER: Henry Brooke of Rantaran, Irish land-owner and writer of plays; said to have been a cousin of the Sheridans.

BEAUMARCHAIS: his *Figaro* appeared in 1784.

PARVISOL: a Dublin Huguenot family.

GRATTAN: Henry Grattan, the Irish statesman.

SURFACE'SH: Thomas Sheridan said his son 'dipped his pen in his own heart' to draw both Joseph and Charles Surface; but Betsy assumes that Joseph was drawn from their elder brother Charles.

LETTER 9

LUKE YARKER: born 1753, son of the Yarkers mentioned in letter 1. He was ordained in 1776 and married in 1777.

LADY RUSSELL: the character in Hayley's play 'Lord Russell'.

HANDEL COMMEMORATION: the second annual celebration in Westminster Abbey. The first in 1784 was fully recorded by Dr Burney.

ROUND CHURCH: St. Andrew's Church, Dublin. The old church was burned down in 1860.

MADAME MARA: Gertrud Mara (1749–1833), the leading German singer of the time.

NORRIS: Thomas Norris; he had been an admirer of Elizabeth Linley.

REINHOLD: the principal bass singer.

FISCHER: J. C. Fischer, the famous oboe player; there was a German bass singer Ludwig Fischer (1745–1825), but he is not known to have been in England at this time.

THREE PRINCESSES: Charlotte, Augusta, and Elizabeth.

TWO OF THE YOUNGER CHILDREN: there were three princes and three princesses younger than Princess Elizabeth.

DR CLEAVER: William Cleaver (1742–1815), became Bishop of Chester in 1787.

LETTER 10

PATTY: Patty Whyte, a cousin of the Sheridans.

TREMBLESTONE: Thomas, 13th Lord Trimleston.

LETTER 11

ROBERTSON: James Robertson (1720–88), formerly Governor of New York, was promoted Lieutenant-General in 1782.

MRS BELLAMY'S MEMOIRS: George Anne Bellamy was acting in Thomas Sheridan's company in Dublin at the time of the Kelly riot in 1746 when the 'bucks' wrecked his theatre and attacked her. Her *Memoirs with all her intrigues* were published this year 1785.

The Mirror: edited by Henry Mackenzie at Edinburgh 1779–80.

DR MILLMAN: Francis Milman (1746–1821), M.D. 1776, President of the College of Physicians 1811–13, created a baronet in 1800. His children, mentioned in the next letter were William (b. 1781), Francis (b. 1783), Frances Emily, and Henry (b. 1791), afterwards Dean of St Paul's.

LETTER 13

HACKMAN'S LETTERS: fictitious letters published by Sir Henry Croft in 1780 as *Love and madness*, supposed to have been written by Francis Hackman, the clergyman who murdered Martha Ray, the singer and mistress of Lord Sandwich, outside Covent Garden Theatre in 1779.

LADY ANSTRUTHER: Sir John Anstruther was a political friend of Sheridan's, and afterwards one of the Managers of the trial of Warren Hastings.

LADY ELIZABETH YORKE: one of the three Ladies Lindsay, daughters of the 5th Earl of Balcarres – Lady Ann Lindsay, the poetess, married Andrew Barnard in 1793; Lady Margaret Fordyce was the reigning beauty at Bath in 1770 when Sheridan wrote *Clio's Protest* for her; Lady Elizabeth married Philip Yorke, later 6th Earl of Hardwicke.

LETTER 14

Lady Barton: 'A novel in letters' by Elizabeth Griffith (1771). She made her name by her autobiographical *Letters of Henry and Frances* published in 4 volumes between 1757 and 1769.

HERON'S LETTERS: *Letters of Literature* 1784, by John Pinkerton (1758–1826), the Scottish antiquary, but attributed to Robert Heron (1764–1807), a Scottish journalist.

LETTER 16

PALMIRA and MAHOMET: *Mahomet the Impostor*, a play adapted from Voltaire by James Millar, produced at Drury Lane in 1744 and long popular. It was the political application of a speech in this play by the actor West Digges which provoked the second wrecking of Thomas Sheridan's theatre in 1754.

CHARLES IN SWEDEN: he was an attaché at the British Legation in Sweden in 1772, and wrote a successful account of the revolution there.

THE PRINCE: George, Prince of Wales (born 1762).

THE PAMPHLET: one of Charles Sheridan's many anonymous political pamphlets.

LETTER 17

LORD SACKVILLE: Lord George Germaine (originally Sackville) was created Lord Sackville in 1782. He died on 29 August 1785 aged 70. He had been a patron of Thomas Sheridan.

MR ERSKINE: Thomas Erskine (1750–1823) afterwards Lord Erskine, soldier, politician and lawyer.

MR HUNTER: John Hunter, F.R.S. (1728–93), the great surgeon and naturalist; he married Anne Home in 1771. She was a poetess, and patroness of Josef Haydn the composer.

ANNEFIELD: near Ballymore Eustace. The home of Alicia's first cousin Mrs Dexter, daughter of Mrs Thomas Sheridan's sister Mrs John Fish.

MASTER OF TONBRIDGE SCHOOL: Vicesimus Knox (1752–1821), headmaster 1778–1812.

LETTER 19

SIR JAMES TYNTE: James Stratford Tynte, created a baronet 1778.

[203]

MRS HASTINGS: Warren Hastings married in 1777 the divorced wife of Baron von Imhoff. She left India in 1783, and Hastings followed, arriving in England on 13 June 1785.

ST. LEGER: William StLeger, a cousin of Lord Doneraile, married Ann Angelo (see letter 1). He became a General.

LETTER 20

SIR RICHARD RYCROFT: Rector of Penshurst, a baronet.

LETTER 21

The Heiress: by General John Burgoyne, based on Diderot's *Père de Famille.* Touched up by Sheridan, it was produced at Drury Lane on 14 January 1786.

The Country Girl: Garrick's adaptation of Wycherley's *Country Wife* first produced 1766. Revived 18 October 1785 with Mrs. Jordan 'peculiarly comic but perfectly natural' in the title-role.

The Romp: a farce, adapted from Isaac Bickerstaff's *Love in the City,* first performed 1778; Mrs. Jordan made a great success of it in this winter season 1785–86.

CHARLES FOX'S BROTHER: Colonel Henry Fox.

THE DUKE: 4th Duke of Rutland, Lord Lieutenant of Ireland 1784–87.

MR ORDE: Thomas Orde (1746–1807), Chief Secretary for Ireland 1784–87, afterwards created Lord Bolton.

LETTER 22

GAINSBOROUGH: Thomas Gainsborough had been a close friend of the Linleys at Bath, and painted several portraits of them, now in the Dulwich Gallery. He took Schomberg House, Pall Mall, in 1774 and arranged his own exhibitions there in the late summer of 1784 and afterwards.

The portrait of Mrs Sheridan was sent to the Royal Academy exhibition in 1783, but Gainsborough worked on it again in 1785 and 1786. It belonged to Mrs. Sheridan's friends the Edward Bouveries, then to the Rothschilds, and now is in the Mellon bequest at the National Gallery in Washington.

DR PARR: Samuel Parr (1747–1825), schoolmaster and Latinist. He had been a senior boy at Harrow when R. B. Sheridan went to school and a master at the end of Sheridan's schooldays, and remained his friend. He wrote the epitaph for Thomas Sheridan's

[204]

tomb at Margate, describing himself in it as 'the well-known Dr Parr'. His private school was at Stanmore.

MRS ROSS: Elizabeth, wife of David Ross. She was the daughter of Thomas Adderly, M.P., and his wife, widow of the 3rd Viscount Charlemont, and thus was a half-sister of the 'Volunteer Earl'. Adderly was a friend of Thomas Sheridan and one of his trustees. Mrs. Ross's son General Robert Ross won the victory of Bladensburg in the British-American war of 1812–14 and was the ancestor of the family of Ross-of-Bladensburg.

MR DRAKE: Francis Drake (1766–1847), son of Francis Drake, D.D., a Fellow of Magdalen and rector of Winestead-in-Holderness, himself became D.D. and rector of Langton.

LORD NUGENT: Robert Nugent (1702–88), created Baron 1767 and Earl Nugent 1776, 'a jovial and voluptuous Irishman, a convert to Protestantism, money and widows, unprincipled but amusing'. His eldest daughter and heiress married George Grenville, first Marquis of Buckingham.

KING'S MEAD STREET: the Sheridans had lived there when Bath was their home about 1770.

KEARNEY: Michael Kearney, D.D. (1734–1814), Archdeacon of Raphoe, and John Kearney, D.D. (1742–1813), both Fellows of Trinity, Dublin. John was afterwards Provost of Trinity and (1806) Bishop of Ossory.

THE ABBEY: Westminster Abbey, for the third Handel Commemoration.

LADY GLARAWLEY: Mary Grove, 'an heiress of £30,000', wife of Francis Charles Annesley, 2nd Viscount Glerawly, created Earl Annesley in 1789.

'No Castles': Charles Sheridan's official residence in Dublin Castle.

MISS BOWDLER: Jane Bowdler (1743–84), elder sister of the editor who 'Bowdlerised' Shakespeare. Her *Poems and Essays by a lady lately deceased* were privately printed at Bath in 1786. Her sister Harriet (died 1830) also published *Poems and Essays* in 1786.

LADY DENBIGH: Mary Cotton, wife of Basil Feilding, 6th Earl of Denbigh.

BOGLE: probably James Bogle (1740–1804) the miniaturist.

The Lounger: a weekly magazine published at Edinburgh 1785–87, taking the place of *The Mirror* (see letter 11).

COWPER'S POEMS: the first collection was published in 1782, and the second in 1785.

THICKNESS: Philip Thicknesse (1719–92), eccentric adventurer, a patron of Gainsborough. He built St. Catherine's Hermitage, Bath, about 1770. He put up the first monument to Thomas Chatterton (died 1770) in 1784.

POPE'S LINES: From the 'Elegy to the memory of an unfortunate young Lady' –

> What though no sacred earth allow thee room
> nor hallow'd dirge be mutter'd o'er thy tomb?
> Yet shall thy grave with rising flowers be dress'd
> and the green turf lie lightly on thy breast.
> There shall the morn her earliest tears bestow,
> there the first roses of the year shall blow;
> while Angels with their silver wings o'ershade
> the ground now sacred by thy reliques made.

THE GREEN: Stephens Green, the principal square in south Dublin.

LETTER 26

HOBNOBS: informal drinking.

LETTER 28

LORD CUNNINGHAM: the 3rd Lord Conyngham, afterwards created 1st Marquis (1766–1832).

PRINCE'S BIRTHDAY: the Prince of Wales's 24th birthday.

MRS JEFFERIES: wife of St John Jefferies of Blarney Castle, Co. Cork; Thomas Sheridan with both his daughters stayed with them there in 1776.

MR COBBE: possibly James Cobb (1756–1818), secretary of the East India Office; he wrote comic operas.

MRS FITZHERBERT: Maria Anne (1756–1837), daughter of William Smythe, secretly married to the Prince of Wales.

THE KING'S SAFETY: Margaret Nicholson, a religious maniac, stabbed the King in August 1786; he called out 'Don't hurt this poor woman, she hasn't hurt me'. She was treated as a lunatic, and not tried.

CAROLINE: *Caroline of Lichfield*, a novel from the French by Thomas Holcroft, published 1786 in 3 volumes.

LAVATER: Johann Kaspar Lavater (1741–81), pastor at Zürich. His work on 'physiognomy' achieved European fame.

LETTER 30

W. W. GRENVILLE: William Wyndham Grenville, youngest brother of Lord Buckingham, who had been Lord Lieutenant in 1782–83 and was re-appointed when the Duke of Rutland died in 1787.

'The labour we delight in physics pain', *Macbeth* II, 3; said by Macbeth to Macduff on the morning after the murder of Duncan.

LETTER 31

MRS CREWE: Mrs Crewe and her relation Mrs Lane had crossed from Ireland with the Sheridans. She was Frances, daughter of Fulke Greville of Wilbury (see letter 47, for her mother), and married in 1766 John Crewe of Crewe Hall, M.P. for Cheshire 1768–1806 and then created Lord Crewe. She was a fashionable Whig hostess, and Sheridan's 'Amoret'.

PARGATE: Parkgate, ten miles north-west of Chester, the Irish mail port on the north shore of the Dee estuary. The longer sea passage avoided the dangerous road to Holyhead through north Wales.

STONE, ETC.: the stages of their journey were – 25 miles to Stone which is 4 miles beyond Crewe, between Stafford and Macclesfield; 28 miles to Lichfield; 27 miles to Coventry; 19 miles to Daventry; 52 miles to St. Albans; 21 miles to London.

MISS SEWARD: Anna Seward (1747–1809), the 'Swan of Lichfield'.

LETTER 32

MR BEAUFOY: see above, letter 7 and next letter (33).

'My Lords I have done': Sheridan's concluding words after the four-day speech, in which between 3rd and 13th June 1788 he had indicted Warren Hastings in Westminster Hall. See letters 57 and 58 for his later speeches.

HOOD: Lord Hood's was an Irish peerage, so that he was eligible as an M.P.

TOWNSHEND: Lord John Townshend (1757–1833), second son of the 1st Marquess Townshend. For his wife see letter 50.

LETTER 33

MR BEAUFOY'S YOUNGEST BROTHER: the brothers were Henry (1750–1795) for whom see letter 7, John Hanbury (1761–1809) killed at the battle of Talavera, and Mark (1764–1827), F.R.S., the first Englishman to climb Mont Blanc.

ANTHONY ANGELO: half-brother of Betsy's friends, born in Italy 1747 before his father Domenico came to England (see letter 1). He went to India, but returned to London about 1785 and married Martha Bland, usually said to have been an actress. Their son and grandson were distinguished soldiers in the Indian Army.

DIBDEN: Deepdene, the Duke of Norfolk's house near Dorking.

LORD ROBERT SPENCER: son of the 3rd Duke of Marlborough, a lifelong friend of R. B. Sheridan. Brother of Lady Diana Beauclerk and Lady Pembroke. He married Mrs. Bouverie after her first husband's death.

LETTER 34

ONE STAGE SHORT OF CANTERBURY: probably Faversham, which is ten miles short.

THE HERALD: the *Morning Herald*, a London newspaper.

SIR SAMSON WRIGHT: on 22 July 1788, the fourth day of polling in the Westminster election, Townshend's gang of butchers' porters killed one of Hood's gang of sailors. Sir Sampson Wright, the Bow Street magistrate, called for a platoon of the Guards from the Savoy and posted them in front of the Whig headquarters, the Shakespeare tavern. Townshend, Fox and Sheridan forced their way to Bow Street. Two of the Guardsmen were committed for assault but bailed out by their officers. Sheridan was reputed to have seized Wright.

The print by Gillray was published before the end of July. It is fully described in Mrs George's *Catalogue of political and personal satires in the British Museum*, no 7353. Fox is in the centre with two soldiers thrusting at him with their bayonets. At the left Wright kneels before Sheridan, whose appearance is not much travestied. Sheridan has hold of Wright's collar and threatens him with his left fist.

LORD HOLLAND'S HOUSE: Kingsgate, built in 1760 by Charles Fox's father, the first Lord Holland, and satirised by Gray in his well-known verses:

Here seagulls scream and cormorants rejoice
and mariners, though shipwreck'd, dread to land. (etc.)
SCARBOROUGH: the Sheridans visited it when Betsy was a child.

LETTER 37

'Her Poor Sister': Mary Tickell died in the spring of 1784.
MISS LINLEY: Jane, see the list of characters at page x.

LETTER 38

DUKE OF NORFOLK: Charles, 11th Duke. He married (1) in 1767 Marian Coppinger, who died 1768; (2) in 1771 Frances Scudamore.

Microcosm: the famous Eton magazine, published from November 1786 to July 1787.

YOUNG CANNING: George Canning (1770–1827), a nephew of Mrs Sheridan's friend (see letter 41), afterwards Prime Minister.

MISS BURNEY: Fanny Burney, novelist and diarist. She was second keeper of the Queen's robes 1786–90.

MME DE STAAL: lady in waiting to the Duchesse de Maine. She had been Mlle de Launay (1684–1750).

SWAN'S SUICIDE: Edward Bellingham Swan, Commissioner of the Irish Stamp Office.

LETTER 39

PRATTON: he practised as an apothecary in Bond Street.

LETTER 40

TESSIER: also called Le Tessier and Texier. A French actor who settled in London in 1775 and gained great popularity by his recitals of plays in which he represented all the characters himself, varying 'his voice, countenance and manner'.

MAINAUDUC: an Irish doctor of Huguenot extraction, John Bonniot de Mainauduc.

DUCHESS OF DEVONSHIRE: Lady Georgiana Spencer, daughter of the 1st Earl Spencer, married in 1774 William, 5th Duke of Devonshire. She died in 1806. The central figure of the 'Devonshire House circle'.

LADY SALISBURY: Lady Mary Emily Hill (1750–1835), wife of the 1st Marquess. She died in the fire at Hatfield.

FARCE OF *Animal Magnetism*: by Mrs Inchbald, produced at Covent Garden in the spring of 1788.

[209]

HARRIS: actor and manager at Covent Garden.

MRS MATTOCKS: Isabella Mattocks (1746–1826), first appeared as a child actress in 1753 and regularly at Covent Garden 1761–1808.

L'Avocat Pathelin: a play by D. A. de Brueys and J. Palaprat (1706) based on the famous medieval farce.

DR FORD: James Ford (1718–95), a fashionable obstetrician, and physician extraordinary to the Queen. A principal shareholder in Drury Lane Theatre.

MR KING: Thomas King the actor (see letter 1), resigned the management because he found Sheridan's methods impossible.

MR LOCK: William Lock of Norbury Park, praised by Boswell for his 'knowledge, taste, elegance, and virtue', and called by Johnson 'an ingenious critic'.

Dictionary: Thomas Sheridan's *English Dictionary*, published by Charles Dilly, who was renowned for his generous patronage of literary men.

STAMP OFFICE: Richard Tickell was one of the Commissioners.

LETTER 41

MRS CANNING: Mehetabel Patrick, widow of Stratford Canning, a London banker of northern Irish family. Sheridan's and Mrs Sheridan's most loyal friend, and called by them 'Sister Christian'. She lived first at Putney and then at Wanstead. She had four sons, Henry, William, Charles Fox, and Stratford who became Lord Stratford de Redcliffe.

MRS BOUVERIE: Harriet Fawkener, married in 1764 Edward Bouverie, brother of the first Lord Radnor. They lived at Delapré Abbey, Northampton.

LETTER 42

RICHARDSON: Joseph Richardson (1758–1803) barrister, and Whig journalist and politician.

SIR WATKIN: Williams Wynn, 4th baronet of Wynnstay. He married Charlotte Grenville, sister of Lord Buckingham and of Thomas Grenville, the politican and bibliophile who was a close friend of Sheridan's.

DUKE OF YORK: Prince Frederick (born 1763), the King's second son.

LETTER 44

RESTRICTIONS: during the King's illness the 'Regency crisis' was deliberately prolonged by Pitt in discussions of the restrictions to be placed on the Regent, supposing the Prince of Wales were appointed: the King recovered before any appointment was made.

MR GRENVILLE: William Wyndham Grenville.

LETTER 46

DR TURTON: James Turton (1736–1806), M.D. Oxford 1767, physician to the Queen 1782 and to the King 1797.

BISHOP DIXON: William Dickson (1745–1804), an Eton friend of Charles Fox, Bishop of Down from 1783. His wife was a Miss Symmes.

LETTER 47

MRS GREVILLE: Frances Macartney, Mrs. Fulke Greville, mother of Mrs Crewe (see letter 31). She wrote the 'Prayer for Indifference' (1762) which was a very well-known poem for many years, and Sheridan dedicated *The Critic* (1781) to her.

A FLEMISH ACCOUNT: this cant word for 'unsatisfactory' came in about 1785 (Oxford English Dictionary).

KEW: the King was moved from Windsor to Kew Palace on 29 November 1788.

WILLIS: the Rev. Francis Willis, the alienist who treated and cured the King.

WARREN: Richard Warren (1731–97), the fashionable Whig physician (see letter 1).

PRINCESS ROYAL: Princess Charlotte (b. 1766).

SIR GEORGE BAKER: President of the College of Physicians 1785–90, 1792–93, 1795. Born 1722, created a baronet 1776, died 1809.

LORD DERBY: The 12th Earl.

MISS FARREN: Elizabeth Farren, acting at Drury Lane from 1778, married Lord Derby in 1797.

LETTER 48

MR CRAWFORD: 'Fish' Crawford, a Whig politician of the older generation, and a patron of art.

LETTER 49

KITTY'S INTENDED: Kitty Angelo married in 1790 the Rev. Mark Drury, a Harrow master.

DICK SHERIDAN: Richard, an Irish M.P., son of Thomas Sheridan's brother Richard.

LADY ELIZABETH FOSTER: daughter of the 4th Earl of Bristol, the Bishop of Derry, and wife of John Thomas Foster, M.P., of Dunleer, Co. Louth. After the deaths of her husband (1796) and of Duchess Georgiana (1806) she married the Duke of Devonshire in 1809.

SPEAKER: W. W. Grenville was elected Speaker of the House of Commons by a great majority on 5 January 1789, but resigned on 5 June following.

5 JANUARY 1789: Alicia's 36th birthday.

LADY WILLIAMS: see the note on Sir Watkin Williams Wynn at letter 42; the surname Wynn had been added by his father. See also letter 62.

'Beyond the Year 40': there were nine weeks' hard frost in 1740 and the Thames was frozen over; 1766 was nearly as cold, and this was the next really severe winter (November 1788 to January 1789).

LETTER 50

J. BOILEAU: probably John Theophilus Boileau (b. 1755) of Dublin, uncle of Sir John Boileau, 1st baronet.

LADY JOHN TOWNSHEND: Georgiana Poyntz, a first cousin of the Duchess of Devonshire, married William Fawkener, Mrs Bouverie's brother, but eloped in 1786 with Townshend (for whom see letter 32).

LADY JULIA HOWARD: Juliana (1749–1849), youngest daughter of the 4th Earl of Carlisle. She never married and lived to be nearly 100. For her sister Lady Betty Delmé see letter 59.

'The Play': at Drury Lane on 21 January 1789, Young's *Revenge* with John Philip Kemble in the name part. Kemble had become manager in 1788.

LETTER 51

DUKE OF GLOUCESTER: the King's brother, Prince William Henry.

GALLINI: 'Sir' John Gallini, a papal chevalier; director of the Italian Opera at the King's Theatre, Haymarket.

LADY PEMBROKE: Lady Elizabeth Spencer, daughter of the 3rd Duke of Marlborough, had been deserted by her husband the 10th Lord Pembroke. She was a lady in waiting to the Queen.

Coriolanus: Kemble's adaptation. He acted the name part, and his sister Mrs Siddons acted Volumnia mother of Coriolanus.

MR PELHAM: Thomas Pelham, Chief Secretary for Ireland 1795–98, and from 1805 second Earl of Chichester.

LETTER 53

MISS BOUVERIE: eldest of the five daughters of Edward and Harriet Bouverie.

THE DELEGATES: from the Irish Parliament inviting the Prince of Wales to assume the Regency – but the King had already recovered.

LETTER 54

Mrs Foresight: in Congreve's *Love for Love*.

LADY BUCKINGHAMSHIRE: wife of John Hobart, 2nd Earl.

LETTER 55

QUILCA: the farm in Co. Cavan where Thomas Sheridan's father had entertained Swift and Stella. Thomas Sheridan had improved it, but was forced to mortgage it in 1756 to his brother-in-law Sheen and to William LeFanu. It descended to Alicia's grandson Joseph Sheridan LeFanu, the novelist, and was sold after his death in 1873.

BALL AT THE PANTHEON: the Tory celebration of the King's recovery, organised by White's Club on 31 March 1789.

BROOKS'S GALA: the Whig celebration was held in the Haymarket Opera House.

'Part of a Play': *Twelfth Night*, with Kemble as Malvolio, Drury Lane, 14 May 1789.

CUMBERLAND HOUSE: the Duke of Cumberland was the King's brother, Prince Henry Frederick.

LETTER 57

THE TRIAL: Warren Hastings was indicted by the House of Commons before the House of Lords. The Commons appointed a Committee of Managers.

JE NE SÇAIS QUOI: a fashionable social club.

THE PRINCES: the King had seven sons living, four of whom were now grown up.

MISS LEE: Sophia Lee (1750–1824), schoolmistress and authoress. Her novel *The Recess* was read by Betsy (letter 63).

DUKE OF CLARENCE: Prince William (b. 1765) afterwards King
William IV.

AMBASSADOR: the Spanish Ambassador.

BOOTLE'S: Boodle's Club celebrated the King's recovery at Ranelagh
on 26 May.

LETTER 59

HORNE TOOKE: Radical and philologist.

LADY BETTY DELMÉ: Elizabeth, fifth daughter of the 4th Earl of
Carlisle, married in 1769 Peter Delmé.

LETTER 60

LORD MELCOMBE: George Bubb Dodington (1691–1762) created a
peer in 1761; his house was called La Trappe.

DEVICES OF PROFESSIONS: the Duke of York was a soldier and the
Duke of Clarence a sailor.

DUCHESS OF ANCASTER: Mary Layard, wife of Brownlow Bertie,
6th and last Duke.

LADY DUNCANNON: Lady Harriot Spencer, sister of the Duchess of
Devonshire, married Frederic Ponsonby, Lord Duncannon, son
of the Earl of Bessborough. Their daughter Caro (Lady Caroline
Lamb) was born in 1785.

LADY JERSEY: Frances Twysden, wife of the 4th Earl. Her daughter
Charlotte married Lord William Russell a month after this
masquerade.

DUCHESS OF RUTLAND: Lady Mary Somerset, daughter of the Duke
of Beaufort, and widow of the 4th Duke of Rutland, for whom
see letter 21.

MISS CHOLMONDELEY: Mary Henrietta, daughter of the Rev. and
Hon. Robert Cholmondeley and his wife Mary Woffington, a
sister of the actress and a close friend of Mrs Thomas Sheridan.

LADY PALMERSTON: Mary Mee, wife of Henry Temple, 2nd
Viscount Palmerston, and mother of the statesman.

LETTER 62

LADY WILLIAMS: Sir Watkin seems to have been unaware that he
was mortally ill; he died on 29 July. (See letter 42.)

MR GILBERT: a Dublin bookseller (publisher) of this name was a
friend of Thomas Sheridan; a Mrs Gilbert is mentioned in
letter 5.

'Our future Habitation': Tickell's rooms at Hampton Court.

LADY DIANA BEAUCLERK: daughter of the 3rd Duke of Marlborough, she married the 2nd Lord Bolingbroke, but was divorced in 1768 and married Topham Beauclerk. Her son George Richard StJohn, 3rd Viscount Bolingbroke, married in 1783 Charlotte Collins.

BROOKS'S BALL: On 23 April, see letter 55.

LETTER 63

COCKER: John Cocker of Cocker and Fonblanque, solicitors.

The Recess: historical novel by Sophia Lee (see letter 57) published 1785.

DELPH: the usual word at the time for cheap earthenware, derived from Delft.

LETTER 64

MRS CROUCH: Anna Maria Crouch (1763–1805), a singer at Drury Lane, her husband was a naval officer.

KELLY: Michael Kelly, the distinguished singer, and later a friend of Sheridan. He left amusing memoirs.

WILLIAM CHAMBERLAIN: son of Betsy's mother's brother Richard Chamberlain. Father and son were general practitioners in north London.

MISS LEE: Sarah Ley.

LETTER 67

GREEN BOXES: the upper boxes.

MISS WALLACE: a Covent Garden actress, usually called Miss Wallis. She first appeared at Bath as Rosalind in *As You Like It* on 17 October 1789.

YORK STREET: Betsy's Aunt Hester (Sheridan) Knowles kept a girls' school in York Street, Dublin.

VERSES TO PATTY WHYTE: Alicia's 'Verses to Miss Whyte on her performance of Anna in the tragedy of Douglas' were published in Samuel Whyte's *Poems*, Dublin 1795.

The Conscious Lovers: Steele's adaptation of Terence's *Andria* (The woman of Andros), first produced in 1722.

LADY JOHN TOWNSHEND: Betsy mentions seeing her at the Sheridans' house in the previous January (letter 50).

'Different Causes': because Lady John Townshend had run away with Lord John from her first husband.

[215]

MISS LEE: Sophia Lee, see letter 57.

MR G. CRAUFURD: George, son of Patrick Craufurd, see letter 1.

GENERAL BURGOYNE: John Burgoyne, author of *The Heiress* (letter 21).

DUKE OF LUXEMBOURG: head of the Montmorency family, he was chairman of the States General at the beginning of the French Revolution.

PINDEMONTE: Ippolito Pindemonte (1753–1828), a Veronese poet. He had been living in Paris and came to England on account of the Revolution.

LA TOUCHE: the most prominent Huguenot family in Ireland.

LETTER 70

The Dramatist: a play by Frederic Reynolds, first produced at Covent Garden in 1789.

TESSIER: see letter 40.

LETTER 71

Jane Shore: the play by Nicholas Rowe, first produced at Drury Lane in 1714.

PHARAOH TABLE: Pharaoh or Faro was a purely gambling game; the betting was on the order in which certain cards would turn up as the pack was cut.

LADY DUNCANNON: the Duncannons (see letter 60) went to Brussels on 27 March 1790 to join the Duchess of Devonshire. Betsy resented Sheridan's attachment to Lady Duncannon.

Index

OXFORD

MORE OXFORD PAPERBACKS

Details of a selection of other books to follow. A complete list of Oxford Paperbacks, including The World's Classics, Twentieth-Century Classics, OPUS, Past Masters, Oxford Authors, Oxford Shakespeare, and Oxford Paperback Reference, is available in the UK from the General Publicity Department, Oxford University Press (JH), Walton Street, Oxford, OX2 6DP.

In the USA, complete lists are available from the Paperbacks Marketing Manager, Oxford University Press, 200 Madison Avenue, New York, NY 10016.

Oxford Paperbacks are available from all good bookshops. In case of difficulty, please order direct from Oxford University Press Bookshop, 116 High Street, Oxford, Freepost, OX1 4BR, enclosing full payment. Please add 10% of published price for postage and packing.

THE ROMANTIC IMAGINATION

Maurice Bowra

This is a classic, illuminating study of the major poets of the Romantic movement and their followers; Blake, Coleridge, Wordsworth, Shelley, Keats, Byron, Poe, Christina and Dante Gabriel Rossetti, and Swinburne. Originally delivered as a series of lectures at a time when the Romantics were to some extent in critical opprobrium, *The Romantic Imagination* sought to reassess the literary values of these poets.

ROMANTICS, REBELS AND REACTIONARIES

English Literature and its Background 1760–1830

Marilyn Butler

This book takes a fresh look at once of the most fertile periods in English literature, a half-century which produced writers of the stature of Blake, Keats, Coleridge, Wordsworth, Byron, Scott, and Jane Austen. Marilyn Butler questions the validity of grouping such diverse talents and personalities under the critical label 'Romantic', and instead presents them to the reader both as individuals and as part of a larger cultural landscape.

This is a highly original book which is sure to enlighten and stimulate students of the period as well as the general reader.

'Dr Butler is brilliantly acute . . . at restoring to literary works the subdued political ticks and rumblings which the alarmed ears of their first readers would have picked up.' John Carey, *Sunday Times*

'Why has it not been done before? one asks of Marilyn Butler's excellent new book, which analyses the diverse writers of the Romantic period exclusively—but also exhaustively and subtly—in political and ideological terms.' *Listener*

An OPUS book

WORDSWORTH
Peotical Works
Revised by Ernest de Selincourt

This edition of Wordsworth's poems contains every piece of verse known to have been published by the poet himself, or of which he authorized the posthumous publication. The text, which Thomas Hutchinson based largely upon the 1849–50 standard edition—the last issued during the poet's lifetime—was revised in 1936 for the Oxford Standard Authors series by Ernest de Selincourt.

COLERIDGE
Poetical works
Edited by Ernest Hartley Coleridge

This edition by Ernest Hartley Coleridge, grandson of the poet, contains a complete and authoritative text of Coleridge's poems. Here are his earliest extant teenage poems, his masterly meditative pieces, and the extraordinary supernatural poems—'The Rime of the Ancient Mariner', 'Kubla Khan', and 'Christabel'.

The text boolows that of the 1834 edition, the last published in the author's lifetime. The poems are printed, so far as is possible, in chronological order, with Coleridge's own notes as well as textual and bibliographical notes by the editor.

SHELLEY
Poetical Works

Edited by Thomas Hutchinson
New edition, corrected by G. M. Matthews

This edition by Thomas Hutchinson (1905), corrected and updated by G. M. Matthews (1970), contains every poem and fragment of Shelley's verse that had hitherto appeared in print. The text, based on Mary Shelley's own editions of 1839 has been freshly collated by Thomas Hutchinson, who had indicated in footnotes every material departure from the originals. Shelley's antiquated or eccentric spellings have been modernized except where required by rhyme or metre. The original pointing has been retained except where it tends to obscure or distort the poet's meaning.

There are also headnotes to each poem, detailing its composition and publication, and a list of the principal editions of Shelley's works.

EARLY MODERN FRANCE
1560–1715

Robin Briggs

This book provides an overall interpretation of a decisive period in French history, from the chaos of the Wars of Religion to the death of Louis XIV. A clear but economical narrative of the major political events is combined with an analysis of the long-term factors which decisively moulded the evolution of both State and society.

'A very fine, thorough and conscientious study of a formative period of French History . . . his account of the French provinces in the age of Richelieu and Louis XIV . . . is one of the best things of its kind in English.' *Sunday Telegraph*

'this vigorously-written book deserves wide use as an introduction to absolutist France' *History*

An OPUS book